The Hunger War

The Hunger War

Food, Rations and Rationing
1914–1918

Matthew Richardson

Pen & Sword
MILITARY

First published in Great Britain by
PEN AND SWORD MILITARY
an imprint of
Pen and Sword Books Ltd
47 Church Street
Barnsley
South Yorkshire S70 2AS

ISBN 978 1 47382 749 3

A CIP record for this book is available from the British Library.

Printed and bound in England by
CPI Group (UK) Ltd, Croydon, CR0 4YY

Typeset in Times by CHIC GRAPHICS

Pen & Sword Books Ltd incorporates the imprints of
Archaeology, Atlas, Aviation, Battleground, Discovery,
Family History, History, Maritime, Military, Naval, Politics,
Railways, Select, Social History, Transport, True Crime,
Claymore Press, Frontline Books, Leo Cooper, Praetorian Press,
Remember When, Seaforth Publishing and Wharncliffe.

For a complete list of Pen and Sword titles please contact
Pen and Sword Books Limited
47 Church Street, Barnsley, South Yorkshire, S70 2AS, England
E-mail: enquiries@pen-and-sword.co.uk
Website: www.pen-and-sword.co.uk

Contents

Acknowledgements

No work of this nature could ever reach print unless the author had received assistance from numerous sources. The book you are about to read is no exception to this rule, and in particular I wish to thank my friend and former colleague Richard Davies at the University of Leeds for his help in relation to the Russian experience of the First World War. Similarly, Christian Greissinger assisted me with German research. Jori Wiegmans in Holland was again immensely helpful in supplying images and other research material, whilst the work of Dr Martin Kraaijestein, and his website *Nederland in de Eerste Wereldoorlog*, were invaluable to me in helping to understand the Dutch experience of the First World War. I would also like to thank Xining Guo, correspondent for China Central Television Europe, whose translation work proved to be most valuable. Naturally, having paid due acknowledgment to those above, it also goes without saying that any mistakes or misinterpretations within this book are entirely my own responsibility.

Other assistance came from Margaret Holmes and I would like to thank her for her kindness in allowing me to use material relating to her father Frank Richards, likewise Ray Scroby for permission to quote from his father's unpublished diary. Gillian Lighton sent me extracts from unpublished notes on her family and early life by her mother Margaret 'Margot' Elaine Cliff, which again were immensely useful. My friend and colleague John Caley assisted with a number of illustrations, and for these I thank him warmly.

Rupert Harding at Pen and Sword once again supported my ideas, and offered his encouragement. I thank him for this, and for his assistance over a number of years. To my family once again I extend my apologies, in that the preparation of this book kept me chained to my desk for so many hours, however I hope that in time you may feel that the end result was worthwhile.

Matthew Richardson,
Douglas, 2014

Introduction

The First World War was a total conflict, and food would be one of its major battlegrounds. Blockade tactics had been a feature of warfare for centuries – starvation had been used as a weapon at many medieval sieges, and the North had imposed a blockade on the South during the American Civil War. However, what was different about the First World War was the sheer magnitude of the conflict. Victory or defeat would hinge as much upon which side could keep their troops in the field supplied and fed – whilst at the same time avoiding starvation on the home front – as much as it would upon which side could produce the most shells and guns.

In this conflict, whole societies were at war, and household brands, many of which are still familiar to us today, were mustered to play their part in it. At the same time, the war provided the impetus for and the arena in which some societies attempted to resolve long-running social questions over alcohol and its control. The legacies of some of these experiments are still with us today.

As the war progressed, the ability of the respective combatants to marshal their food resources effectively would become a key component of victory. Those who could not meet this challenge – firstly Russia, but eventually also the Ottoman Empire, Austria-Hungary and Germany – would fall by the wayside. The Western Allies, by contrast, eventually pooled their food resources, and by forming a bloc were better able to manage what food they had available. These eventual outcomes were not easily discernible or predictable before the war. Germany had spent much time before 1914 preparing a siege economy; the Russian Empire (especially its province of Ukraine) was a vast breadbasket, and Ottoman Turkey was primarily agrarian, whilst on the other hand Britain was heavily reliant upon imported food, and might have been considered to be the state which was most vulnerable to food shortages.

The effects of this total war upon the neutral countries has previously been a neglected and under-researched area, but the impact of the regulations imposed by the Allies and their restrictions upon free trade and the freedom of the seas would have far-reaching consequences for the non-combatant nations also. These consequences, for Denmark, Sweden, Norway, Holland, Switzerland and Spain, are also explored in this book.

Food is a universal constant – we all know what hunger feels like, no matter what nationality we are, where we were born or what language we speak. The part played by food – and hunger – in the First World War deserves closer examination, and this book seeks to chart that role at both national and individual level. Wherever possible it uses eyewitness testimony, and also in a number of cases introduces the modern reader to some now almost forgotten writers, whose work is surely worthy of re-examination.

Chapter 1

On the Battlefronts:
The Western Front

During the First World War, feeding soldiers in the front line became a major logistical challenge. Ensuring an adequate and palatable food supply to the troops was crucial not only to their health, but also to their morale. At times, due to battle, this supply became haphazard; the British also faced the challenge of feeding South Asian troops with special dietary requirements, and POWs often faced particular food hardships, but on the whole soldiers of both sides were inventive, and inveterate, scroungers. Tinned products were a central part of the soldiers' diet: sometimes these were monotonous, but they were often supplemented by supplies from family at home. This chapter examines the differences in food supplies between officers and men, and between differing armies, on the Western Front as the First World War progressed.

Prior to the war a considerable amount of scientific work had been carried out to establish what was the optimum daily calorie intake for a front-line soldier, and each combatant nation had based its daily ration for the ordinary fighting man upon what it believed this quantity of food to be. When they entered the war in 1917, soldiers of the United States were the best fed, with a daily quota of 4,714 calories. Next were the French with a quota of 4,466 calories, then the British with 4,193 calories and finally the Germans with 4,038. Of course, these figures were only ever an ideal, because everything depended upon the food being able to reach the soldier, and at times this simply was not possible. Things also changed during the course of the war; as the conflict went on and shortages began to bite, official rations were reduced. In June 1916 the meat portion of the German soldier's ration was cut, and in April 1917 his bread portion followed suit. By the opposite token, under certain circumstances soldiers found themselves able to supplement their rations, either by buying or taking food from civilians.

Once the front line had settled into a static trench system, supplying the fighting man was in theory much easier, but in the first months of the war, during the retreat from Mons and the subsequent race to the sea, food supply could be erratic to say the least. At Mons on 24 August 1914 a sharp rearguard action was fought amid the slag heaps of the mining town of Frameries, in which the Germans were roughly handled by the South Lancashire and Lincolnshire Regiments. Captain Herbert Stewart of the Army Service Corps (ASC) was tasked with supplying rations to the defenders whilst under fire here, a duty he performed most gallantly. He recounts in his memoir:

> Overhead was the incessant crack of the shrapnel, and as fast as one group of the little white clouds, caused by the burst of the shells, dissolved into the still morning air, another group appeared. Fortunately the shells were bursting high, and so were not as dangerous as they might have been, but they brought down pieces of chimney-pot, slates, tiles, bricks, and lengths of telegraph wire, which were showered into the streets and about our ears. The continuous rattle of rifle fire, the cracks of the bursting shells, and the discharges of our own artillery, made a babel of noise which I found very distracting . . . The first groups of soldiers we met were waiting in support under cover of houses and walls; later we turned down towards the barricades or hastily constructed breastworks made from the pave torn up out of the road, and met some companies on their way to reinforce the fighting line, while others were working at a fresh line of barricades to be occupied when the advanced ones could no longer be held. To each I distributed such bread as they wanted: some were glad indeed to get the hot fresh loaves, others were too occupied or too anxious to eat, while most were still in possession of the iron ration carried by every soldier in his haversack to meet such an emergency as the present, when it is impossible or very inadvisable to bring forward the Supply Train.[1]

The efforts of the ASC to supply fresh food to the troops in this chaotic period should not be underestimated. A Distinguished Conduct Medal was even awarded to one member of the ASC in recognition of his determination to ensure that his comrades were fed; the citation of Staff Sergeant A. J. Steele stated that the award was:

> For great zeal and devotion to duty as Master Baker during the early part of the campaign at Boulogne, when, working under the greatest difficulties in the open, and exposed to all weathers, he successfully carried out the work of the First Bakery, never failing to turn out the maximum output from the ovens.[2]

During the Retreat from Mons, however, most British soldiers were left to their own devices in terms of rations. Discipline almost as hard as the food itself prevented most of these Regular soldiers from breaking into their iron rations of corned beef and biscuits, and many men resorted to what they could find or scrounge instead. Gunner John Trusty from Sunderland was serving with a Royal Field Artillery 4.5in howitzer battery on the Retreat. He remembered:

> The roads were crowded with refugees. Old men and young people there, pushing their prams and beds . . . I remember there . . . we were feeling hungry and we saw a French farmer and he told us to come and help ourselves to his sheep. There were several of us there who got hold of sheep and we slaughtered them ourselves . . . of course we had our iron rations but we weren't allowed to eat them without being ordered to do so and we mostly relied upon what we could get from the French people or what we could pick up in the fields and it did very often happen that we could get carrots, turnips and onions and we used to very often make a stew ourselves, which was a very simple thing to do but with regards to meat we saw very little of it, with the exception of Bully Beef, and there wasn't any bread of any description. It was all biscuits . . .[3]

British soldiers pause for a hastily-cooked roadside meal, possibly on the Retreat from Mons, 1914. (Library of Congress: Bain collection)

Of course in a situation where an army was in rapid retreat, it was often a source of considerable frustration that deliveries of the ample food supplies which were available could not be made to coincide with the rest halts of the men who needed them. Frederick Bolwell, of the Loyal North Lancashire Regiment, who was also on the Retreat, recalled:

> On several occasions we passed food-supplies left on the roadside – left for the Germans: whole cheeses, tins of mustard, one of which I carried for four days, but, on getting nothing to eat with it, I threw it away. We would arrive outside a village, allotted for billets, perhaps about 7.30 pm, and, after having marched the whole of the day, we were not allowed to enter the village until eleven or twelve o'clock at night to make ourselves comfy. The reason, I believe, was that it might be shelled by the enemy. No one was allowed to touch a thing – not even fruit – or he would be punished for looting; yet we knew very well that, perhaps on the morrow, the Germans would secure it all.[4]

This last aspect was taken very seriously by the British military authorities and it was a point of honour that nothing was taken from French and Belgian civilians which was not paid for. The Germans of course had no such qualms, but at this stage in the war they were equally well supplied by their own commissariat department. In August 1914, Musketier Karl Storch was in the front line near Le Cateau. The German soldiers here had missed their lunch the day previously because of the hectic nature of their advance, but now at last they were allowed to pause for a meal; Storch recounts:

> Now here we had yesterday's ration: peas and bacon. This was splendid and tasted delicious, but we did not get to enjoy as much as we would have liked, very suddenly we were fired upon once again by the enemy, and bullets and food do not get on with each other. The thoughtless enemy, who had spoiled our well-earned pea soup, drove us into a rage.[5]

Musketier Karl Storch, a German soldier whose meal of peas and bacon was rudely interrupted by British fire. (From Storch, Vom feldgrauen Buchhändler)

This was typical German army fare, often supplemented with bread or *wurst* (German pork sausage). The field kitchens which travelled with the German army were almost always close at hand, so the Germans were generally assured of a hot meal. Gerd Leberecht, a

A German field butchery preparing food. Note the animal carcasses hanging in the background. (Author's collection)

reserve officer and journalist from the *Täglichen Rundschau*, was near Antwerp in October 1914 when:

> Into the garden of a large house is driven the 'Gulaschkanone', the mobile army kitchen, and makes noodle soup with pork. The beasts were still alive a half hour ago; they got here very quickly. Unfortunately it is usually very difficult to get such freshly slaughtered meat; because naturally one cannot carry along meat for days at a time. The dessert is shaken down from a pear tree.[6]

As might be expected of a nation with such a fine culinary tradition, French officers generally took their food very seriously, but at times like this it was necessary to eat whatever came to hand. At Montigny-les-Conde, on 9 September 1914 during the Battle of the Marne, a French officer named Marcel Dupont and his comrades rested in a temporary billet, whilst in pursuit of the now-retreating Germans. After their exertions that day, the Frenchmen were pleased enough with simple country fare:

What a dinner we had that evening! It was in a large room with a low open roof supported by small beams. The walls were smoke-blackened and dirty. On a chest placed near the door I can see still a big pile of ration loaves, thrown together anyhow; and leaning over the hearth of the large fireplace, lit up by the wood fire, was an unknown man who was stirring something in a pot. Round the large table a score of hungry and jaded but merry officers were fraternally sharing some pieces of meat which the man took out of the pot. The Captain and I ate out of the same plate and drank out of the same metal cup, for crockery was scarce. The poor woman of the house ran round the table, consumed by her eagerness to make everybody comfortable. And in the farthest corner, away from the light, a very old peasant, with a dazed look and haggard eyes, was watching the unexpected scene. The company heartily cheered Captain C. for his cleverness in finding and bringing to light, from some nook or other, a large pitcher of rough wine.[7]

As the Western Front settled down into trench warfare, it became easier to ensure that adequate supplies of food were at least within reach of large bodies of troops. However, at this early stage there were often as yet no communication trenches, and it was still a hazardous and difficult operation to get hot food to the front lines; the troops of both sides whilst in the trenches would come to rely mainly on what they could carry in with them. Occasionally a ration party could get food up to the front line. Near Messines in October 1914, the German writer Paul Oskar Hocker was in command of a company of Landwehr soldiers. He described the arrival of one such party near his position around midnight, the cloak of darkness being necessary in order to conceal the ration wagons from sharp-eyed enemy observers:

Gottschalt, the sergeant cook – at home he is a teacher – crawls over to me along the hedge, and as he reaches my dug-out reports to me in a whisper that the provision wagon has now appeared on the road nearby. We can now receive bread and bacon. The company is ravenous and quickly the word spreads of the presence nearby of the food carriers. Canteens begin to rattle and deep voices murmur. 'Silence, silence, children!' I quietly exhort. With bread and bacon for [Leutnant] Rochlitz and myself comes Gefreiter Kern, quite a fearless man. We occupy the cellar of a shelled house, surrounded by rubble and debris. A box of sardines, a box of pineapples and six bottles of salvaged wine form the stock of our underground larder.[8]

The crystallisation of the trench systems allowed soldiers – particularly officers – greater scope for formal meals when they were out of the front line in reserve positions. In contrast with Dupont's hastily-arranged meal described previously, in October 1914 another French officer named André Cornet-Auquier was able to lay on a far more lavish spread, something more in keeping with stereotypical Gallic good living:

André Cornet-Auquier, the French soldier who prepared such a lavish spread for his fellow officers. (From Cornet-Auquier, *A Soldier Unafraid*)

> Yesterday, as we were behind the firing-line having our periodic rest, I took advantage of this and invited to lunch the commander of our battalion and a captain whom I like very much. We gave them a fine meal. Here is the menu: Entree: sausage and ham, preceded by a delicious soup; a round of beef with a famous sauce, canned peas, which were most palatable; a roast with fried potatoes . . . browned to a golden yellow; salad, apple fritters, a tart, cakes, pears; wine: Bordeaux white grapes; coffee and chartreuse! The major nearly fell off of his chair at the sight of all this and of course we were highly complimented. And all this was done by my cook, a miner from Saint-Etienne, aided for the occasion by my landlady. In addition, we had a large white tablecloth, plates changed every second course, etc., etc. We didn't know ourselves with all these frills. It is odd how here at the front, for weeks at a time, we eat like pigs, and on the whole badly, when we suddenly start gormandizing and are idiotic. For instance, yesterday's lunch was simply an idiotic thing to do. But then you will admit that we might have done something worse.[9]

For the British army as well as the French, the advent of trench warfare brought more stability and routine to the supply of the men in the front line or just behind. Cecil W. Longley was a member of a Territorial artillery battery in 1915. He wrote:

> As for food, the gunners who are in their dug-outs by day and sleep in a barn at night have it cooked mid-day (hot tea morning and night) and brought to the gun position, where they line up to receive it in mess tins. We signallers sleep in a passage floor in the farm

where we have all our wires (more in number than the hairs of my
head) and do our own cooking in an outhouse where Madame has
the pigwash tub! The latter being most useful and saves us digging
a waste pit for scraps. Poor pigs – tea-leaves, bacon fat, biscuit and
jam all go towards the local dairy-fed pork. We do little cooking
now, as we can't get all the signallers together for any-given meal,
and meat is often of tremendous altitude! So we live on tea – bread
and jam and parcels – rarely a day passes without one of us or more
getting a parcel to 'whack' round. Signallers on distant or night duty
take a loaf of bread (which we get four days out of six) and jam.
Bully beef is taboo. You cannot get anyone to eat it – one portion of
our trenches that I have seen has a pavement of unused bully tins
. . . the stretcher men are a very decent lot, and will always offer the
artillery signaller some hot tea, which they seem to keep going day
and night; good stuff, strong mother's meeting sort of tea with a
lavish supply of sugar in it, but it is the drink and the one we all live
on here. Sometimes we take them an egg or two from our position
and exchange it for one of their Maconochies (issued only to
infantry, a thing to dream of) – lumps of meat, vegetable and gravy
all cooked together in a tin that only needs heating and opening; and
Solomon in all his glory never had such a meal.[10]

Longley's aversion to 'bully' (or corned) beef was probably based upon its
monotony rather than anything that was actually wrong with it. The British
Army imported vast quantities of this easily portable and nutritious
foodstuff from South American producers, and it has become uniquely
associated with the First World War. There was no corn used in the
preparation, instead the name comes from the 'corns' of salt with which the
beef was boiled. As a staple ration it was unparalleled: it could be eaten
cold straight from the tin, or warmed up, or mixed with other ingredients to
form a stew. Longley's admiration for Maconochie's rations, however, are
harder to explain and do not chime with other contemporary accounts, of
which more later. The French army as well as the British issued their troops
with emergency rations, only to be consumed on the orders of an officer;
generally speaking, French soldiers were rather disparaging of their corned
beef ration, often referring to it as *singe* ('monkey'). However, French
soldier Jacques Roujon wrote of an inspection of such items by an officer
on 19 November 1914, at which it transpired that they were too much for
one hungry soldier to resist:

In the afternoon the lieutenant reviews each man's supplies of food:
his haversack, spread open at his feet, must exhibit to the officer's

vigilant eye two tins of corned beef, a dozen biscuits, two little bags containing sugar, coffee, and two tablets of condensed soup. One of our men has neither biscuits nor corned beef. Questioning glance of the lieutenant. Evasive gesture of the man, who immediately stands at attention.

'Have you eaten your two tins of corned beef?'

A sign of assent.

'Your biscuits too, naturally?'

Another sign of assent.

'Ah! And why did you eat your tins of corned beef?'

'Mon lieutenant, one evening I was hungry. . . .'

'Better and better! If the men begin to eat their reserve supplies whenever they are hungry, there will be no army left!'

That evening we laughingly relate the incident to Belin. Being an old soldier, he cannot get over it.

'Eat one's reserve supplies without orders! If he had been in the Foreign Legion he would have received eight days' prison for every biscuit missing.'[11]

'The Language of the Trenches' – a cartoon illustrating various aspects of the life of the French soldier. Among other things, it states in regard to corned beef, 'Singe: very poorly regarded by the troops.' (Author's collection)

In late 1914 and 1915 the British Expeditionary Force in France contained two divisions drawn from the Indian Army, and this added somewhat to the difficulty of victualling British forces at the time. The situation was all the more complex because the personnel of the Indian Corps had such widely differing dietary needs, even across this relatively small formation. A British officer wrote at the time of a visit to the stores at the base depot, where these items were held:

> . . . the feeding of the Army is a delicate business and complicated. It is not enough to secure that there be sufficient 'caloric units' in the men's rations; there are questions of taste. The Brahmin will not touch beef; the Mahomedan turns up his nose at pork; the Jain is a vegetarian; the Ghurkha loves the flesh of the goat. And every Indian must have his ginger, garlic, red chilli, and turmeric, and his chupattis of unleavened bread. One such warehouse we entered and beheld with stupefaction mountainous boxes of ghee and hogsheads of goor, rice, dried apricots, date-palms, and sultanas. Storekeepers in turbans stood round us, who, being asked whether it was well with the Indian and his food, answered us with a great shout, like the Ephesians, 'Yea, the exalted Government hath done great things and praised be its name.' To which we replied 'Victory to the Holy Ganges water.' Their lustrous eyes beamed at the salutation. Great, indeed, is the Q.M.G. He supplies manna in the wilderness, and like the manna of the Israelites it has never been known to fail.[12]

However, this account belies the complications involved in feeding the different religions and indeed castes which made up the Indian contingent. A. M. Beatson, an ASC driver, noted:

> One of the commissariat problems, which, however, has been solved satisfactorily, was the question of 'Native meat,' or the ration of meat for Indian troops serving in Europe. The solution has been found in the institution of 'Native butcheries'. A Native of high caste in India would, of course, not eat any meat that even the shadow of a European had passed over. In coming to France the Native troops have, however, been granted certain religious dispensations, not only with regard to food, but, in the case of Hindus, in being allowed to leave the boundaries of their own country. Nevertheless, their caste rights as to food are as strictly observed as the exigencies of active service allow. The goats and sheep, chiefly Corsican and Swiss, purchased for their consumption, are sent up in a truck to railhead alive, and are

INDIAN SOLDIER COOKING — IN FRANCE

An Indian soldier on the Western front in 1915, cooking his rations in the traditional manner. (Library of Congress: Bain collection)

slaughtered by men of their own caste in a butchery arranged for the purpose, generally in a field or some open place in close proximity to the railhead. The Mohammedan will eat only goats or sheep slaughtered by having their throats cut, and the Hindu, by their being beheaded. The latter method is carried out in the abattoir by a Native butcher with the aid of a cavalry sword at one fell swoop, and of the two methods is certainly to be recommended as being the most rapid and instantaneous death. I need hardly add that the Native butchery is always looked on as an object of awe and interest, if not of excitement, by the French inhabitants, and none the less by English soldiers.

The Natives do not object to their meat being handled by English soldiers, or to it being brought to them in the same lorry which also perhaps carries British ration beef, although the cow is a sacred animal to the Hindu and in the form of beef is naturally distasteful. The only point is that the goat's meat or mutton intended for their consumption must not actually come into contact with the beef, and this is arranged for by a wooden barrier between the two, erected in the interior of the lorry. On one occasion, however, the native rations for a certain regiment had just been dumped on the side of the road, and were being checked by the Daffadar, or Native Quartermaster-Sergeant, when at a critical moment an old sow, followed by her litter, came out of a farm gate and innocently ran over the whole show. A lot of palaver followed amongst the Natives, and there was no alternative; they would not have these rations at any price, and back they had to be taken to be exchanged. The pig is, of course, abhorrent to the Mussulman.[13]

The Muslim soldiers were not the only ones for whom special provision was necessary. Beatson continues with an account of an incident which occurred near Ypres in the summer of 1915:

The cow being a sacred animal to the Hindu, it became necessary to replace the usual tins of bully beef by a suitable substitute. With this end in view, quantities of tins of preserved mutton were sent up for the consumption of Hindu personnel. The tins in which it was packed, however, unfortunately bore the trade mark of the packers, Messrs. Libby – a bull's head – and in consequence of this the Hindus would not have it that their contents could be anything but beef, until their own Native officers convinced them that such was not the case. It will be seen that the organization for rationing Native troops is such that they are able to be fed in accordance with the rites of their caste, surely a not unimportant factor.[14]

Nevertheless, the difficulty in supplying the Indians, along with the effect of the north European climate upon their health and morale, was one of the reasons for which the Indian Corps was eventually withdrawn from the Western Front.

Feeding Empire troops from the Dominions presented less of a challenge, and these soldiers were nothing if not resourceful. With the settlement of the Western Front into fixed lines, opportunities to supplement official rations soon presented themselves. Canadian sapper George Clark wrote to his brother in January 1916:

I am writing this in the 'Dug Out' where I have been for the last four days. I am sitting on an empty cartridge box watching the supper cook. I am going into camp to night. I have been the cook this turn in the trenches. By the way, I want to thank you for the big box of eats you sent me. They were fine. I didn't open the box at camp where there is so much of that kind of good eats, but brought it out to the dug out where it is appreciated. We certainly did enjoy it; everything was so well packed it was all in good order when it arrived. It is all eaten except what is in the little sealed box. I am taking that back to camp.

I have just turned the bacon. We will have bacon and French fried potatoes tonight, besides bread and jam, butter, tea and milk and sugar. We have had some great meals. Today for dinner I had beefsteak and onions, carrots, turnips, potatoes, bread, tea, and jam for the boys. That doesn't look as if we are suffering much, does it? and we are not! At the 'dugout' we have great meals. We put in a mess fund, a franc a piece for the six men – and that brings us Ideal canned milk, oatmeal, and extra vegetables – then it is up to the cook. For three days I gave the boys stews; besides the meat, there were carrots, turnips, potatoes, pea-meal, onions and cabbage, also several oxo cubes. It surely made a very savory mess. I can understand how a woman loves to cook and have her cooking appreciated. I don't cut the wood or haul the water, the boys rustle the wood out of old destroyed barns, and we get our water out of a little creek nearby.[15]

Of course, officers especially had opportunities to supplement their rations in other ways. Charles Doudney, a Chaplain to the Forces serving near Ypres, wrote in his diary for 8 July 1915:

Kinnear brought out a small 28 bore shotgun with him and the other day he shot five pigeons with it. D____ (my servant) cooked 'em and burnt three to ashes, and as we sat down to eat the other two, two officers came in, and we had to ask them to stay, so we each had one bite and a half![16]

This incident was by no means unique; pigeons were often kept by the Flemish farmers with whom British soldiers were billeted, and often made their way into the cooking pot. One group of Tommies in particular compensated the farmer at the rate of one tin of corned beef for each pigeon they took. Others were probably less scrupulous. In the line, men were as resourceful as it was possible to be, but there the corned beef usually had to be eaten rather than traded. One British soldier wrote in 1916:

> Without his tea Tommy was a wretched being. I do not remember a day, no matter how serious the fighting, when he did not find both the time and the means for making it. Shorty was a Ph.D. in every subject in the curriculum, including domestic science. In preparing breakfast he gave me a practical demonstration of the art of conserving a limited resource of fuel, bringing our two canteens to a boil with a very meager handful of sticks; and while doing so he delivered an oral thesis on the best methods of food preparation. For example, there was the item of corned beef – familiarly called 'bully'. It was the piece de resistance at every meal with the possible exception of breakfast, when there was usually a strip of bacon. Now, one's appetite for 'bully' becomes jaded in the course of a few weeks or months. To use the German expression one doesn't eat it gem. But it is not a question of liking it. One must eat it or go hungry. Therefore, said Shorty, save carefully all of your bacon grease, and instead of eating your 'bully' cold out of the tin, mix it with bread crumbs and grated cheese and fry it in the grease. He prepared some in this way, and I thought it a most delectable dish. Another way of stimulating the palate was to boil the beef in a solution of bacon grease and water, and then, while eating it, 'kid yerself that it's Irish stew'. This second method of taking away the curse did not appeal to me very strongly, and Shorty admitted that he practiced such self-deception with very indifferent success; for after all 'bully' was 'bully' in whatever form you ate it. In addition to this staple, the daily rations consisted of bacon, bread, cheese, jam, army biscuits, tea, and sugar.
>
> Sometimes they received a tinned meat and vegetable ration, already cooked, and at welcome intervals fresh meat and potatoes were substituted for corned beef. Each man had a very generous allowance of food, a great deal more, I thought, than he could possibly eat. Shorty explained this by saying that allowance was made for the amount which would be consumed by the rats and the blue-bottle flies. There were, in fact, millions of flies. They settled in great swarms along the walls of the trenches, which were filled

to the brim with warm light as soon as the sun had climbed a little way up the sky. Empty tin-lined ammunition boxes were used as cupboards for food. But of what avail were cupboards to a jam-loving and jam-fed British army living in open ditches in the summer time? Flytraps made of empty jam tins were set along the top of the parapet. As soon as one was filled, another was set in its place. But it was an unequal war against an expeditionary force of countless numbers. 'They ain't nothin' you can do,' said Shorty. 'They steal the jam right off yer bread.'[17]

The flies of course were a major factor in spreading disease, moving freely between the latrines, corpses in no man's land, and the food consumed by the men in the trenches.

Alexander McClintock was serving with a Canadian battalion in France in 1916 and wrote vividly of his experiences in the front line. To McClintock's account may be added the fact that in addition to most of the food coming up to the front line in sandbags, much of the time fresh water was carried up in disused petrol tins. These being almost impossible to clean completely, the water always tasted strongly of petrol. This was a memory of the Western Front which many veterans carried with them to their dying day. McClintock writes:

Our rations in the trenches were, on the whole, excellent. There were no delicacies and the food was not over plentiful, but it was good. The system appeared to have the purpose of keeping us like bulldogs before a fight – with enough to live on but hungry all the time. Our food consisted principally of bacon, beans, beef, bully-beef, hard tack, jam and tea. Occasionally we had a few potatoes, and, when we were taken back for a few days' rest, we got a good many things which difficulty of transport excluded from the front trenches. It was possible, sometimes, to beg, borrow or even steal eggs and fresh bread and coffee.

All of our provisions came up to the front line in sand bags, a fact easily recognizable when you tasted them. There is supposed to be an intention to segregate the various foods, in transport, but it must be admitted that they taste more or less of each other, and that the characteristic sand-bag flavor distinguishes all of them from mere, ordinary foods which have not made a venturesome journey. As many of the sand bags have been originally used for containing brown sugar, the flavor is more easily recognized than actually unpleasant. When we got down to the Somme, the food supply was much less satisfactory – principally because of transport difficulties.

Right: An empty bottle of Mason's OK Sauce, found behind the British front line on the Somme. Bottled sauces and preserves were frequently sent to the Tommies in France by families at home. Above: The remains of British army food tins found at White City, on the Somme battlefield. The round ones probably contained jam or condensed milk. The British made extensive use of tinned food in the First World War. (Courtesy of John Caley)

At times, even in the rear, we could get fresh meat only twice a week, and were compelled to live the rest of the time on bully-beef stew, which resembles terrapin to the extent that it is a liquid with mysterious lumps in it. In the front trenches, on the Somme, all we had were the 'iron rations' which we were able to carry in with us. These consisted of bully-beef, hard tack, jam and tea. The supply of these foods which each man carries is termed 'emergency rations,' and the ordinary rule is that the emergency ration must not be touched until the man has been forty-eight hours without food, and then only by permission of an officer.[18]

McClintock's account is paralleled by that of another American in the British army, Arthur Guy Empey, who wrote:

[Tommy] carries in his haversack what the government calls emergency or iron rations. They are not supposed to be opened until Tommy dies of starvation. They consist of one tin of bully beef, four biscuits, a little tin which contains tea, sugar, and Oxo cubes (concentrated beef tablets). These are only to be used when the enemy establishes a curtain of shell fire on the communication trenches, thus preventing the 'carrying in' of rations, or when in an attack, a body of troops has been cut off from its base of supplies. The rations are brought up, at night, by the Company Transport. This is a section of the company in charge of the Quartermaster-Sergeant, composed of men, mules, and limbers (two-wheeled wagons), which supplies Tommy's wants while in the front line. They are constantly under shell fire. The rations are unloaded at the entrance to the communication trenches and are 'carried in' by men detailed for that purpose. The Quartermaster-Sergeant never goes into the front-line trench. He doesn't have to, and I have never heard of one volunteering to do so. The Company Sergeant-Major sorts the rations, and sends them in. Tommy's trench rations consist of all the bully beef he can eat, biscuits, cheese, tinned butter (sometimes seventeen men to a tin), jam, or marmalade, and occasionally fresh bread (ten to a loaf). When it is possible, he gets tea and stew. When things are quiet, and Fritz is behaving like a gentleman, which seldom happens, Tommy has the opportunity of making dessert. This is 'trench pudding.' It is made from broken biscuits, condensed milk, jam – a little water added, slightly flavored with mud – put into a canteen and cooked over a little spirit stove known as 'Tommy's cooker'. . . This mess is stirred up in a tin and allowed to simmer over the flames from the cooker until Tommy decides that it has reached a sufficient (gluelike) consistency. He takes his bayonet and by means of the handle carries the mess up in the front trench to cool. After it has cooled off he tries to eat it. Generally one or two Tommies in a section have cast-iron stomachs and the tin is soon emptied.[19]

The other staple of the front-line Tommy was the rum ration, issued each morning from earthenware jars. The rum was produced in Jamaica and shipped to France in large vats, from which it was diluted and decanted into the jars for its journey to the front line. These jars were marked 'S.R.D.' which is variously understood to have represented Special Ration Distribution, Service Rum Diluted or more probably Supply Reserve Depot. For the Tommies the initials were an endless source of fascination and humour. To them, the letters stood for 'Soon Runs Dry' or 'Seldom Reaches Destination'. It was supposed to be issued by an NCO under the supervision of an officer to ensure both that the allocation was fair and also that the men consumed it on the spot, rather than hoarding it. The issue of rum to the men was deeply controversial at the time, for the temperance movement had spent many years in Victorian and Edwardian Britain campaigning against alcohol and its damaging effects upon the poorest sections of society. Now, as they saw it, the army was placing temptation in the path of honourable young men who had signed up to do the right thing by their God and country. Some of those in senior positions in the army felt the same way, and one general in particular was notorious for abolishing the rum issue in his division. This earned him the disdain of men like Frank Richards, who labelled him a 'bun punching crank'. However, some of the men in the ranks also had temperance tendencies. The memories of one young soldier named Fred Smith, serving with the East Yorkshire Regiment remained fresh as late as the 1980s. Despite the fact that he was, in his words, 'shaking like a leaf' during his first spell in the front line, he refused to countenance rum as a nerve stiffener, in the process earning the ire of the veteran under whose wing he had been placed:

> The listening post was a slit trench about thirty yards in front of the trenches . . . There were two of us in there. This other fellow was an old soldier, he was a regular soldier, he belonged to the 2nd battalion East Yorkshires, and he was a 21 year man. I was only a recruit in those days, I'd only been in the army about four months, and he said, 'You come with me, I'll volunteer then you volunteer to go out on listening post' . . . Anyhow, that night we had about four or five hours in this slit trench, and our time was up and we got relieved . . . And along came the rum ration. Me being a staunch tee-totaller in those days – I was only seventeen and I belonged to the Independent Order of Good Templars, and I never used to drink any alcohol or anything like that because I was a staunch tee-totaller. Anyhow I threw mine away, and this fellow, Drummer Carney his name was, he played into me because I threw it away. He said, 'Why didn't you give it to me?' I said I didn't want it, I told him I was a tee-totaller, well he said, 'Next time it comes round, I'll have it, don't throw it away!' They just poured it into your dixie, you got about half a cupful . . .[20]

Other men, who did partake of rum, deplored the suggestion made by teetotallers on the home front that they were drunk when going into action. Another young soldier, Jack Horner of the Leicestershire Regiment, remembered an incident which took place whilst he was home on convalescent leave in 1916:

> I was in the Market Place [in Leicester] – a man on a traditional soap box was telling the world at large that the troops and soldiers were made deliberately drunk, to force them to go into action. I listened with amazement, and I asked him if he had been in France, and in action. He said, 'No.' I asked him who had told him the story

Drummer Thomas Carney, of the East Yorkshire Regiment, who berated Fred Smith for throwing away his rum ration. (Author's collection)

of soldiers being made drunk. He replied that it was common knowledge. I pressed him to say where he had all his information from. He could not give a reply.

Then I let him have a few choice words, and told him he was a bloody liar (and I really meant that), and to keep his mouth shut, or I would shut it for him, as I had just been in the Battle of the Somme where I was wounded and sent to Hospital, and was now on leave, and I told him (and by now a rather large crowd of people were listening to what I had to say), that if he thought that two jars of rum of one gallon each between seven or eight hundred men would make any man drunk, then I would pour the bloody lot down his throat. He got off his perch and walked off with a flea in his ear. Some of the people thanked me, including a policeman who had been listening to all that I told this man, and he told me that he had said the same thing about the troops and soldiers many times, and was very pleased indeed that I had put the teetotal fanatic in his place. He said he would keep an eye on him in future.[21]

Nevertheless, with so many soldiers in France, and so many jars of rum going up to the front line, it was inevitable that there would be some instances of drunkenness. There were stories for example of soldiers finding a full jar of rum which had been abandoned by a ration party caught in a shell burst, and drinking it all to themselves. There is also evidence contrary to that of Horner, which suggests that sometimes rum was indeed liberally used as a 'stiffener' for troops about to go into action. Private Leonard Wilkinson of the 15th Battalion London Regiment (Civil Service Rifles) went over the top on 15 September 1916 near High Wood. Wilkinson remembered the tension in the hours leading up to zero hour (for him it was at 6.30 a.m.) and the fact that the men had had no sleep as they awaited the order to attack. The rum ration was passed around, and Wilkinson's substantial portion was further augmented by that from men who had abstained. He freely admitted to having had 'plenty', and that this had more than put him in the mood for killing Germans.

It was more common for British officers to carry whisky or brandy, usually in a hip flask. As a nerve tonic, or to assuage the effects of shock, it was undoubtedly invaluable at times. Exactly how many officers came to rely upon it as a crutch is something of a moot point. The fictional character of Captain Stanhope in R. C. Sherriff's play *Journey's End* is depicted as just such a man, one who has seen too much of the war and now can only function with the aid of whisky. The French soldier more or less lived on cheap white wine, and British soldiers were amused by the fact that 'ving blong' was almost universally carried in their canteen by French *polius*; the Germans for their part mostly consumed either beer or wine, or on occasion schnapps. In early 1915 an American journalist, visiting a Bavarian regiment in the front line near Ypres, only 800 yards from the French positions, was invited to dine with the colonel at a nearby farmhouse. He wrote:

A comfortable yellow light falls from the yellow lamp in the center of the table. We begin to feel as snug as a fireside cat. 'Our knives and forks are rather limited,' apologizes the Adjutant, who introduces himself as Hauptmann Koller, a tall handsome Bavarian with a scraggy black growth on his chin. 'However, there are dishes enough to go around.' I begin to have a suspicion that our sympathy has been absurd. Black bread and army wurst never gave out the odors that are coming from those pots on the stoves, and then our surprise is complete when the Colonel offers us a cocktail. Cocktails, and the French trenches eight hundred meters away!

'A German cocktail,' smiles the Colonel, as he pours out the white schnapps, 'not like the kind you have in America. One of my friends had a bottle of them in München – Bronx cocktails,' and the Colonel makes a grimace. There are only two cordial glasses, but by passing them around, we succeed in drinking the Colonel's health . . . Hauptmann Koller, who is opposite, is hacking off chunks of bread from a round rye loaf. On my other side Reed is looking at the bottle of schnapps and wearing his unextinguishable smile. A soldier brings a pot from the stove and the Colonel serves us. It is an oxtail stew, canned of course, but smells appetizing. 'The Colonel hasn't any left for himself,' exclaims Poole; but the Colonel is holding up his hand. 'There is plenty,' he says, and the soldier

A German Steinhäger *schnapps bottle, found on the Somme battlefield.* (Courtesy of John Caley)

brings another steaming pot. Magically, tall, dark liter bottles make their appearance and on the labels I see 'Hacker-Brau.' 'Münchener Beer,' cries Reed. 'Isn't this amazing?' The Colonel looks at Hauptmann Koller and grins. I think that from their viewpoint they are enjoying it as much as we. Canned boiled beef follows the stew; more of the tall, dark bottles appear.[22]

Out of the line, in the towns and larger villages, soldiers had the opportunity to buy foodstuffs to supplement their rations. Empey continued:

At the different French estaminets in the village, and at the canteens, Tommy buys fresh eggs, milk, bread, and pastry. Occasionally when he is flush, he invests in a tin of pears or apricots. His pay is only a shilling a day . . .[23]

In October 1916 an American lady, Mrs Waddington was visiting wounded at Hazebrouck, a major base town behind the British lines, and describes an incident which she witnessed in one of the shops there:

British soldiers buying extra rations from French civilians at Etaples, the location of a major British base camp. (Library of Congress: Bain collection)

The shops are what one would find in any English provincial town – food (jam, of course, of all kinds), clothes, beds, illustrated papers. The 'Tommies' seem on the best of terms with the townspeople. They pay well for everything they take . . . There are a great many Anzacs (Australians and New Zealanders) in the streets . . . I was amused with some of them I met the other day in a shop. I and several other people were buying fruit, grapes, pears. The patronne showed us a fine bunch of white grapes. They looked very good, firm and yellow where the sun had touched them. 'How much?' said one of the men. ''Three francs fifty,' replied the woman. Upon which the man broke into a loud peal of incredulous laughter, saying: 'You won't sell any at that price. In my country, we get a big basket full for one shilling,' and he and his companions went off whistling and laughing, but declining absolutely any purchases.[24]

Whilst out of the line, in bivouacs or billets in more or less damaged French villages, British troops were generally fed from field kitchens. Robert Derby Holmes was an American serving in the British army, and had a keen eye for the eccentric ways of the Tommy when it came to food. He wrote:

I had the job of issuing the rations of our platoon, and it nearly drove me mad. Every morning I would detail a couple of men from our platoon to be standing mess orderlies for the day. They would fetch the char and bacon from the field kitchen in the morning and clean up the 'dixies' after breakfast. The 'dixie', by the way, is an iron box or pot, oblong in shape, capacity about four or five gallons. It fits into the field kitchen and is used for roasts, stews, char, or anything else. The cover serves to cook bacon in. Field kitchens are drawn by horses and follow the battalion everywhere that it is safe to go, and to some places where it isn't. Two men are detailed from each company to cook, and there is usually another man who gets the sergeants' mess, besides the officers' cook, who does not as a rule use the field kitchen, but prepares the food in the house taken as the officers' mess. As far as possible, the company cooks are men

British soldiers in a rest camp behind the lines in France. Note the large dixies in which stew was prepared. (Author's collection)

Imp. et Edit. J. Bouvere – Le Mans

Souvenir de la Guerre Européenne 1914. — Troupes Anglaises (au 1er plan un Ecossais)

who were cooks in civil life, but not always. We drew a plumber and a navvy (road builder) – and the grub tasted of both trades. The way our company worked the kitchen problem was to have stew for two platoons one day and roast dinner for the others, and then reverse the order next day, so that we didn't have stew all the time. There were not enough 'dixies' for us all to have stew the same day.

Every afternoon I would take my mess orderlies and go to the quartermaster's stores and get our allowance and carry it back to the billets in waterproof sheets. Then the stuff that was to be cooked in the kitchen went there, and the bread and that sort of material was issued direct to the men. That was where my trouble started. The powers that were had an uncanny knack of issuing an odd number of articles to go among an even number of men, and vice versa. There would be eleven loaves of bread to go to a platoon of fifty men divided into four sections. Some of the sections would have ten men and some twelve or thirteen. The British Tommy is a scrapper when it comes to his rations. He reminds me of an English sparrow. He's always right in there wangling for his own. He will bully and brow-beat if he can, and he will coax and cajole if he can't. It would be 'Hi sye, corporal. They's ten men in Number 2 section and fourteen in ourn. An' blimme if you hain't guv 'em four loaves, same as ourn. Is it right, I arsks yer? Is it?' Or, 'Lookee! Do yer call that a loaf o' bread? Looks like the A. S. C. (Army Service Corps) been using it fer a piller. Gimme another, will yer, corporal?'

When it comes to splitting seven onions nine ways, I defy anyone to keep peace in the family, and every doggoned Tommy would hold out for his onion whether he liked 'em or not. Same way with a bottle of pickles to go among eleven men or a handful of raisins or apricots. Or jam or butter or anything, except bully beef or Maconochie. I never heard any one 'argue the toss' on either of those commodities. Bully is high-grade corned beef in cans and is O.K. if you like it, but it does get tiresome. Maconochie ration is put up a pound to the can and bears a label which assures the consumer that it is a scientifically prepared, well-balanced ration. Maybe so. It is my personal opinion that the inventor brought to his task an imperfect knowledge of cookery and a perverted imagination. Open a can of Maconochie and you find a gooey gob of grease, like rancid lard. Investigate and you find chunks of carrot and other unidentifiable material, and now and then a bit of mysterious meat. The first man who ate an oyster had courage, but the last man who ate Maconochie's unheated had more. Tommy regards it as a very inferior grade of garbage. The label notwithstanding, he's right.[25]

An advertisement for Maconochie's tinned stew, one of the commonest tinned food products in use by the British army. (Author's collection)

Empey was equally scathing about the product, and gave a tongue-in-cheek definition of it as follows:

> Maconochie. A ration of meat, vegetables, and soapy water, contained in a tin. Mr. Maconochie, the chemist who compounded this mess, intends to commit 'hari kari' before the boys return from the front. He is wise.[26]

Sometimes Maconochie was used as the basis for a stew with other items added. A Canadian officer named Wells wrote home describing one such concoction in 1916:

> I took a great responsibility upon myself to-night. The cooks of my party are rather in-experienced. They have on hand to-night some fresh vegetables, some tins of baked beans, and some tins of Macconachie [*sic*] (tinned Irish stew). The two latter require to be heated only before being eaten, while the vegetables (turnips and

Oxo was a British brand which frequently made use of its popularity among soldiers in France in its advertising, in order to increase domestic sales. (Author's collection)

Welco Cocoa, one of many 'comforts' sent to British soldiers at the Front by families at home. (Author's collection).

cabbage) of course require a thorough cooking. We have no facilities for cooking the three things separately, so I have told the cooks to cook the vegetables, and then add both the beans and the Macconachie. They are very unwilling to mix the three ingredients in this manner, but I cannot see why the result should not be very good indeed. As I do not want to have a sick party on my hands, I am waiting anxiously for the result of the experiment.[27]

The official rations of the British soldier were also supplemented by whatever was sent to him in parcels from home. In some cases, if the family of the soldier was wealthy, these could be inordinately extravagant. The London department store Fortnum & Mason would send hampers to the Western Front and these were apparently common among the aristocratic offers in guards regiments. For the ordinary Tommy, however, a cardboard box, tied up with string and containing perhaps a homemade cake was as much as they might expect. Robert Derby Holmes, the American serving in a British regiment, wrote revealingly of those other items which were most eagerly sought in parcels from home:

Many people have asked me what to send our soldiers in the line of food. I'd say stick to sweets. Cookies of any durable kind – I mean that will stand chance moisture – the sweeter the better, and if possible those containing raisins or dried fruit. Figs, dates, etc., are good. And, of course, chocolate. Personally, I never did have enough chocolate. Candy is acceptable, if it is of the sort to stand more or less rough usage which it may get before it reaches the soldier. Chewing gum is always received gladly. The army issue of sweets is limited pretty much to jam, which gets to taste all alike.

It is pathetic to see some of the messes Tommy gets together to fill his craving for dessert. The favorite is a slum composed of biscuit, water, condensed milk, raisins, and chocolate. If some of you folks at home would get one look at that concoction, let alone tasting it, you would dash out and spend your last dollar for a package to send to some lad 'over there'.[28]

After the close of hostilities, the nutritionist Arthur Knapp, writing on the history of chocolate and its production, commented specifically upon its value to the soldiers of the First World War. Indeed, he went further and stated that many men who had previously not encountered chocolate before (either because it was a luxury item and out of their reach, or because they were not interested, perceiving it as being merely for children) were introduced to it for the first time during the war. This resulted in increased consumption of chocolate by men in the post-war years. Knapp added:

During the war chocolate was valued as a compact foodstuff, which is easily preserved. Dr. Gastineau Earle, lecturing for the Institute of Hygiene in 1915 on 'Food Factor in War', said: 'Chocolate is a most valuable concentrated food, especially when other foods are not available; it is the chief constituent of the emergency ration.' Its importance as a concentrated foodstuff was appreciated in the United States, for every 'comfort kit' made up for the American soldiers fighting in the war contained a cake of sweet chocolate.[29]

Much of this chapter thus far has dealt with food supply during the static conditions of trench warfare. Difficult though this may have been, it was as nothing compared to the erratic nature of the food supply – and the consequent hardships endured by the troops – during a major battle. During the Somme offensive in 1916, soldiers might have to survive for several days just on what they could scrounge, for ration parties were sporadic at best. One German soldier in the front line here wrote of being cut off by the British advance and, with two comrades, surviving on 'ersatz' or substitute foodstuffs:

> In the evening of 6 July the company had sent possibly sixteen to eighteen men to fetch rations from the sugar factory near Longueval. The ration party did not return. Who knows, what became of them? The next day the sergeant comrade from Elberfeld produced a mess tin in which were the remains of a sordid lard substitute. He warmed up the contents with help of a candle stub, and thus we three held a banquet with tiny servings.[30]

It was not only the Germans who were struggling to find enough to eat in the shattered wilderness of the battlefield. British author Frank Richards served with the Royal Welsh Fusiliers on the Somme and remembered the situation near High Wood in July 1916. In his book *Old Soldiers Never Die* he writes:

> Just inside the wood, which was a great tangle of broken trees and branches, was a German trench, and all around it our dead and theirs were laying. I was in luck's way. I got two tins of Machonochies and half a loaf of bread . . . The bread was very stale and it was a wonder the rats hadn't got at it.[31]

Frank Richards, who wrote frankly in his memoirs of the reality of food supply in combat conditions – including the fact that soldiers were often forced to survive on food taken from dead comrades. (Courtesy of Margaret Holmes)

German POWs in a camp in the south of France, cooking their rations in the open air. (Library of Congress)

In the same brigade as Richards' battalion was the 20th Royal Fusiliers, the Public Schools Battalion. Many of these well-educated young men would have been better employed if commissioned as officers, rather than serving in the ranks as private soldiers, but Richards comments that they received more food parcels than all the other battalions in the brigade combined. After an attack, it was customary to distribute the parcels intended for those who had been killed among the survivors. After the battle for High Wood the Public Schools Battalion had suffered such heavy casualties that their parcels were distributed throughout the brigade. Richards commented that he and his comrades lived on luxuries for the next few days.

By the winter of 1916, the official rations of the German front-line soldier had already been reduced once and were about to be reduced further. Small wonder then that Allied propaganda emphasised the fact that those Germans who were living the best now were those who had been taken prisoner and who were held in Allied POW camps. There was of course a considerable element of truth in this. In French POW camps behind the lines, food was certainly plentiful for German prisoners. An American diplomat, Lee Meriwether, had special responsibility for inspecting the conditions in which prisoners were held. In November 1916 he visited a camp near Rouen, commenting afterwards:

> In Biesard's kitchen we saw eleven German cooks standing beside as many huge cauldrons; the cooks ladled out soup into the tin bowls of the prisoners as they filed by, and so expert were they, the line did not halt – it moved slowly, but continuously, so that the twelve hundred men were served in less than half an hour. As each man passed out of the kitchen he went to his barrack and there ate his dinner of steaming soup, bread, coffee and water. The soup, filled with potatoes and beef, tasted good to me, but no doubt after two years I would have as great a distaste for it as some of the prisoners told me they have. But none said the food was insufficient in quantity or that it lacked nourishment.[32]

For the British front-line soldier, this winter was to be the hardest yet experienced in France. For many living in the open on the devastated Somme battlefield, conditions were harsh in the extreme. There were no intact villages for several miles behind the line, and hot food had to be carried across the morass for hours by struggling ration parties. By the time it got to the men freezing in waterlogged shell holes, it was usually cold. No wonder then that a particular innovation took hold at this time. A journalist named Basil Clarke reported upon the conditions which he found on several of the war fronts, and in his memoirs he recounted something which he had observed whilst in France:

> One excellent little idea I noticed gaining ground among our men in the winter of 1916–1917, one which I think the authorities might have looked upon more helpfully. It was the 'Primus stove club' custom. Three or four 'pals' of a company would club together to buy a Primus stove. It has an oil reservoir, a little hand-pump to create air pressure, and a burner. You heat up the burner with some loose oil, pump up the pressure, prod the burner holes with a pin to clear them of burnt oil and away goes the stove burner into a circle of blue flame, which burns with a pleasing little drone of its own that is quite companionable – and not loud enough to be overheard by 'Fritz' in the enemy's trench. There is no smoke at all, just a little ring of roaring blue flame. Very 'devilish' it looks, down in the blackness of a trench on a dark night. As these stoves and the fuel

for them were not an Army 'issue' the trouble was to get your oil fuel up to the trenches. You might carry up a small supply begged, borrowed, bought or stolen, from someone down in your rest billets, but there was nothing like regularity of supply, and such small private supplies as could be taken up to the trenches by soldiers having many other things to carry, soon gave out. Paraffin is the right fuel, but it was not easy to get, even behind the lines; and you found daring young campaigners using petrol obtained (irregularly, of course) from friendly motor drivers 'away behind'.

A Primus in a trench was invaluable, not because a soldier could warm himself on a cold day by its modest heat, but because he could prepare on it hot drink and could warm up rations, which in their turn warmed him. One little Primus club that I came across warmed up all their tinned food before they opened it. The method was to put the food tins into water boiling on their Primus. Bully beef, Maconachie stew, salmon, and the rest, were all served hot in this club. One genius of the party heated even tins of jam, vowing that no other food was really so hot and so warming as hot jam. They dipped spoons into the tin and ate their jam so hot that tears ran down their cheeks. Still you could stand heat in 'quantities' in the trenches of the Somme![33]

It was also possible for soldiers to cook bacon using a primus stove, and the writer Robert Graves noted in his memoirs that for him, the all-pervading smell of the front-line trenches was that of bacon frying.

As noted earlier, water usually came up to the front lines in petrol tins, but there was another source available to soldiers. Frank Richards, serving on the Arras front in 1917, tells us:

At night we used to pop over the parapet of the trench and into any shellhole when we wanted to go to the latrine. We also got our drinking water from the shell holes. On the third night we discovered that the water we had been drinking and making tea with had been brought from a shell hole which a couple of us had used for another purpose. I asked the man who had brought the jars of water the night before to come and show me which shell hole he had brought it from, as it seemed better water than the stuff we had the day before. He replied, 'You come with me and I'll show you the best shell-hole water in France.' We hopped over the top and he took me to a shell hole which I knew very well. When I told him so he exclaimed, 'Hell, how was I to know?' I also took a jar of water from this hole for the officer's cook, who gave me a packet of

Woodbines and a piece of bread for it. He told me during the day
that the officers had complimented him on the excellent tea he had
made with it. I didn't fill my jar out of that hole but went to another,
and the same thing may have happened there for all I knew.[34]

This was to become a particularly dangerous practice later in the war, after
the introduction of mustard gas on the Western Front in the autumn of 1917.
This type of gas tended to settle in shell holes, and could be absorbed by
standing water. There were reported instances of numbers of men poisoned
by tea made from water contaminated with mustard gas. A few days after
the shell hole incident, Richards' battalion was in support in an attack on
the Hindenburg Line. In an extraordinary paragraph, he writes in his usual
matter-of-fact way of the grisly steps which men would take to find
sustenance in such a situation:

> The following day we were without food and water and during the
> night some of us were out searching the dead to see if they had been
> carrying any with them. I was lucky enough to discover a half-loaf
> of bread, some biscuits and two bottles of water, which I would not
> have sold for a thousand pounds.[35]

Getting food up to the troops in the front-line trenches was fraught with
danger, not just for the British, but for all those on the Western Front.
Georges Lafond was a sergeant in the French Army, who described one
typical incident:

> The time for supplying the company in the lines comes. The men of
> the field kitchens come by groups of three or four from the trenches
> just behind us. The first two have a long rod on their shoulders and
> rolls of bread on this. Others carry in canvas pails and kettles come
> from nowhere the coveted wine and the aromatic brandy. Others
> bend under the weight of pots which hold lumpy black bean soup,
> which splashes out at every jolt in the path. It is already cold and
> greasy. Finally, the mess corporal reaches the end of his trip and
> draws out of his sack the desserts bought with the mess balance and
> the commissions given to him the day before by the men in the
> trenches.
>   The pockets of his jackets are full of letters he has just received
> from the officer with the mail, and which he delivers to the men
> who have been waiting for them hungrily. When he gets as far as the
> fatigue party he stops and hesitates. He must go over a space of fifty
> yards, absolutely exposed, to the edge of a group of trees where

A humourous French postcard, showing a well-fed poilu. *French propaganda made much of the fact that their soldiers ate* pain blanc *(white bread), whilst the Germans ate inferior* pain k.k.*(koningen kriegsbrot – war bread).* (Author's collection)

there is a first-line trench taken from the Boches in the last attack and not yet connected with the communication trench. He has reason for his hesitation, for the last two days the Boche trench on our left has been firing on it heavily. Day before yesterday an entire fatigue party was killed. We can see there in front of us the abandoned sacks and scattered packages. Five men out of eight were killed yesterday. The others were able to get over some of the provisions and the bad news by crawling, and at the price of a thousand risks. They also took the rest of the provisions from the bodies of their comrades who carried them. To-day they advanced the time of bringing the supplies an hour in order to foil the enemy's vigilance.[36]

A tin of Dejeuner de L'Aumonier, a malted drink similar to Ovaltine, and advertised as being popular with French soldiers. The uniform depicted on the tin dates it to mid- or late war. (Author's collection)

In early 1917 the Chinese Labour Corps began to arrive in France. In total some 140,000 Chinese indentured labourers would serve on the Western Front before the end of the war. Like the Indians before them, they had their own dietary requirements, though these seem to have been by no means as rigid as those of their Asiatic neighbours. In a remarkable book, the title of which can be rendered in English as *Memoirs of European War Work*, a young translator by the name of Xingqing Gu who served with the Corps

Members of the Chinese Labour Corps. These workers were recruited by the British for construction duties behind the lines from 1917 onwards, and great efforts were made to supply them with food to which they were accustomed. (Author's collection)

records the only known account of the First World War by a Chinese national. In the book, he gives the following description of the dietary arrangements for the Chinese:

> We had three meals a day, sitting on the ground in the field to eat bread and butter for lunch, because it was not easy to cook outside camp, but we had breakfast and dinner in the camp. The British gave a great deal of consideration to our diet. Some of us from north China were in favour of foods made from flour, but the others from south China favoured rice. Initially, the British provided us with cheese, cereal, and so on which we were not used to eating. Later they supplied us with cream, rice, noodles, and other things which we all liked to eat very much. Without the consideration of the British, we could not have had meals which we liked. The food was sufficient and delicious. Most of the food was imported, as the United Kingdom is an industrial country. Our daily meal consisted of:

> Beef or lamb, 4 ounces
> Rice, 10 ounces
> Flour, 6 ounces
> Vegetables (potatoes and onions), 8 ounces
> Sugar, 1 ounce
> Ham, 2 ounces
> Oil, 1.5 ounces
> Cheese, 1 ounce
> Tea, 0.8 ounces.[37]

To the kaleidoscope of nations represented on the Western Front would soon be added American troops, of both the black and white races, as in mid-1917, units of the US army began to cross the Atlantic. One of these men, travelling on the liner *King of Italy*, was named Edward Trueblood. His account reminds us that blacks and whites serving in the US military at this time were segregated, and nowhere was this more apparent than at mealtimes, when blacks ate after the whites had first been fed:

> The kitchens and mess rooms of the transport were on the top deck. Meal tickets were issued to the men, and when they went to mess, the tickets were punched. This is the way the Government kept track of the number of meals served, as these tickets were collected when we left the boat. The white men were fed first, and the colored troopers afterwards. This was done so as to keep free of any possibility of racial trouble, and apparently it worked well.[38]

However, Trueblood was less than thrilled with the standard of fare served to his countrymen. His account reminds us that in the supposedly democratic United States, at this time as well as racial distinctions there were also differences between the officers and the men in terms of standard of food:

> The beef that we were given consisted of only the poorest and toughest parts. The good cuts went to the mess for the army officers and for the officers and crew of the ship. The potatoes that we were fed were the poorest that I have ever seen. They were served about half cooked, and were small, wet, soggy and unpalatable. It was seldom that a potato fit to eat was given to the men. We received rice several times, but it was only about half cooked. During one meal we were given bologne sausage, and after some of the boys had eaten their allotment, the discovery was made that the sausage was full of maggots. The soup was like water with neither flavor nor body. The bread served was Italian-French bread made with sour dough, and not at all palatable to an American, who has been accustomed to sweet and wholesome bread. The coffee was of the poorest quality – probably mostly chickory – and we were given neither milk nor sugar for it. The result was that most of the boys did not touch their coffee at all. The only seasoning given our food was an insufficiency of salt. Everything served was tasteless, unpalatable and unwholesome. That there was better food on the boat, we knew, for we could see it going to the officers' tables. They were served chicken two or three times a week – the men never. Officers were given fresh fruit at every meal – the men not at all. Officers were given palatable, sweet bread; the men only when they would pay for it out of their own pockets and then at a big price.[39]

Arriving in France, units of the American Expeditionary Force began the march from their disembarkation ports to the front line. One of these 'doughboys' wrote of his early experiences, and it seems that food once in France was an improvement on that at sea:

> Every mile we advanced our spirits climbed higher and so did our appetites. In the middle of the hike we stopped for chow, which was served from a rolling kitchen. Beans, bacon, rice, bread and coffee was the menu, and we devoured the rations like a pack of hungry wolves.[40]

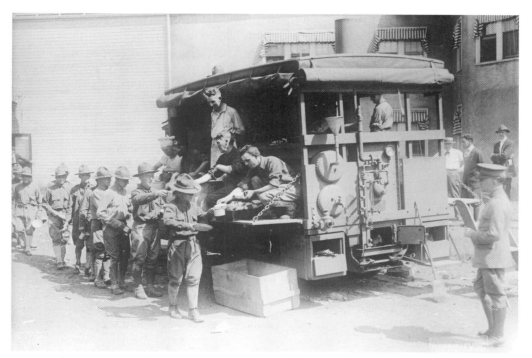

American 'Doughboys' receive a meal from a mobile field kitchen, around 1918.
(Library of Congress)

Quartered in billets in the winter of 1917/18, the same soldier, Osborne De Varila, continued:

> Breakfast was our best meal, consisting of bacon, hardtack, coffee and potatoes with the jackets on. At noon we had a sandwich and at night beef stew, coffee and hardtack. The food improved wonderfully after the raising of the second Liberty Loan over in America.[41]

In the spring of 1918, movement returned to the battlefield as the Germans launched a series of major offensives designed to win the war before the Americans could arrive on the front line in sufficient numbers to make a difference. Alcoholic drink once again influenced events on the battlefield when the last of these great offensives, near Rheims, petered out as the Germans overran well-stocked cellars of champagne. The empty bottles littering the streets in the wake of the attacking troops told their own story. Nevertheless, thousands of British soldiers were taken prisoner in the offensives on the Somme, near Ypres and at Soissons, and they would now find themselves dependent for their survival upon whatever rations their German captors could spare them. The British POWs were now at the back of a metaphorical queue behind the German army and German civilian population, neither of which had enough food for their own requirements. This situation would require all the ingenuity which the British prisoners possessed. Like many of those men captured in the spring of 1918, George Scroby of the Cheshire Regiment was not taken to Germany proper, but was held behind the German lines in France and was employed on labouring duties. He wrote afterwards of the hardships which he and his fellow POWs endured:

> [We] managed to make the food spin out by various additions and substitutes such as gathering Nettles and Dandelions old Cabbage Etc which we were able to gather whilst out working. I had a host of old cooking utensils which I found in the ruined villages we passed through, such as frying pans, saucepans, bowls, and tin mugs and bowls which were all very useful. On returning to our ramshackle billet I used to cook the nettles Etc over a fire in the yard to make a bit of a meal. Another meal was made better by an idea which very soon spread until everyone had caught it. The Bread ration was broken up by us into small pieces and put into a pan and boiled in the coffee that we were issued with. This we used to stir over our fire until a thick paste or pudding was made and any jam or meat that we had managed to be issued with was added and made a more appetising and filling meal then the dry German Black Bread.
>
> We often found useful articles when we were salvaging dug-outs and trenches and these were allowed to be kept by us. I found two towels, four handkerchiefs and a shirt and a pair of pants which I washed on a Sunday and made good. Besides the Herbs mentioned, some of the fellows driven by hunger even went to the extent of gathering snails from the trees and cooking them like winkles and any time that a dead horse was found there was always a rush for a slice or two and it was a common sight to see a crowd of them kneeling round one and cutting lumps off which they took to the billet to cook.[42]

The contrast in experience that summer, between these POWs in German hands and the prevailing conditions just a few miles away behind the Allied lines, is striking. Food supplies from the United States were now reaching France in quantity. Chewing gum had first been introduced in France by the

French POWs in German hands receive a ration of soup. (Library of Congress)

British army in 1917, as it was believed that it helped steady the nerves before an attack. It was also, not surprisingly, widely issued to US soldiers, Benedict Crowell writing of the quantities which were shipped to France by producers in America:

> The winter consumption of gum was heavier than that of summer, the average monthly supply being only 1,500,000 packages. A total of 3,500,000 packages represent the overseas shipment in January, 1919. The shipment for February was 3,200,000 packages. Chewing gum came to be seen as a necessity by the men in France and has been found to be an invaluable aid to keep up their spirits in the midst of hardships.[43]

In June 1918 an American girl working with a canteen attached to a US field hospital found herself stationed near a French hospital, which was also treating wounded Tommies. One afternoon the Americans entertained some of the French and British, and the higher standard of American food was soon evident:

> . . . the water boiled and we made the tea and carried cups and bowls of it around with canned milk and commissary sugar. The Frenchmen, true to type, with the scarcity of sugar in mind would only take one lump, until you invited them to have another, when

Two advertisements for Wrigley's chewing gum. First used on the Western Front by the British and Canadian armies, the product was also enormously popular with US forces. (Author's collection)

each, with evident pleasure, took a second. As we could only muster six teaspoons between our two canteens to supply the whole company, we had to pass the spoons from guest to guest allowing each man just long enough for a good stir and then on to the next. The men with wounded arms got their neighbors to stir for them. With the tea we served sandwiches; these were a special treat to the poilus because they were made with American army bread. Now to my mind our white army bread is very poor and tasteless stuff in comparison with the grey well-flavored French war-bread, but the French, probably on account of the novelty, prize highly any scraps of the pain Americain that they can obtain. 'Why, they eat it just like cake!' one boy said to me. Besides the sandwiches, there were little cookies and candies and cigarettes and finally, the gift of an American officer who happened in, an orange for each man to take home with him.[44]

Another American soldier, Bob Hoffman, was following up the German retreat that summer and autumn. Those American troops on the front line did not always have the luxury of eating bread baked by their own ovens. Ironically it was French bread that Hoffman remembered best, and the conditions in which the men received it were far from ideal:

> Our bread rations during most of the war consisted of the big round French loaves which were quite palatable. The bread was brought up to the front, piled high in open trucks. It was handled, time and time again, by men who almost never had the opportunity to wash. It was piled along the road, fell off the trucks to roll through the excrement of animals, then back on the trucks. But we ate it with relish when we received it. Dirt seldom kills.[45]

The German troops falling back ahead of Hoffman and his comrades had abandoned a wagon with a broken wheel. On board, Hoffman and his comrades found some German bread, which by this stage in the war contained a fair amount of sawdust, and some evidence of German foraging – a barrel of recently-made apple butter. Hoffman recounts:

> It was packed in big crocks, open at the top; it would not have remained preserved for long in that condition, so it must have been intended for immediate consumption by the German troops. Not

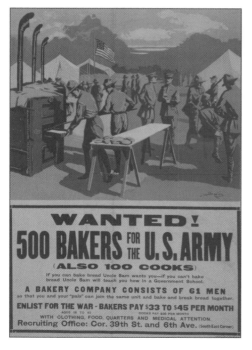

An American recruiting poster, illustrating the scale of the task of feeding the enormous army which the US raised between 1917 and 1918. (Library of Congress)

knowing what minute the whistles would blow again, we hastily filled our drinking cups with apple butter – a full pint each – helped ourselves to some of the bread and were enjoying a late midnight supper when we received the order to go forward. The apple butter was good – the black bread hard and quite unpalatable. I covered the bread with apple butter and managed to get it down. But that wasn't the last I knew of it. It remained in my stomach all the next day as a lead-like, indigestible mass. I had a cast-iron stomach, and could barely keep this bread down; what digestions the Germans must have developed to eat this sort of food for years! Perhaps they had gradually become accustomed to it.[46]

There was no official issue of alcoholic drink in the American Expeditionary Force. US soldiers were officially permitted to buy ordinary wines and beer but other drinks, such as champagne, whisky and brandy, were banned, and any establishment where such spirits were sold was off-limits to American troops. Of course this rule was bent whenever opportunity presented itself, and despite General Pershing's claim that what little drinking there was among his men reduced dramatically after Prohibition became law, this was seldom borne out by reality. However it was another item of French fare which made the deepest impression on the American 'doughboys' of the First World War. The thinly-cut chips, or 'frites' frequently encountered in French or Belgian estaminets, were hugely popular, and it is said that the American appetite for 'French Fries' stems from this era.

Thus whilst it was relatively easy for all armies in France and Belgium to feed their soldiers whilst out of the line, and parcels from home added greatly to the comfort of the troops in this regard, the real culinary challenge of the Western Front was how to get an adequate supply of warm and nutritious food to their men whilst in the front-line trenches, and more particularly whilst in battle. Naturally this could have a critical effect both upon their morale, and upon performance in combat. To some degree this problem was overcome by extensive use of tinned food, such as bully beef and Maconochie's, and sometimes brave ration parties were able to get through with supplies for their comrades, but often the food of the fighting man in France and Belgium was lacking in quantity, and usually less than appetising. Even supplying fresh drinking water was difficult under battle conditions. Yet, given the scale of the task of feeding the enormous armies on the Western Front, it would perhaps be more accurate to consider it an achievement that it was accomplished as well as it was.

Chapter 2

On the Battlefronts: Other Fronts

Having previously examined the food and rationing situation on the Western Front, this chapter seeks to examine the circumstances which prevailed for British, Empire and other troops in theatres of war beyond Europe, where conditions for storing food were in many cases considerably harsher than those in temperate northern France or Belgium, and indeed in many cases the distances over which that food had to be transported to reach the front line were also far greater. At Gallipoli and Salonika, heat and flies were a constant threat to provisions, whilst those soldiers besieged in Kut-al-Amara in Mesopotamia were reduced to a starvation diet. In some theatres such as East Africa, the normal chains of supply were simply not able to support the troops in the field, and the armies of both sides in this area were often forced to live off the land, and to feed themselves with anything which was locally available.

One of the first British operations in the First World War outside of Europe took place in Turkish-held Mesopotamia (modern Iraq), where a mixed Anglo-Indian force landed in late 1914 to attempt to secure the oil supplies in that region. The force, which was equipped and controlled by the Indian Government at Simla, was to begin with at least comparatively well supplied with food and rations, particularly when this was contrasted with the parsimonious quantities supplied in India in peacetime, and a British officer at Amara in southern Iraq wrote:

> If I ask my men how they like it [here] compared to India, they all say they like it better. 'Why, you gets a decent dinner here, Sir.' My experience quite confirms that of Sir Redvers Buller and other great authorities. If you feed T.A. [Tommy Atkins] well you can put him in slimy trenches and he'll be perfectly happy: but he'd never be contented in Buckingham Palace on Indian rations. Here we are of course on war rations, cheese, bacon and jam, bully beef and quite

decent mutton, and condensed milk. Vegetables are scarce, so lime juice is an issue: and they are said just to have made beer one, which would be the crown of bliss.[1]

The same officer described his own daily routine and rations in another letter home:

As to our mode of existence, my day is almost uniformly as follows:
6.30. Am called and drink 1 cup cocoa and eat 4 biscuits.
7.15. Get up.
7.45. Finished toilet and read Times till breakfast.
8.0. Breakfast. Porridge, scrambled eggs, bread and jam, tea.
8.30-9.15. Read Times.
9.15-10.15. Parade (or more often not, about twice a week I parade).
10.15-1.0. Read and write, unless interrupted by duties.
1.00. Lunch. Cold meat, pudding, cheese and bread, lemonade.
1.30-4.0. Read and write.
4.0. Tea, bread and jam.
4.30. Censor Civil Telegrams.
4.45-6.15. Take exercise, e.g., walk, ride, fish, shoot, or play football.
6.15. Have a bath.
6.30-7.30. Play skat, or talk on verandah.
7.30. Mess. Soup, fish, meat, veg., pudding, savoury, beer or whisky.
8.45-10.15. Bridge.
10.15. Go to bed. Such is the heroic existence of those who are bearing their country's burden in this remote and trying corner of the globe![2]

This officer, however, was in a reserve formation at the time, and once troops moved forward into the front line and thence into battle, the food supply could break down just as easily as on the Western Front, if not more so. A force under Major General Townshend advanced as far as Ctesiphon, but weakened by casualties and outnumbered by Turkish reinforcements, it was forced to retire upon the small Mesopotamian town of Kut-al-Amara. Here, one of the most infamous sieges in British military history took place as, protected as they were by a bend in the River Tigris, the garrison attempted to hold out against the surrounding enemy. That they did so from December 1915 to April 1916 is quite remarkable when one examines the appalling mismanagement of the town's food supplies during the campaign.

The town of Kut-al-Amara, Mesopotamia. Its besieged Anglo-Indian garrison would suffer extreme food privations in the winter of 1915/16, a situation made worse by poor management of supplies. (Library of Congress: Bain collection)

No proper assessment of the provisions available was carried out at the beginning of the siege, and the system of rationing applied to both civilians and military personnel in Kut was haphazard to say the least. By the end, the garrison was reduced to a situation of appalling hardship, whilst at the start of the siege grain had actually been allowed to spoil through being left out in the open. Here again, the force comprised a significant number of Indian troops, whose dietary requirements brought their own complications.

British officer E. L. Mousley kept a diary of the siege, which was later published as *Secrets of a Kuttite*. Not surprisingly, many entries contained references to the food question, which became more critical as time went on:

> 21 January 1916: As to food, we have eaten up some very tough bullocks, and I much prefer donkey to mule. We are down to horse in a day or so. The floods have put our meagre fires out, and for dinner we had half-raw donkey, red gravy, and half-cooked rice with some date stuff that made me feel like an alarm clock just set off.[3]

19 February 1916: Food may be made to stretch, but the casualty list of sick will be very high. Even now some [Indian] castes will not eat horseflesh, and the Mohammedans have refused to touch it.[4]

24 February 1916: The Mussulman soldiers here will not eat horseflesh. Among their excuses is one that the signature from India of their High Priest's permission to eat it is not authentic. It came by wireless! Generally speaking, the native soldier for first-rate work in the field is only third class if he has no *khana* (food).[5]

5 March 1916: As for food it matters not. Dysentery and rheumatic cases can be safely starved, I believe, and if this is the chief way of getting well there is every facility here for rapid recovery. Two small portions of Mellin's food and one egg with a small piece of white bread are the daily ration. A few extra things came for me, but I could not eat them.[6]

Captain E. L. Mousley, whose meticulous diary charts the hardships suffered by the Kut garrison as their food supply dwindled. (From Mousley, *Secrets of a Kuttite*)

21 March 1916: It is needless to remark that the only foodstuffs now for secret sale are those that have been stolen or illicitly concealed. But even these have long since been purchased, and it is only by secret-service methods that an Arab is fossicked out who will sell a tin of milk for fifteen rupees, a pound of rice for five rupees, or atta for ten rupees. Officers and men, we are all on the same footing, and the extra that one can buy is, after all, such a very small supplement. There are many besides myself who have to starve completely if eggs or milk are not obtainable. Of the latter I have had one on issue per day when they are available. This just keeps one going, and after a few days of it one can manage with potato meal and a small portion of horse.[7]

30 March 1916: This morning I paid the men and did some office work, and brought the war diary up to date. After that I found time to try a longer walk around our first line, but felt too seedy to go into the Fort. I heard that the sickness is rapidly increasing, and the condition

of the troops is so bad that the chief dread of the whole routine is the marching to and from the trenches. This being so, regiments are now allowed to remain out there permanently. In one Indian regiment man after man has simply sunk down in his tracks and died through want of food. And an extraordinary number of soldiers wretchedly ill won't report sick, partly through a horror of entering the crowded and unhappy hospitals, and also from a sense of duty.[8]

31 March 1916: Native rations, except for meal, have ceased altogether. This may induce them to eat horse. There is nothing against it now as they have the full permission of the Chief Mullahs in India.[9]

2 April 1916: We tried some green weed or other the Sepoys gathered on the maidan. Boiled and eaten with a little salad oil that Tudway fished out from heaven knows where, it seemed quite palatable. After all, as he says, all we want is something of a gluey nature to keep our souls stuck on to us . . . I am carver and taster, both useful functions in a siege. Tudway likes it thin, but with Square-Peg it is necessary to cut it thick. After the third helping Square-Peg has to carve for himself. We inaugurated that last week. If by accident the horse is extra tough, and Square-Peg gets splashed, he gets four helpings, but Tudway does not, for he can take cover under the table. As regards the vegetables, 'Sparrow-grass' and potato meal or beetroot and rice, I divide, and we all cut cards for first pick. There is always plenty of horse, but vegetables are a great delicacy. Tudway and I conspire to do Square-Peg out of his greens so as to keep him up to the scratch in procuring or in 'pinching' vegetables from the garden of which he is C.O. It works admirably, and I am only sorry his small pockets necessitate his making several trips. On wet days we have 'encore' in the vegetables, for then he wears a top coat with big pockets. He refuses to do so on fine days as he says it looks suspicious. If we have an issue of a spoonful of sugar I barter it for milk, and the date juice, when we get it, is measured out with a spoon.

For pudding we have kabobs, fried flour and fat, two each, and we cut for choice. An excellent idea which we have lately followed is to get the fat off a horse – there is very little now, poor things – and render it into dripping, which is quite excellent. I have sometimes waited for hours to get this from the butchery. While we had sardines our bombardier produced a savoury with toast, but that is long ago. Instead we have coffee, which is mostly ground-up roots, plus liquorice powder, if you're not careful in buying. The date juice goes into the coffee, but Square-Peg complains that he can't 'feel it that way,' so he drinks his like a liqueur. I prefer bad tea, as the coffee is generally atrocious, but Tudway likes it for the sake of 'the smell'.[10]

Early in 1915 the British and French opened up another front against the Turks, this time in the eastern Mediterranean, at Gallipoli in the Dardanelles. This was to be a campaign in which the heat of summer would play havoc with the ration supply for the troops ashore. Everything on this barren peninsula had to be landed by boat, even drinking water. Here, shortage of rations was not the only problem; rather, the insanitary conditions in which the troops lived in many cases conspired to rob them of any appetite. Joseph Murray, an AB in the Hood Battalion of the Royal Naval Division at Gallipoli, was always hungry and wrote in his diary in June 1915:

> I cannot understand why our rations are so meagre. One would have thought that as our numbers are reduced to less than half each time we leave the firing line there would be additional rations, at least for a day or two, but they seem to get less. Surely they don't cut the ration requirements on the assumption that we shall need only half the previous amount as only half will return each time? I did not think it was possible for a man to exist, let alone live, on such meagre portions of fly infested oily cheese, a few hard biscuits and a daily billy-can of bully beef stew flavoured with millions of blue-black flies. I don't know what the other troops get but this is all we have. My stomach aches for food and aches even more after I have eaten the food that is given me.[11]

Murray went on to describe the canteen which he and his comrades visited behind the firing line, on the beach:

> With apologies to the nursery rhyme – 'When the door was opened, the flies began to hum'. The dainty dish set before the king was a dozen or so figs on a string. I asked for a tin of condensed milk. The Greek made his face even uglier than it normally was, and with a characteristic shrug of his shoulders, offered me a string of figs. It was Hobson's choice, figs or nothing. Lovely juicy chunks of dysentery, covered with the usual layers of flies. I came away delighted; however bad they were they would certainly be easier on the teeth than the biscuit diet.[12]

In fact these flies were so numerous that they represented a serious hazard to the effectiveness of the fighting force at Gallipoli. Migrating back and forth between corpses, open latrines and foodstuffs, they were soon responsible for a near-epidemic of dysentery and diarrhoea, and many men left the peninsula unnecessarily, evacuated sick rather than injured by Turkish bullets. Geoffrey Sparrow, who also served with the Royal Naval Division, remarked of the:

> . . . ubiquitous flies. How those flies pervaded everything! Food became black with them immediately it was uncovered. They swarmed around the unburied dead and infested the habitations of the living. They spoilt the temper of the healthy and added greatly to the sufferings of the wounded and sick. No wonder men ate little. Unopened bully beef tins were stuffed in the parapet for want of a better use – meat for the asking, and yet few had any desire to touch it. Tins of jam in plenty, but none cared to sample them, except perhaps the Turks, to whom we slung them over in our catapults. Tickler's artillery, named after a firm of jam makers, soon became famous.[13]

It was often the case that bully beef, in the heat of the Mediterranean summer, turned to a liquid with the consistency of treacle, which could almost be poured from the can. Rock-hard ration biscuits, sometimes flavoured with liquid plum and apple jam, were responsible for the loss of numerous teeth among men who often had poor dental health to begin with, making food even harder to consume. Murray and his comrades had a way of supplementing their ration allowance. When on a working party unloading lighters bringing supplies onto shore, it was an unwritten law that anyone carrying a broken box of condensed milk tins would 'accidentally' drop it into the sea. It would then be an easy enough job to swim back later and retrieve individual tins from the broken box undetected. Murray was at pains to stress, however, that this kind of pilfering would never be carried out if it left other comrades going short:

> I must make it plain to my reader that this business only operated between the lighters and the beach. Rations carried from the Quartermaster's Store to the front line always got there intact. It is true that biscuits were sealed in tins but cheese, bacon, tea, sugar and the inevitable apricot jam could become 'lost' but never were. That would be sacrilege. We would trudge through what seemed to be miles of trenches to deliver the rations to the lads in the line. They did the same for us but, even so, it seemed to be a wasted

effort to carry tea and sugar, mixed in a sandbag, to the firing line. You had to have water to make tea and the lads had precious little. [14]

During several of the ill-fated offensives at Gallipoli, survivors record their agonising thirst under a broiling sun, as provision of drinking water had not been properly planned. As often as not, once they had finished the meagre supply in their water bottle, there was nothing more for several days. Even in quieter times water was often scarce at Gallipoli.

The French army was also present at the Dardanelles campaign, and its soldiers relied heavily on wine as a substitute for water – hardly surprising when one considers the unpalatability of the water obtainable on the peninsula. One French officer wrote after a day's exertions: 'I was very thirsty. The water is almost salt, and makes one thirsty.'[15] This same officer added in a later comment the observation that the water was also strongly tainted by the potassium compound which was used as a sterilising agent to disinfect it for drinking purposes: 'When I returned to the camp Corporal

French Senegalese troops about to embark at Mudros for Gallipoli. Note what appear to be loaves of bread on the right of the picture. (Library of Congress: Bain collection)

A British army rum jar, holding a gallon of the spirit which was issued as part of the soldier's ration. (Courtesy of John Caley)

Riffat got me something to eat. I had a craving for some wine, but there was nothing but water, which was salty and flavoured with permanganate!'[16]

The British Army issued rum, but the ration was curtailed as the campaign went on, adding further hardship. Only when the order was given to evacuate the Gallipoli Peninsula were foodstuffs suddenly available in quantity, as the garrison was gradually reduced in number. New Zealander C. J.Walsh recorded in his diary for 14 December 1915: 'Heard that good things were to be had on the beach, got loaded up with jam and cheese and also a bag of cabbage and onions.'[17]

The following day, much to his chagrin, he discovered that food supplies were actually being destroyed:

> On the beach the authorities are tipping out rum and whisky in Mule Gully and a terrible lot of rum etc was tipped out and formed a pool. All hands were there with jam tins, dixies etc lapping it up.[18]

It is hardly surprising that some troops were rather the worse for wear when finally leaving the peninsula and in occasional cases this was in fact almost their undoing; one officer leaving the Gallipoli trenches for the last time under cover of darkness remembered casually kicking aside what he assumed was a pile of old clothes or rubbish, only to discover that it was his cook, scarcely conscious and hugging a rum jar.

British troops also fought against the Turks in Palestine, and one of the officers who served in this theatre was Eliot Crawshay-Williams, of the Leicestershire Royal Horse Artillery. The base for the Palestine campaign was Egypt, and in one passage in his memoirs, Crawshay-Williams provides a description of the officers' mess – probably typical of many at this time – as it existed whilst his unit was stationed in tent lines in Egypt. The position of mess-president, whilst not a particularly enviable one, nonetheless carried with it considerable perks:

> One cannot always dine 'in town.' Means would not stand it, nor would health, for dining 'in town' usually means returning after midnight, and one must be on parade at 6.15 a.m. So, perforce, the Mess dinner must be faced. Our C.O. is very keen on our being able to 'do for ourselves', and consequently no caterer is allowed, but the Mess cook must manage. In the opinion of some, he will 'do for us' in more senses than one before long. As a matter of fact, he is not at all so bad. His materials are not all that might be desired, and he contrives to make as much out of them as one could expect. This is what he is provided with: 1. Rations i.e., the beef (or bully beef), bread, vegetables, and 'grocery ration', for each officer, which is precisely the same as for each man. 2. Extras provided, when he can remember about them, by the Mess President. 3. Private supplies; e.g., if Lieutenant Smith buys a tin of sausages for his personal breakfast, or Major Jones produces a bottle of beer for his own (and perhaps 'a friend's') delectation. Of course, the Government ration is not enough in some ways, though it is equally too much in others. There is more meat than is wanted; but one tin of Nestle's Swiss Milk cannot possibly last nine officers three days. Hence the necessity for item 2 on the programme. The meat is good, but hard (the effort of the cook to roast it without previously boiling it to get it a bit soft was cried down unanimously, and one officer broke his false teeth). The bread is hard, but good, except for a persistent flavour of acid. The biscuits are hard. In fact, their chief flavour is hardness, if one may say so. Bacon, sugar, tea, marmalade, salt, pepper all satisfactory. Vegetables good, but not really sufficient. Rice, flour, etc., are all counted as vegetables, and if you want them they have to be taken out of the small daily allowance. The supplementary things provided by the Mess President vary considerably. Everyone wants his own pet delicacy, and as a rule no one gets anything. The C.O. introduced a suggestion-book, which

was largely used by everyone except the Mess President, whose attention it apparently entirely escaped, since the sixth suggestion was, 'That suggestions be sometimes paid some attention to.' However, later such luxuries as fresh rolls, more vegetables, pickles, eggs, oranges, and, for one brief day, bananas, made their appearance. It has been found almost impossible, however, to break the Mess President of his predilection for tinned fruit, which is, as we have unanimously pointed out, both more costly and less desirable than the fresh variety.[19]

Eliot Crawshay-Williams, of the Leicestershire Royal Horse Artillery. (From Crawshay-Williams, *Leaves from an Officer's Notebook*)

Also serving in Palestine at this time were several Jewish battalions of the Royal Fusiliers, raised during the First World War and known as 'Judeans' or the 'Jewsiliers'. Lieutenant Colonel J. H. Patterson was the commanding officer of one of these battalions. Patterson had considerable empathy with the men under his command. In his mind, the Jewish religion of most of those in his battalion was a key aspect of its identity. It was fundamental to recruiting the formation, and to morale within it, and in its early days he had to fight several times with the military authorities to ensure that Kosher food was provided for his men. When the battalion was later posted to the Middle East, Patterson records that:

> The Feast of the Passover was celebrated during our stay at Helmieh. Thus history was repeating itself in the Land of Bondage in a Jewish Military Camp, after a lapse of over 3,000 years from the date of the original feast. I had considerable trouble with the authorities in the matter of providing unleavened bread. However, we surmounted all difficulties, and had an exceedingly jovial first night, helped thereto by the excellent Palestinian wine which we received from Mr. Gluskin, the head of the celebrated wine press of Richon-le-Zion, near Jaffa. The unleavened bread for the battalion, during the eight days of the Feast, cost somewhat more than the ordinary ration would have done, so I requested that the excess should be paid for out of Army Funds. This was refused by the local command in Egypt, so I went to the H.Q. Office, where I saw a

Jewish Staff Officer, and told him I had come to get this matter adjusted. He said that, as a matter of fact, he had decided against us himself. I told him that I considered his judgment unfair, because the battalion was a Jewish Battalion, and the Army-Council had already promised Kosher food whenever it was possible to obtain it, and it would have been a deadly-insult to have forced ordinary bread upon the men during Passover. I therefore said that I would appeal against his decision to a higher authority. He replied, 'This will do you no good, for you will get the same reply from G.H.Q.' He was mistaken, for I found the Gentile, on this particular occasion, more sympathetic than the Jew, and the extra amount was paid by order of the Q.M.G., Sir Walter Campbell.[20]

By contrast, in the trenches opposite, the food of the ordinary Ottoman soldier at this time was poor. Alexander Aaronsohn was a Jewish conscript from Palestine, who served in the Turkish army. He tells us of his first encounter with military cuisine, on the day after he was enlisted:

The black depths of the well in the center of the mosque courtyard provided doubtful water for washing, bathing, and drinking; then

Ottoman Turkish infantrymen share a meal of soup from a communal bowl. (Library of Congress)

Ottoman army mobile bake ovens, producing bread at Tel es Sheria, southern Palestine, around 1917. (Library of Congress)

came breakfast, – our first government meal, – consisting, simply enough, of boiled rice, which was ladled out into tin wash-basins holding rations for ten men. In true Eastern fashion we squatted down round the basin and dug into the rice with our fingers. At first I was rather upset by this sort of table manners, and for some time I ate with my eyes fixed on my own portion, to avoid seeing the Arabs, who fill the palms of their hands with rice, pat it into a ball and cram it into their mouths just so, the bolus making a great lump in their lean throats as it reluctantly descends.[21]

This was meal-time at a depot. For the Ottoman troops on campaign, sparseness of food would grow to be the norm. The Turkish commander Kemal Pasha, writing of the ill-starred campaign to capture the Suez Canal from the British in 1915, describes the almost starvation rations upon which his men were expected to march and fight:

The 8th Corps reported that as the supply of food for officers and men right through the desert to the Canal was impossible, we must adopt a new system and call it the 'desert ration'. It was based on a list of comestibles, the weight of which was not to exceed one kilogram per man, and comprised biscuits, dates, and olives. As regards water, no man must carry more than contents of a gourd.[22]

In the Balkans, British, French and Serbian troops fought against the Bulgarian Army, in particular on the Salonika front in northern Greece and Macedonia. Again, one of the greatest problems at Salonika was availability of clean drinking water. Joseph Marguerite Jean Vassal, who had previously served at Gallipoli, was later posted to this front with the French forces. As a medical officer he was astonished by casual way that men put their health and even their lives at risk by drinking dirty water. He wrote:

> [An] unheard-of paradox, there is no drinking water! I saw a soldier to-day take water in his mug from a hole in the ground made by a horse-shoe! I spoke to him. He had not seen me come up. He confessed that it had an earthy taste.[23]

Another similarity with Gallipoli came in the form of the pestilential insects which in the summer made the lives of the soldiers a misery. A Royal Engineers officer, Captain M. J. Rattray, wrote:

> The greatest pests both as disease producers and causing acute physical discomfort, making life a torment, are the flies and mosquitos. Flies simply teem in millions, they are a regular plague and a source of disease and dysentery. Any food or refuse left in the open is immediately covered with them. This is no mere exaggeration. A piece of food left on the ground for a few minutes could not be seen with the black swarm of flies on it. The British fly usually leaves human beings in peace, but his Balkan relative is no respecter of persons. Unless protected by netting it is almost impossible to obtain rest or sleep during the heat of the day, for the flies persist in crawling over hands and face, and when driven away simply return to the attack, until one gives up through sheer exhaustion. As we had no netting during our first summer months in 1916, it can be readily understood that we had not a joyous life of it. When eating a meal, flies would cluster on the jam on one's bread almost till it was put in one's mouth.[24]

One British officer, Captain Harold Lake, remembered that the British army's canteens were established behind the lines here in much the same way as they were behind the front in France, providing a boost to morale by selling small luxuries which were not part of the normal ration:

> To every man there comes each day the food required to keep him fit for his work. It comes in generous measure, and in really wonderful variety, considering the difficulties of the business. But

the variety cannot be great enough to satisfy the very human craving for an occasional change, for sharp flavors, and for sweetness. With jam and with onions the authorities do their best for our palates, and their achievements are really wonderful, but they do not reach to the end of healthy desire. Filling the gap there comes the work of the Expeditionary Force Canteens, those glorified tuck-shops of the army. Here and there in Macedonia there stand great marquees with signboards bearing the words of cheer, 'Expeditionary Force Canteen.' There are not many of them. There is, of course, a big head-quarter place in Salonika. There is one at Hortiack, and another, I believe, at Stavros. At the forty-fifth kilo on the Seres road there is a kind of branch establishment, and there is one at Janes.[25]

Lake also tells us of the recreations enjoyed by officers not on duty, which occasionally produced a welcome addition to the menu when those same officers sat down to dine:

One other amusement we had which called for plenty of exertion, and was occasionally profitable to the mess. We used to get our revolvers and go out looking for hares. Macedonia is simply alive with game in certain areas. It seems impossible to walk a couple of hundred yards without putting up a covey of partridges or a great, galloping hare. To go hunting hares with a revolver is quite amusing, though of course it is not regarded with favor by those aristocrats who have shot guns and treat themselves seriously as purveyors of game. But if you have no gun, and are very weary of seeing large quantities of desirable food escaping from you it is soothing to take your Webley for a walk round the hills. Of course it is more a matter of luck than anything else. A service revolver is a wonderful weapon with a great range, but it takes a crack shot to put a bullet into a retreating hare, and so to hit it, moreover, that the animal shall not be reduced to a shapeless mash of fur and flesh and splinters of bone. But if by some fluke the bullet just chips the head, the prospect for tomorrow's dinner is suddenly and wonderfully improved, and there is ample recompense for three hours of scrambling over rocks and through thickets of brambles.[26]

Britain and France supported the Serbian army in the Balkans. As well as being militarily weak, the Serbs were also particularly poorly fed. Research has shown that at this time the average daily ration for a Serbian soldier was between only 2,000 and 2,500 calories, but in the early stages of the Balkan campaign, when the Serbs were in retreat through Albania, their soldiers were virtually starving. Retreating through Montenegro and in Albania, the Serbian army passed through poor and inaccessible regions, where, according to a physician in the Serbian army named Stevan Ivanic: '. . . As for the great mass of the army, and its deserters, there was no longer anything to be had either for purchase or for plunder.'[27] Thus the army had to rely almost solely on its own sparse rations. The same author records that from 13 December 1915 to 21 January 1916, the average intake per soldier per day was now only between 500 and 1,670 calories. Food consumed by the Serbs consisted at this time mostly of rice, flour, bread, bacon, canned meat and oil, sometimes beans, but generally with no or few vegetables (occasionally just twenty grams a day of onions and cabbage). In a meticulously-kept diary Ivanic noted that on 27, 28 and 29 December and 19 January the army received nothing in the way of rations. All in all, during the two outbreaks of scurvy which affected the Serbian army in the First World War some 300 soldiers contracted the disease in 1915 and 3,223 men in 1917. Today it is understood that it is necessary to suffer a lack of Vitamin C in the diet for a long time, around two or three months, in order to develop scurvy, and it is no coincidence that both of these epidemics broke out before the end of winter and in early spring, from April to May, after months of shortages of fresh vegetables.

On 22 January 1916, Ivanic's unit boarded a ship bound for French controlled Corfu for a respite, and there, according to his testimony, '. . . for the first time [we] received appetising cooked food'.[28] The stay in Corfu was intended to provide the troops with much needed rest and proper food in order to restore their energy, and for them to be supplied with clothes, boots, and other essentials. However, starvation and malnutrition-related deaths continued to affect the soldiers even whilst at Corfu. Since the meat ration was relatively small (comprising 100 grams of canned or frozen Australian beef per man), the troops were in the habit of keeping the meat from one day to the next, in order to eat a decent portion at least once every two days. The temperature in Corfu at that time of year is quite high, and in such circumstances unrefrigerated meat is of course quickly spoiled; the soldiers suffered significant outbreaks of food poisoning as a result of this habit, and after the intervention of military doctors, on 8 February the Serbian Supreme Command ordered that henceforth meat must be cooked immediately on arrival.

This measure, despite the difficulties which the Serbians faced in the form of a lack of appropriate vessels and cooking equipment, and even a shortage of wood for fires, led to a reduction in the number of patients with gastroenteritis, and thus the troops were fed adequately up to the middle of March, for as long as it was possible to provide a regular supply of meat.

Serbian infantry with a wounded comrade, on the Salonika front. (Library of Congress)

Then, however, fresh and frozen meat began to run out, and bacon began to replace it in the daily ration. It was noted that after almost a month of eating bacon instead of meat, during which time high-value proteins were replaced with animal fat, there was a corresponding increase in the number of cases of jaundice.

Perhaps the most extraordinary campaign of the First World War, certainly in terms of diet and rations, was that waged in East Africa between the German *Schutztruppen* (colonial troops) and their native allies in German East Africa, and the British and other local troops which tried for four years to suppress them, without success. At the war's end, German troops under their commander General Paul von Lettow-Vorbeck remained undefeated and only surrendered after the collapse of the Imperial German regime in Europe. The fighting here was the complete antithesis of that in Europe. Instead of a stalemate as in France, in East Africa the war was characterised by extensive movement and mobility. After a short, sharp engagement with the enemy, the German force (usually a mixture of a handful of European officers and NCOs, together with native Askaris) made off at the last moment in order to fight another day. The British expended huge effort and resources in chasing von Lettow-Vorbeck around, but this was always his objective – he knew that he could not hope to defeat the Allies but instead tried to occupy as many troops as possible in pursuing him. He wrote of his experiences in this campaign, and in particular of the raids mounted in 1914 and 1915 from German-controlled territory deeper and deeper into British East Africa and Uganda. He tells us that the troops on these expeditions were often forced to live almost entirely off the land:

> The patrols that went out from the Kilima Njaro in a more easterly direction . . . had to work on foot through the dense bush for days on end. The patrols sent out to destroy the railway were mostly weak: one or two Europeans, two to four Askari, and five to seven carriers. They had to worm their way through the enemy's pickets and were often betrayed by native scouts. In spite of this they

A German propaganda postcard, showing the Governor of German East Africa, Heinrich Schnee, together with his army commander, von Lettow-Vorbeck, and the African Askari soldiers who made up a large percentage of the German forces here. (Author's collection)

mostly reached their objective and were sometimes away for more than a fortnight. For such a small party a bit of game or a small quantity of booty afforded a considerable reserve of rations. But the fatigue and thirst in the burning sun were so great that several men died of thirst, and even Europeans drank urine.[29]

Later on, large game provided sustenance for the German troops in action in this campaign. They were not, however, deer and antelope as might have been expected:

> Owing to the general demand for fat, hippopotamus shooting became a question of existence. One has to watch until the animal's head is clearly visible, so as to hit in a spot that will cause instantaneous death. The animal then sinks, and comes up again after a little time when it can be drawn to the bank by means of a rope, quickly made of bark. There it is cut up, and the expert knows exactly where to find the white, appetizing fat. The quantity varies: a well-fed beast provides over two bucketfuls. But one has to learn, not only how to prepare the fat, but also how to kill immediately with the first shot. Some foolish people had been reckless, and in many places the dead bodies of wounded animals were to be seen, which quickly decompose and become unfit for food. The elephant also was now regarded in a new light; ordinarily the elephant hunter gauges the length and weight of the tusk before firing; now the pressing question was: how much fat will the beast supply? For elephant fat is very good, and possibly tastes even better than that of the hippo.[30]

At other times the diet of the Germans was more mundane, *mtama* being the Swahili name for a kind of millet, which can be ground and the flour made into a kind of stiff porridge widely eaten in East Africa:

> The country along the river Malema in which we had our camp was quite extraordinarily fertile. The mtama was perfectly ripe, and there was an abundance of tomatoes, bananas, sweet potatoes (batatas) and other fruits. The food was also very varied. Game and fish were plentiful. The natives knew the German troops from previous acquaintance, and were very friendly.[31]

As 1915 gave way to 1916, South African General Jan Smuts took over command of what was by now a reinforced and multinational force, comprising not just his own countrymen but also Belgian and Portuguese troops, a large number of locally recruited troops in the form of the King's African Rifles, and in addition Indian troops who were deployed because they were accustomed to warfare in this kind of climate. One of the British officers with the Indian contingent, Francis Young, wrote of the tendency of his men to help themselves to the food belonging to the African tribesmen (indeed the African civilian population suffered the greatest privations of any group during this four-year campaign, having their crops and fodder raided by both sides) but also of his concern that the British should be seen to pay their way, and not just act as looters:

> The old man was loud in complaint. He said that some of our troops, and from his description we recognised the Kashmiris, had driven away two of his sheep while they were grazing down by the swamp. We told him that if he applied at our camp he would be paid for the damage done. He shook his head, saying that he was afraid to enter such a great camp, and then, to show him that we were in earnest, we offered to pay him there and then, and handsomely, for any fruit or vegetables that he might bring us; but he swore that there were none in his village, that the Germans had stripped their mealie-fields and plantain groves bare, and that as it was his people were starving. Certainly the natives who came with him were very thin, but I think they were more probably wasted by fever than by lack of food. With a certain melancholy civility, he bade us farewell, and when they had moved a little way from us, the others, who had kept silence throughout the interview, began to talk excitedly. They seemed to be upbraiding the old man for what he had said, though we could not imagine why. I suppose it was quite likely that the Kashmiris had indeed driven away his sheep. The problem of feeding a Hindu regiment on active service is not easy, for strenuous work calls for a meat diet, and to them the slaughter of oxen is an impious act – so that the temptation to loot sheep or goats for food was great. And yet, on the whole, I do not suppose any invading army in the history of war has behaved better in this particular than the Indian troops of the East African force.[32]

It seems, however, that the Indian soldiers in East Africa were inveterate consumers of local supplies, and Young implies that neither crops nor animals were safe from their attentions in this campaign:

> At the bottom of a little valley, where a trickle of water ran, I found a small but fertile garden in which French beans, asparagus, and tall globe artichokes were growing. It was evident that no Indian troops

British officers and soldiers of the Nigeria Regiment in East Africa. (Winterton collection)

had passed that way, or else the place would have been stripped of all its eatable green; for vegetable food is what the Indian on active service misses most. Here, too, I picked two pocketsful of that red-leaved flower, rosella, whose fleshy bracts make a stew that is like rhubarb, but more acrid.[33]

The following year, West African troops joined Smuts' force. In the pursuit of a German raiding column a mixed Allied force, including soldiers of the Nigeria Regiment, covered several hundred miles as the Germans led them a merry dance through some increasingly inhospitable terrain. Then, in January 1917 the rainy season in this part of East Africa began. It was to be the wettest such season in this part of Africa for many years. The Nigerians, holding recently captured positions around Mkindu in the Rufiji Valley, were to suffer serious privations as a result. Recently-built roads and bridges were washed away, vast tracts of country became swamps and the low-lying valley was infested with horse sickness and tsetse fly. The only food which reached these forward troops now came to them from the railhead over 80 or 90 miles of difficult country on foot, by porter alone. At first, the problem was one simply of monotony as bully beef was increasingly relied upon, but as the season progressed, things became much worse. A British officer of the regiment, Captain Walter Downes, has provided a graphic description of the state that his men were soon in, and the desperate measures that they went to, in order to find food:

> February, March, and April 1917 were all black months for the Nigerian Brigade. The hardships passed through during these three months must be unparalleled in military operations of our time. Our condition could not have been worse even if we had been in a siege. The men got terribly thin and wretched, till they became almost unfit to take the field in any active operations. The men went sick, and many died from eating poisoned roots and herbs, twelve men dying in the 2nd Battalion early in May from this cause. To give an instance or two of the state the men got into, will no doubt interest the reader, besides, if they were omitted, this record would be most incomplete. A donkey died of horse sickness and was buried. Two days later the body was dug up and eaten by certain men. This happened several times with condemned cattle, till it was found necessary always to burn carcases.
>
> A bridge was built over a stream between the main position at Mkindu and a detached position known as Stretton Hill. The spars forming the bridge were lashed together with strips of raw hide, dating back to the days of plenty, when a large herd of cattle supplied the meat for the troops at Mkindu. The bridge had been standing about two months, when one night all the hide was stolen, and the bridge left in a very tottering state. The hides were cooked down into soup, and so disposed of by the starving men.[34]

Downes went on to describe how the European officers fared in these circumstance. They were somewhat better off than their soldiers, but there can be no doubt that they too were facing increasing food hardship as time went on. The local supplies with which they sometimes supplemented their rations will no doubt turn the stomachs of some readers!

> Below is given a fair example of a day's rations for Europeans. The following was issued to the officers of the 4th Battalion on 4th April: Bacon, 1/2 oz.; jam, 1 oz.; condensed milk, 1/2 oz.; onions, 3/4 oz.; fresh meat, 2 2/3 oz., the total weight of each officer's ration being 1 lb. 2 1/2 ozs. On the same day to the men was issued half a pound of rice, with nothing in addition. Before leaving this doleful subject I quote a paragraph out of a brother-officer's diary of the 2nd Battalion, dated the 18th April: 'The men are getting thinner daily; Europeans are up against it now, and honestly have barely

enough to keep body and soul together. Rations for Europeans for six days from 15th-20th April inclusive: flour, 3 lbs.; bacon, 3/4 lb.; dried fruit, 3/4 lb.; sugar, 3/4 lb.; tea, 1 7/8 oz.; salt, 1 1/2 oz.; tinned meat, 2 1/4 lb.; onions, 3/4 lb.; ghee, 1 oz.' The troops during all this time of semi-starvation were called upon to carry out many arduous duties, such as trench-digging, construction of dug-outs, house-building, patrols, and other military duties. That they performed their duties cheerfully and thoroughly speaks well for the credit of the black soldier. I am convinced that no other troops, whether they be Indian, East African, or White, could possibly have done better. Whilst on the subject of rations, when a full ration was issued it was ample, for it consisted of 1 lb. of meat, 1 lb. of bread or flour, abundance of vegetables, tea, coffee, cocoa, milk, sugar, salt, rice, condiments, lime juice, and, last but not least, 'dop' (Cape brandy). I have written at length upon this subject of rations, but so far have written nothing of how certain of us increased our food supply from local resources. I doubt if the reader has ever tasted monkey's brains on ration biscuits, bush rat pie, or stewed hippo's sweetbreads, but all three were consumed by the more daring Europeans of the Brigade, and thoroughly enjoyed.[35]

This chapter provides only the briefest of overviews of the situation in some of the 'minor' theatres of operations during the First World War, but even from this short summary it is clear that, certainly in comparison with the relative luxury on the Western Front, troops in the Mediterranean, Middle East and Africa often suffered considerable hardship, in spite of the almost ubiquitous presence of bully beef! What is also of interest is the resourceful nature of soldiers in many parts of the world, their adaption to local conditions, and willingness to eat whatever was to hand, however unpalatable. These difficulties of supply were common factors in all armies fighting in inhospitable climates, and poor diet, and its negative impact on fighting efficiency and morale, was never the sole preserve of just one nation or army.

Chapter 3

Russia and the Eastern Front

It is arguable that in no other combatant nation during the First World War did the supply of food – or more precisely the failure of it – so directly affect the political situation and the course of the war as it did in Russia. When war broke out in the summer of 1914, the Russian government did not feel that providing the army with food was a pressing priority: Russia was after all a major exporter of grain. Germany might have to worry about obtaining enough food to sustain its war effort, but not Russia. Indeed, it was thought that the extra purchases required by the army might prove to be a bonus, since they would help avert a depression in agricultural prices that might be caused by the cut-off of Russian exports. The casualness of the government approach was not justified. Although first regarded as an opportunity, food supply soon came to be seen as a problem, then as a crisis, and finally as a catastrophe. As the war progressed, food shortages in the army, exacerbated as they were by fuel shortages, would drive the soldiers into the arms of the equally discontented urban poor and working classes. These people had, through problems with the food supply chain, become dislocated from the rural communities which before the war had supplied them with food. The result was a revolution, which would ultimately take Russia out of the war. Instead of falling because of a glut on the internal market, agricultural prices steadily climbed until efforts to control them became one of the central questions of domestic politics. Not only was the army poorly supplied, but the cities and the grain-deficit provinces (located for the most part in the north of Russia) began to feel the shortages and to fear for the future. In the last months before the revolution, food-supply policy became the centre of a pitched bureaucratic and political battle that led to drastic shifts of policy but not to alleviation of the people's hardships and insecurity. When the Tsarist government fell in the depths of the winter of 1916/17, it was the Petrograd crowds calling for bread that delivered the final blow.

What went wrong? The explanation must begin with the disruption of normal life caused by the outbreak of war. This disruption first expressed itself in the physical relocation of millions of men, taken from productive

A pre-war photo showing quantities of Russian grain stockpiled for export, at the southern port of Odessa on the Black Sea. (Author's collection)

activity at home and sent to the front. At the same time there was massive redirection of agricultural effort, and almost half of all marketable grain went to the army in 1916. The necessary reorganisation of the national economy was made even more difficult by sudden isolation from the world economy. Losing Germany as a trading partner was a severe blow to Russia, but a more basic problem was that Russia's transport infrastructure simply could not cope with the pressure of war. The strain on the transportation network resulted from the attempt to supply the front in the far west of the country and the swollen capital city of St Petersburg (Petrograd) in the far northwest. The new demands on the transportation network were almost the reverse of the usual pattern of peacetime trade, when grain was mostly shipped to southern ports for export. The Russian rail system matched the river system by having a north-south emphasis; it was simply not set up for east-west traffic. Difficulties were compounded by the enormous length of the front line, and when large-scale troop movements took place, the transport system failed to cope.

To begin with, the rations of the ordinary Russian soldier were not intolerable – and certainly not so when compared to what the soldier might have expected to receive at home. The ranks of the Russian army were overwhelmingly filled from the peasant class, whose experience of luxury goods would in most cases have been slight. Even compared to the poorest classes in Britain at this time, the living standards of the Russian peasantry were basic to say the least. It was said that the Russian peasant ate meat only twice a year, at Easter and Christmas, and the basis of his diet was formed by coarse bread, buckwheat porridge (kasha) and cabbage soup (shchi), indeed so much a part of Russian culture are these foods that a Russian saying runs '*щи да каша – пища наша*' (*shchi da kasha – pishcha nashi*) literally translated as 'shchi and kasha are our food' or, more loosely perhaps, 'cabbage soup and porridge are all we need to live on'. Thus it might be argued that the food served to the Russian other ranks was in many cases an improvement on what they were used to. This assumption is supported by an observer of the Russian army in action in the early part of the war, an American journalist, Robert McCormick, who stated:

On the march the Russian soldier is fed from the field kitchen, a huge cauldron in which the national soup or stew is cooked. This is composed of a ration of meat and grain and potatoes for each man with whatever other vegetables the cook can lay his hands on. There is a specific ration for each man, but in practice during this war the limit has been as much as each man desired. Three advantages of this method of cooking are immediately apparent. Troops can be fed on the march. After the march supper is served to them without their having the further effort of cooking their meals, and hot soup can often be brought up on wheels to the actual firing line or to places in its immediate proximity. In the mountains the kitchen cannot always follow the troops and there an excellent canned stew is substituted.

Where the soldiers are for any length of time in a secure position the kitchen is given a rest and the men cook their own food. 'The food is not as good,' explained a staff officer, 'but the cooking relieves the tedium of life in the trenches.' These field kitchens are kept at a high state of cleanliness and efficiency and are constantly inspected. One day when I was at the front the inspector general, Ci Roberti, tried a sample from every pot of a regiment. Since a Russian regiment consists of four thousand men and every company

'On the march the Russian soldier is fed from the field kitchen, a huge cauldron in which the national soup or stew is cooked.' (Author's collection)

has its individual kitchen, the general had plenty of soup that day. This special kitchen is an innovation which has been copied by other armies. Some say that the German kitchen is better, being divided into compartments and cooking several kinds of food. This may be necessary to satisfy the standard of living of the German soldier, but the extra weight must prove a serious handicap on bad roads. It is the aim of the Russian army to give the soldiers good, and better food, than they are accustomed to at home. There is certainly a military advantage in being a simple people.[1]

Prince Andrei Lobanov-Rostovsky, a Russian aristocrat, wrote of his experiences in the Imperial Russian army in *The Grinding Mill*, and the story of his account is almost as fascinating as the detail which it contains.

Written originally in note form and in French, in the front line, under fire and sometimes on horseback, he worked the notes up into a coherent narrative during the war. This however was lost in Petrograd in the summer of 1917, but by an irony the original notes survived. Lobanov-Rostovsky began his military career in the ranks as an officer-candidate in the Guards Sapper Battalion, just before the outbreak of war. He wrote:

> The food in the regiment was monotonous but wholesome. Bread, tea, and sugar were given out to the soldiers, and every day for

Prince Andrei Lobanov-Rostovsky, a Russian aristocrat, whose writings provide a vivid insight into life in the Russian army. (From Lobanov-Rostovsky, *The Grinding Mill*)

dinner and supper they had the same thing: a bowl of extremely rich cabbage soup (shtchi), a piece of meat, and a plate of barley. This was so seasoned and substantial that it took me some time to become accustomed to it. But there was plenty of it and the men did not complain among themselves. Before every meal a sample of the food was taken to the commander of the battalion for him to taste. Also, there were continuous inspections of the kitchen, and occasionally the general would drop in at night to see if everything was clean.[2]

By way of contrast, an Englishman named John Morse served in the ranks of the Russian army, and offers a useful comparison of what rations were like for the ordinary soldier in his regiment, in the early part of the war at least. He describes food which was unexciting but at least nourishing:

Bread was a species of 'hard tack' compared with which dog-biscuits are fancy food: cheese was a wretched soft mess resembling wet putty, sour and peculiarly flavoured. Meat was plentiful and good, especially German pork, and fowls, many of which were large and fleshy.[3]

The Tsar tasting the food served to his soldiers, in the early part of the war. Much was made by the Russians of the fact that senior commanders would often sample their men's food. Their own fare, however, was far more sophisticated than that of their men. (Library of Congress)

The effect of a full stomach was as heartening and beneficial to the morale of the Russian soldier as it would have been to the British soldier – perhaps even more so. A young corporal in the Russian ranks at this time remembered:

> At last, early in the afternoon we received orders to rest, get out our kitchen, and eat dinner. Never before had borsch (Russian soup) tasted so good to me, and the kasha (corn-meal), the black bread, and the veal were all infinitely better than any kasha, black bread, or veal I had tasted in all my life before. We soon resumed the march, and with our stomachs well lined we were in much brighter spirits, although, if a foreigner had heard us singing as we swung along the snow-bound roads, he would never have guessed how light-hearted we really felt, because the songs the Russian soldiers sing have the most mournful airs imaginable and the words are seldom more than childish nonsense.[4]

Morse served with a Siberian regiment in the campaign in Poland in the first months of the conflict. He goes on to give a more detailed description of the diet of the soldiers of his regiment, which he compared unfavourably with that of the armies of the western powers; the ordinary soldier was generally not issued with coffee, tea being the Russian national beverage:

> The army from 'All the Russias' seems to be considered the elite troops; but in my opinion the Siberians are not in any way inferior to them, and the Tiflis Rifles is one of the finest bodies of light infantry I have ever seen. The physique of the men, generally, is magnificent, and their powers of endurance unsurpassed by that of any soldiers in the world. They can march and fight, too, on rations so scanty and coarse that I much doubt if any other European soldiers would tolerate such food. Many of the regiments for days had no better diet than tea and biscuit. Milk was not drunk in the tea, but sugar was used when it could be obtained. The troops were supposed to have a ration of sugar, and also salt. Some years ago the sugar ration was abolished, but the health of the men deteriorated so much that it was again served out to them with beneficial results.[5]

He also took part in the initial Russian advance into East Prussia in 1914. In this campaign, as in the 1914 war of movement in the west, the ordinary soldier relied heavily on what he could carry with him. Sometimes commissariat wagons had difficulty finding the troops whom they were

A Russian army-issue food tin, containing a meat stew. On the outside of the can are instructions on how to heat it. (Author's collection)

supposed to be supplying, or indeed keeping up with them if the advance was rapid. Morse tells us:

> We had brought three days' rations in our haversacks. The food consisted of biscuit, and fat boiled mutton, which is excellent diet for marching men. Our drink was water only, which we had to procure where we could find it; not an easy task, as the rivers were full of putrid bodies and carcasses of horses, and the Germans had polluted many of the wells.[6]

The Germans counterattacked, however, and drove the Russian army back. Their advance took them into what is now Poland, then part of the Russian Empire. For Polish civilians and Russian POWs alike, life under the German yoke here was harsh in the extreme. Laura de Gozdawa Turczynowicz was a well-to-do Polish woman in Suwalki. Having a large house, German officers were billeted with her, and these men expected also to be fed. She had hidden as much food as she could inside couches in her house, because the German occupying forces had placed a levy upon the civilians of Suwalki, confiscating so much that there was barely enough for the townspeople to eat. She wrote:

German soldiers eating in a looted shop, during the advance into Russia in 1915.
(Library of Congress: Bain collection)

Four officers from the Ober-Kommando took up quarters with us. I
told them there was no more food. I had only macaroni, zwieback,
and a few jars of strawberry and raspberry preserves, no potatoes,
and about a half-pound of coffee and tea . . . Not long after that,
when things were at their very worst in the matter of food, an officer
walked into the room where I was busy with the children, a doctor
of the sanitary service, of Polish blood! Oh! how glad I was to see
him, and how kind he was examining into all the details, not only of
the children's health, but how we lived . . . That afternoon this good
doctor, Sanitats Rat, sent me a loaf of bread and four eggs! Nothing
I have ever seen, no jewels, were ever so precious in my eyes as that
white bread and eggs, for in the town the food had all been taken,
and there was none to buy![7]

Through her cook, Mrs Turczynowicz was able to obtain a little milk, which
was in extremely short supply, though often it was confiscated by German
soldiers. She continued:

Once my cook found a chicken! It also was taken from her. She cried and called down such vengeance upon the thieves, the soldiers of the army of occupation, that I told her she would be shot if they understood what she said. Not long after a Jew brought me five chickens. Five roubles apiece! If I could keep them they meant eggs for the children. So I had them shut up in what had been our beautiful library. They roosted on the pretty old shelves, clawed over the books, and I did not care or have any feeling about it. Those things were finished, passed out of my life. After that we were able to buy more food. Potatoes were to be had [but only] at a ruinous price . . . [8]

Laura de Gozdawa Turczynowicz, who described the suffering of Polish civilians and Russian POWs under German occupation in 1915. (From Turczynowicz, *When the Prussians came to Poland*)

She also did her best to help the Russian prisoners of war in the town, who were harshly treated by their German captors. Emaciated and starving, they were glad of whatever she could offer:

Every day there was the excitement of feeding the two parties of prisoners; once there was nothing but soup made of meal, and a very old and dry ham bone! To make so much soup with one small bone! The prisoners found it good, hot at least. The Jews knew I was feeding prisoners and so brought anything they could get to me, knowing they would be paid, the Germans taking things without the ceremony of paying! . . . The look of those men is burned, seared in, upon my mind. That sound of their voices when they saw us coming, for there was no one else but me to help my cook carry the pot of soup; then . . . I doled out whatever there was to those reaching, trembling hands.

One day a company of prisoners were passing. Just in front of our windows one fell to the ground . . . The poor creatures instantly begged me for food . . . 'Little Sister, give us something to eat. We have been kept in the forest, near the trenches, working; there was nothing to eat [and] many of us died like our comrade!' My cook did not need to be told what to do; she had the samovar already going, and the usual soup for the prisoners was cooking . . . I gave them each a half cupful of soup; they protested at the amount, but after taking a few sips they suffered pain.[9]

Many of these ill-nourished, indeed starving, POWs would inevitably die. Those Russian soldiers still fighting against the Germans were immeasurably better off in terms of food, but as the war progressed the food supplies for these men also became more haphazard. Lobanov-Rostovsky again describes the Russian advance into Galicia, against the Austro-Hungarian army, between October 1914 and May 1915. Due to difficulties of supply, the food available to the men of his battalion was often erratic, and they were reduced to raiding the supplies of the local peasantry:

> After a day at Ilja the advance proceeded, and once more our movement was so rapid that we lost touch with our ordnance service. This meant great hardships as far as food was concerned. We were short of bread, meat, sugar, and salt. The absence of salt was the most painful of all as it left food without any taste whatsoever, and, notwithstanding my hunger, I could not force myself to eat it. At one time the only thing we could find in the fields around us was potatoes and so potatoes we had for breakfast, dinner, and supper for over a week.[10]

Very often, for the Russian soldier it was a case of living off the land and foraging for whatever he could find. In the same campaign was a Cossack officer, Sergei Kournakoff, who wrote:

> We had been sitting at the bottom of a little valley for several hours, in a drizzling rain. The men had caught one of the numerous half wild sheep which roamed the sides of the mountains. This was our only food because the supply train could never reach us in this wilderness. There was no bread, no salt, nothing except mutton. As a substitute for salt, we burned the bones of the sheep and crushed them into powder. It was bitter, but helped a little. The poor horses had to eat the moldy hay which was rotting in abandoned haystacks. With infinite pains, the men had started a fire and were roasting the shashlyk on a big forked stick. There was a mountain range between the Germans and us, and our orders were to stay here until they had occupied the crest. We were cold, wet, and hungry. I watched the sizzling quarter of mutton with mixed feelings of desire and nausea: never had I dreamed before that bread and salt were such important things![11]

Unlike the situation in the British army, where on the whole, in the front line at least the officers ate much the same food as their men, in the Russian army officers could expect a much higher standard of fare than their subordinates. A former Russian officer remembered:

. . . we decided to give a party for the many officers of other squadrons. At such parties there was a lot of food and a lot of drinking, and my squadron had the unusual luck of having among our soldiers a fantastic professional cook. This man was very dedicated; his name was Samsonov. Before having been drafted into the Reserves he had been a secret police agent and a trainer of police dogs. Food was plentiful because there was a supply center for the whole division where one could buy delicacies that had been brought from the city. Otherwise eggs, butter, meat, and poultry could be bought in some of the local villages. So with the delicacies from the city, the local food, and the fantastic cooking of Samsonov, I never ate better than from the moment I went to war.[12]

Another Briton, R. Scotland-Liddell, was serving with a Russian regiment and as late as mid-1917 he recorded that:

In the matter of rations I have found that the Russians have the better of it. A Russian officers' mess with its generous supply of food is a banquet compared with the British officers' mess-room. The cooking is much better. Our English table has much to learn from Russia. Indeed, referring again to the soldiers' food, I am not sure but what the simple fare of the Russians is much more nourishing and much more health-giving than the preserved food with which the British soldiers were rationed in Kars and elsewhere. Perhaps it will be interesting to tell what my rations in the Russian Army are. At the moment of writing (June, 1917) I receive daily the following allowances:

Meat (this includes beef, mutton, ham and sausage) 1 lb.
Butter 2/3 oz.
Eggs oz.
Rice, Kasha, etc. 2 2/3 oz.
Flour 3 1/3 oz.
Macaroni 2 2/3 oz.
Sugar 2/3 oz.
Bread (black or white – usually black) 1 1/2 lb.
Cabbage, carrots, onions or other vegetables 6 2/3 oz.
Potatoes 1 lb.
Milk 1/2 lb.

and each month I receive 5 oz. of tea and 10 oz. of coffee. I find that these rations are ample. It must be remembered that Russians drink their tea very weak, so that the allowance of an ounce and a quarter a week is ample. Jam, as we in England know it, is unknown on the Russian Front. At present (June, 1917) our woods are full of wild strawberries and whortle-berries. The soldiers gather pans of these each day. We put them in our glasses of tea – and sop them before we drink the tea. This is the nearest to jam we ever get![13]

However, he also was aware that the food of the ordinary Russian soldier was by this stage in the war much poorer. He notes:

The Russian soldiers' food was simple and good as a rule – black bread, kasha, cabbage-soup, meat and tea. But there were times when the food was very bad. During the [1916] retreat the Russian soldier very often had only stale black bread – green with mould – to eat . . . The general living conditions were bad, too. In the spring of 1917 I know that a whole regiment was down with scurvy, caused by the unhealthy living quarters and the poorness of the food of the men . . . [14]

The hardships endured by the ordinary Russian soldiers – not least the shortage of food – would lead them ultimately to side with those people who sought to overthrow the Tsarist regime in Russia, and who in the main comprised the populations of the major urban centres, Petrograd and Moscow. In reality, what the war had succeeded in doing was to drive a wedge between the urban populations and the rural communities upon which they depended for their food. The conflict affected the two groups in very different ways, and it is necessary to bear in mind at all times the vast sizes of both the country and of the mass of peasantry in that country, numbering around 160 million. The rural, agrarian communities often maintained an autonomous, self-sufficient existence and as noted previously, lived lives largely devoid of luxury items. One source tells us in more detail of the diet of the rural poor at the time of the First World War:

The food of the [Russian] peasant is . . . simple. By force of circumstances he is essentially a vegetarian. In the first place the Greek Orthodox religion prohibits the use of all animal foods, including egg and milk products, but excepting fish, on Wednesdays and Fridays and at various lengthy intervals during the year. In the second place, meat is rather expensive; the hog or steer which the peasant raises, he is likely to sell in order to obtain the money with which to pay his taxes and debts. Even the well-to-do mouzhik

'The food of the Russian peasant is simple . . .' Russian women sit down to a roadside meal of tea and kasha (porridge), around the time of the First World War.
(Library of Congress)

partakes of meat only on Sundays and holidays and at other special occasions, never every day. The chief articles of food are bread, made out of the whole grain of rye, and potatoes, also the various vegetables in season, cucumbers, beets, onions, turnips, radishes, garlic, and various milk products . . . The most common dishes at the peasant table are shtchui – a vegetable soup, and kasha – a sort of gruel or mush made from buckwheat meal or some other cereal. If these dishes are properly cooked and flavored, they are as delicious and nourishing as anything ever prepared in any kitchen. The shtchui made from cabbage with a generous slice of beef boiled in it, and enriched with a big cupful of cream, will waken hunger in the most dyspeptic Russian – be he mouzhik or grand duke. And the kasha steamed and baked and served hot with a generous layer of golden butter and a cupful of fresh sweet milk poured over it, is a dish for kings.[15]

At the same time, there was another Russia; a wealthy, metropolitan Russia whose inhabitants had more in common with the citizens of London, Paris or Berlin than with their own countrymen in the villages. An American woman, travelling by train through Russia in June 1915, saw glimpses of it:

Opposite us sat a fat, red-nosed man, with a fur cap, though it was summer. Between his legs was a huge, bulky bag. When the train stopped, he put a pinch of tea in his little blue enameled teapot, which he filled at the hot-water tank that is at every Russian station just for that purpose. He pulled out of his bag numberless newspaper packages and spread them out on the newspaper across his knees – big fat sausages and thin fried ones, a chunk of ham, a boiled chicken, dried pressed meat, a lump of melting butter, some huge cucumber pickles, and cheese. With a murderous-looking knife he cut thick slices from a big round loaf of bread that he held against his breast. He sweetened his tea with some sugar from another package, and sliced a lemon into it. When he had finished eating, he carefully rolled up the food again and put it away, and settled back in his chair . . . At noon and night we stopped at railway stations for our meals. After Bulgaria and Roumania it was bewildering to see the counters laden with hot and cold meats and vegetables and appetizing 'zakouskas', and thick 'ztchee' soup, and steaming samovars for tea. Through the open windows came refreshing puffs of wind. At the restaurant tables sat officers, rich Jews, and traveling business men – nothing much in it all to suggest war. Always, on the station walls were bright-colored portraits, in heavy gilt frames, of the Czar and Czarina and the royal family. And always in the corners of the room were ikons with candles lighted before them at night. The train always started before people had finished eating. At supper, one of the priests almost got left and had to run for it, a piece of meat-pie in one hand, the other holding up his flapping gray gown.[16]

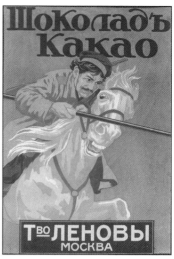

This unusual Russian advertisement for cocoa, dating from 1915, shows a charging cossack. Unlike in Britain, few advertisements in Russia made reference to the war. The Russian economy – and Russian food advertising – were much less developed. (Author's collection)

The war provoked an agrarian crisis in Russia, for reasons that with the benefit of hindsight may appear now to be obvious. In the first place, the mobilisation of about eighteen million soldiers seriously drained the supply of labour in a rural economy that was barely mechanised at all. Secondly, the war caused an acute shortage of agricultural implements, and of materials for their repair. Switched over to war purposes as they were, Russia's industries greatly curtailed their manufacture of farm tools, which was scanty even under normal conditions. At the same time, it was exceedingly difficult to import them. Before the war, every year Russia bought from Germany large quantities of agricultural machinery – of imported ploughs alone Germany supplied some 43 per cent of Russia's requirements – but in 1914 this source was immediately cut off. Other industrial nations, especially among the Allies, had difficulty getting supplies to Russia, and with the blockade in operation in the Baltic and in the Dardanelles, trade with them became more difficult. Besides, their output of agricultural implements was also necessarily reduced by the war. Not having new machinery, the Russian peasant continued to use his old dilapidated tools, which he could not even repair, because the proper material was lacking.

A third cause contributing to the agrarian crisis was the decrease of livestock in the village. The best horses were drafted into the army, and the mouzhik (peasant) was tempted to sell his cattle because of the inordinately high prices they would fetch. Under these circumstances acute suffering was imminent. True, the peasant possessed more money than ever before, but it was paper money – metal coins had practically disappeared from circulation – and its value was constantly diminishing because of the constantly rising prices. In reality the peasant was growing poorer; he was

A Russian peasant ploughs his fields. Russian agriculture in the First World War was greatly hampered by poor equipment, made worse by the curtailment of supplies from Germany. (Author's collection)

disposing of a large portion of his principal commodity, and his paper money could not buy kerosene, iron, leather, oils or sugar. The longer the war lasted the poorer he became. As the Russian economy began to break down, the problem became one of getting the peasants to release their grain. A manufacturer in a Russian town explained the situation facing the authorities:

> How can they get food into the towns? The peasant will not give up his grain, because he cannot get goods in return. He has shut himself up in his village, and gets along quite nicely there. He has plenty of food and forage, and he is making his own clothes. Only in villages near the towns have the peasants been used to ready-made clothes. In all the villages more remote, they still make homespun garments of flax and wool and sheepskin. When the peasant does sell grain

for cash, he soon goes lame on the money he saves; for while we put our money in banks and so keep it in circulation, the peasant stuffs it into his boots.[17]

Throughout 1916, whilst the rural areas of Russia were managing to just about rub along, hardship in urban areas grew. Indeed in some cities it was worse than that being experienced in Germany at the same time. One eyewitness reported:

[In Moscow the] talk is all of the terrible dorogovizna. The pretty word dorogovizna means dearness of living, and it is the commonest in the townsman's vocabulary this season of the war. The price of nearly every commodity in Russia has doubled or trebled since the outbreak of war. One would expect the price of manufactured goods to rise there; but the surprising phenomenon is that, despite the overwhelming abundance of foodstuffs in Russia and Russia's inability to export any of that abundance, food has become, on the whole, dearer than in Berlin. The *Russian Word* has a long list of comparative prices, showing that out of sixteen common articles of food ten have increased more in price in Moscow than in Germany. The price of mutton has increased 180 per cent, in Berlin, but it has increased 281 per cent, in Moscow; pork 114 per cent in Berlin, 142 per cent, in Moscow; white bread 27 per cent, in Berlin, 45 per cent, in Moscow; sugar, 27 per cent, in Berlin, 57 per cent, in Moscow, and so forth. Sugar has in many districts disappeared entirely, and shop windows exhibit the notice 'No sugar whatever,' which means not even the dirty brown soft sugar which has displaced the rafinade. At Archangel there is a fixed allowance of 1 lb. of sugar per person per month, and that is only accessible for settled inhabitants. As a visitor I was lucky to purchase twenty-four lumps at a halfpenny a lump. At the railway stations at many buffets you are offered sugar candy or raspberry drops with your tea, or a wrapped caramel with your coffee. In cases where they have sugar the waiters have the audacity to put it in for you, lest you should secrete what you did not want. Now cards have been introduced for sugar almost everywhere, even in the villages. The possession of a card entitles you to purchase the article specified on it. At first receiving the food card the heart rejoices. But it is one thing to possess a card and another to find a grocer who has anything to sell.[18]

Russian women discussing the worsening food situation, Petrograd 1917. (Library of Congress)

The answer of the Imperial Russian authorities to this crisis was to try to regulate everything. The government tried to take charge of the entire business of supply and issued cards for almost anything; thus it became necessary to present a card at the grocer, another at the butcher, and so on. Every day in Moscow queues the length of the street were a common sight, the people waiting hours with cards in their hands, waiting for a pound or so of sugar. So large were the queues which turned up at the butchers' shops on the mornings of the meat days that the butchers decided to issue tickets the day beforehand – on each ticket was a number designating the holder's turn to buy meat on the following day.

In 1916 the fruit harvest was good. Some evidently made a handsome profit on apples, since the common price in Moscow was the equivalent three or four pence British apiece (about £5 today). Despite the dearth of sugar, jam-making was carried on in the country to an even greater extent than usual. People felt that it was a good way to save sugar for the winter, by putting it into jam. (Russian jam, as described earlier, is unlike its British counterpart, being much sweeter, and was often put in tea as a syrup. It was never spread on bread and butter.)

Early in the war, vodka had been prohibited by order of the Tsar, and by 1916 it had disappeared. Beer had also gone, and wine was sold at chemists' only on presentation of a medical certificate endorsed by the police. Far from being relaxed, by mid-war the alcohol prohibition had actually increased, and districts to which the Tsar's original ukase (edict) did not apply, such as Russian Central Asia, had been taken in. It was not uncommon to see smart officers sitting down to a bottle of citro, and apparently without grumbling. Restaurants served *kvas*, a sort of fruity ginger-beer, which was not allowed to have more than one per cent alcohol and was in no sense a real beer, or birch beer, a sort of empty symbol of ale taken not because it was pleasant but because the diner had to order something with his meal.

There was no wine in restaurants, only grape juice. As regards wine, it must be remembered that in the Caucasus, in Transcaucasia, and in Russian Central Asia there were wine industries, and wine was the popular local drink, not tea as in Russia proper. This wine was usually kept in skins and

Russian meat ration coupons. These examples were issued to an Englishman working for the Russian admiralty in Petrograd. (Courtesy of Richard Davies)

sold in pots. There was also a bottling industry, but the export of this wine from these remote parts of the Empire to Russia proper had been prohibited, except in cases of specially guaranteed orders. In some cases, British and American and other foreign subjects were allowed to purchase wine for their private use on the presentation of a certificate. Russian prohibition was seized upon by advocates of the measure in the USA as evidence of the benefits which it would produce in their own country. One of these prohibitionists was Ernest Gordon, who travelled to Russia to see from himself the results of the ban. He wrote of a visit to a specialist in Petrograd, which it must be said is tinged more than a little with wishful thinking:

> The war Dr. Bechterev believed to have proved helpful to Prohibition in that it had put millions of drinkers under temporary discipline. He anticipated, however, no reaction when they returned home. Opinion favorable to Prohibition has so developed that it will not be possible to break it down later. The movement has, in fact, safely passed the crest of the hill. Then I rode with him to the Psycho-Neurological Institute at the other side of the city and talked with his assistant, Dr. Gorielov. 'The blessings of Prohibition,' averred Dr. Gorielov, 'cannot be exaggerated. They are, in fact, so great and so varied that it is impossible to enumerate them all. The people could not be more satisfied. There was a certain opportuneness in choosing the outbreak of the war as the time for trying the experiment. Everybody accepted the new order as a matter of patriotism. There were no long discussions, no ups-and-downs of agitation. Then when the proofs had been delivered ad oculos for 15 months public opinion was made up both as to the feasibility and the value of Prohibition.'[19]

Nevertheless, there were often surprising positive social results arising from the Russian alcohol ban. It was said that male complexions generally became less red. As a result of over two years' temperance, violent crime practically disappeared from whole regions of the countryside, and it was said that when occasionally some brutality occurred, the police often managed to bring to book not only the direct offender, but also the person who was secretly brewing the liquor which lay behind the crime. The spirit of peace came into the industrial or mining village on the Sunday and Saint's Day, where formerly there were often scenes of outrageous public hooliganism on the part of whole populations. Money had increased in the pockets of the poor, and there was a higher standard of living; butter was now being spread on the black bread. Peasant families were enjoying the eggs which formerly they would have sold for the money to buy drink.

Archangel, North Russia. By 1917 the port was one of the few places in Russia in which alcohol could be obtained, due to illicit supplies entering from Britain. (Library of Congress: Bain collection)

Paradoxically, one of the reasons given for the shortage of food supplies in the great towns was that owing to the fact that the peasants could find nothing on which to spend their money they would not sell their produce. Formerly they would buy vodka. In Archangel city, where there was evidence of drunkenness, the transgressors were often drunk on British whisky obtained from the boats in the harbour. Again, it was said that the pilot taking boats out of the harbour always expected a bottle of whisky as well as his three-rouble tip. All manner of people were, as a British captain expressed it, 'bumming around for whisky', and there were calls for ships bound for Archangel only to be allowed to take in a limited supply of the drink. *Shinkarstvo*, or illicit distilling and sale, had broken out in some places. Alcoholic substitutes were prepared and sold in small quantities, and there were several hundred prosecutions connected with this. The police tried hard to suppress this *shinkarstvo*, though in a few extreme cases incurables took to methylated spirit, eau de Cologne or furniture polish, and some died as a consequence.

What the breakdown in order in Russia also demonstrated was the fact that food was inextricably linked to fuel. The Russians from about 1915 onwards had used up their stockpiles of coal, and were denied fresh supplies either from Britain or Germany, their two pre-war suppliers. Their own coal producing areas were also under German occupation. Thus Russian food supplies were diminished both directly and indirectly; production fell, and the disorganisation of the transport system increased. Moreover, this disorganisation increased exponentially: the more the military needs of the nation demanded of the railways, the less as time went on were the railways able to meet those demands, for the inexorable increase in wear and tear could not be met by the repair shops. Stories of corruption among the railway officials circulated freely from mouth to mouth, and an exasperated public sentiment conveniently assigned the evils of transport disorganisation to this cause. However, corruption, though by no means absent, was far from adequate to cause a national disaster of such magnitude as the breakdown of railway transport in Russia. The number of railway cars under repair at the beginning of 1916 was 20,130, and it had increased to 25,810 by January 1917. The number of locomotives under repair in May 1916, reached the figure of 3,387 out of the 19,951 which comprised the total equipment.[20] The chief cause of the breakdown was a lack of all sorts of materials for repair work. Food supply relied upon railway transport, which was now crippled by the lack of fuel. Towards the end of 1916, the situation in respect of the supply of fuel grew critical. It is no more than the simple truth that Russia, at that time, was face to face with fuel-hunger as well as with food-hunger, and the one exacerbated the other. The consequences of this and the other factors at play were plain to see:

Meat has so risen in price that through-out all Russia four meatless days have been proclaimed, and on Tuesday, Wednesday, Thursday, and Friday you must keep to vegetables, fish, or fowls. On these days no meat may be sold and no cattle may be slaughtered. The meat may not be sold in a smoked state nor as sausage. When this measure was introduced the butchers wailed, if the cows and the calves rejoiced. The chickens suffered for it. But ask a Russian, and he will tell you all suffer for it. The price of vegetables has risen, the price of meat on the days when you buy it has risen, the price of fish and fowl has risen. One day at the National Hotel in Moscow I noticed cauliflowers standing at the superb price of 3 roubles, 50 copecks . . . From scores of districts in Russia petitions have been sent to Petrograd – Cancel the regulations as to meatless days. But the regulations are not likely to be cancelled. At the restaurants such small portions are given that it is difficult to make a good meal even at large expense. And the soups which are made without meat are the same price as they used to be when meat was allowed . . . Sugar has disappeared because the Germans and Austrians are in possession of some of the richest beetroot country of Russia, and also of several sugar factories. Coffee is scarce because there is war with Turkey; butter and eggs because the peasants, being unable to obtain vodka, have no particular use for extra cash, and won't sell their products. Speculators are holding large quantities of provisions in ice-houses and waiting till the prices are pushed higher and higher. The banks are holding quantities of sugar. There are many explanations.[21]

Another eyewitness, also in Moscow, recalled that the hardships were not born fairly by all, and this only served to increase the discontent of the urban poor:

When Christmas [1916] arrived, millions of good pious people could not celebrate that joyful holiday, because of the shortages of fundamental necessities of daily life. According to some of them I knew personally, they could not find the room in their hearts for real Christmas joy at all. There were shortages of bread, flour, milk, sugar, fats, clothing, and particularly of fuel, which was terribly needed by all! Only the wealthy, who were rich before the war, and those who had become rich on war profits, were able to buy food-stuffs and other necessities of life on the black market, for which they had paid fabulous prices. Those of us who knew the realities of life in Moscow, in those days, could not deny the truthfulness of these accusations.[22]

She continued with a description of the worsening situation in January 1917:

Moscow was visited by extreme cold. It crippled the city and paralyzed its entire life for several days. Thousands of families suffered acutely because they did not have enough fuel. Thousands of others had no bread. The neighborhood stores and bakeries did not sell bread for three days. Although housewives had ration coupons and waited in long lines many hours for bread, they waited in vain.[23]

A story circulated in Moscow at this time of a woman standing in a food queue in the freezing cold, carrying a baby wrapped in swaddling clothes. It was customary in these circumstances for other women to allow the nursing mother to proceed to the front of the queue, but when she did so, a nearby policeman happened to glance more closely at the 'baby', only to discover that it was in fact a piece of wood wrapped in blankets! The story

A winter market in Moscow; as food hardship began to bite in the city, supplies in such markets began to dwindle. (Author's collection)

had it that the incident caused such amusement among the weary Muscovites that they overlooked the attempted deception on the part of the woman. In contrast with Britain, however, where strenuous official attempts were made to demonstrate that food hardship was being borne by all classes equally, in Russia, corruption and graft by the authorities served to further stoke a situation which was steadily becoming a crisis. Our eyewitness states:

> . . . there was supposed to be just enough bread in Moscow to fill the small rations of every person. That, however, was not the fact, for many people could not obtain their share, in spite of long waiting. Although not supposed to do so, some newspapers dared to publish that the reason for the precarious situation was that certain individuals, a kind of human parasite, whom the angry mothers of Moscow called 'vultures,' 'hyenas,' and other terms, were shamelessly prosperous on other people's suffering. It was a known

DISCOVER MORE ABOUT MILITARY HISTORY

Pen & Sword Books have over 4000 books currently available, our imprints include; Aviation, Naval, Military, Archaeology, Transport, Frontline, Seaforth and the Battleground series, and we cover all periods of history on land, sea and air.

Keep up to date with our new releases by completing and returning the form below (no stamp required if posting in the UK).

Alternatively, if you have access to the internet, please complete your details online via our website at **www.pen-and-sword.co.uk.**

All those subscribing to our mailing list via our website will receive a free e-book, *Mosquito Missions* by Martin W Bowman. Please enter code number ACC1 when subscribing to receive your free e-book.

Mr/Mrs/Ms ....

Address...

Postcode.............................. Email address..

Website: www.pen-and-sword.co.uk Email: enquiries@pen-and-sword.co.uk
Telephone: 01226 734555 Fax: 01226 734438
Stay in touch: facebook.com/penandswordbooks or follow us on Twitter @penswordbooks

Freepost Plus RTKE-RGRJ-KTTX
Pen & Sword Books Ltd
47 Church Street
BARNSLEY
S70 2AS

fact that they operated a so-called black market, selling bread and other foodstuffs, including sugar, butter, and flour, for such high prices that only wealthy people could afford to buy them. When I inquired about the manner in which bread and other food was obtained by the people operating black markets, I was told that the high officials in the food department, as well as in the police department, were co-operating with the black-market operators, and even protecting them. The people appeared to know this situation, and their anger against the higher-ups was growing every day.[24]

The Russian Revolution of March 1917 broke out first in the city which, though not literally besieged, was suffering most from the effects of blockade; Petrograd. The setting-up of the Commune in Paris in 1871, and the outbreak of revolution in Petrograd in 1917, were both produced by the same force, namely, the power of blockade. However, the term 'blockade' as applied to Petrograd requires a little explanation. The external blockade of Russia, together with the internal process of economic disintegration, disorganised the system of internal communications so much as to transform Russia from being one economic whole into a congeries of separate provinces; they were separate because of the great difficulty of communication between one and another. Province was cut off from province as much as though the enemy had really penetrated deeply into Russia and by force had isolated part from part. Petrograd suffered from

Russian women protesting about food shortages outside the Duma (Parliament) in Petrograd. (Library of Congress)

this 'internal blockade' most of all, and it was significant that the revolution began in urban rather than in rural Russia. An eyewitness to the events which took place in Petrograd in March 1917 wrote:

> Workmen were running through the streets carrying huge signs bearing such inscriptions as: 'We want bread!' [and] 'Down with the lines!' The latter demand referred to the annoyance and suffering caused by the food and clothing rationing system. Ever since the early days of the war practically all commodities had been distributed by the card system. We had to have cards for everything – bread, meat, butter, sugar, clothes, coal, in fact, all the necessities of life. Luxuries were almost entirely barred. These restrictions, while necessary, bore particularly hard on the poor. The rich found ways of evading them. Through various channels they succeeded in getting more and better things than they were entitled to, and even when they took their place in line it was their servants and not themselves who had to endure the personal discomfort of the long, weary wait. For the poor, however, it was a case of wait in line or go without.
>
> In those days, coming home late at night, I had sometimes seen the bread-line forming for the following morning's allotment. The poor devils were preparing to stand in line all through the night so as to be served as quickly as possible in the morning when the distribution began. If this had happened only occasionally, it would

Protests and revolution engulf Russia, March 1917. The placard reads: 'Long live the Provisional Government; Long Live Democracy; Freedom for Russia'. (Author's collection)

A typical peasant village in Russia around the time of the First World War. Life in such places had changed little in hundreds of years, and the villages were largely self-sufficient. Although the peasant villages avoided food hardship during the war, famine would strike much of Russia as civil war followed revolution. (Author's collection)

perhaps have made little impression, but it had been going on for months now and began to look like a permanent institution. The demand 'down with the lines' meant far more than it signified on its face. It was a demand for equality and freedom, a protest against privilege, an appeal for the leveling of classes.[25]

One young Russian officer was perceptive enough to see that Russia's problems in 1917, and the subsequent revolution were largely the result of transport difficulties rather than actual food shortage (though he blamed this on deliberate sabotage rather than incompetence):

Contrary to what people said and heard, food in Russia was in plenty. The whole problem was in getting that food to the big cities. Most railroad boxcars were requisitioned for the transportation of troops. The rail road tracks had been, since the beginning of the war, in disrepair, trains rolled slowly, and among the railroad personnel there were many Socialists who exercised plain sabotage. All of this created an artificial shortage of food supplies in the big cities like Moscow and Petersburg.[26]

Yet the March Revolution did little to bring about positive change, and the Provisional Government which took control of the country in its wake was weak and ineffective. It lacked both the will and the capacity to tackle Russia's food shortages, and a bad situation became critical. Further evidence of the growing division between town and city even after the March Revolution comes from Ernest Poole, an English journalist:

Last summer, as the new government proclaimed and proclaimed, month after month, and still did not meet the peasant's needs, he grew bitter toward the government. Disgusted with the cities because of the disorders there, he made up his mind to stick to his village, grow his own flax and make his own clothes. Roubles, he said, were worthless, for they could buy him nothing now. But bread he could eat, and bread he would keep until the towns starved and so came to their senses. In Petrograd, although I was stopping at one of the best Russian hotels, often in the morning the waiter would come up to my room with the cheerful tidings, 'No sugar today, no butter, no eggs, no milk.' And he would set before me a pot of clear bitter coffee and a small chunk of soggy 'black bread'. But when I made trips to the villages, in the huts of the more prosperous peasants I would be regaled by my hosts with white bread, milk and eggs and butter. I would fatten on the land for a time, and then would return to my meagre life in that starved elaborate hotel.[27]

Thus, Russia was the first of the major powers to suffer a serious collapse, largely brought about by her difficulties in food supply. Although food concerns would be a key element in the arguments and slogans of the Bolsheviks, who in October 1917 seized power from the Provisional Government, with such statements as 'We Want Bread and Peace and Freedom' and 'Land for the Peasants, Bread for the Workers, Peace for the World', Russia's trials were not yet over. The Bolshevik revolutionaries of October 1917 took a weary and battered Russia out of the war with

Germany by signing the treaty of Brest-Litovsk, but led her only as far as a bitter and protracted civil war which exacerbated the existing problems. The food crisis in Russia was by no means over, and by 1918 it had worsened to become an all-out famine, which was to last until the early 1920s.

Chapter 4

The Home Front in Britain

Food rationing and food shortages on the home front were an aspect of the First World War which was entirely new to the British people. Never before in warfare had an enemy of those people possessed the military capability of starving them into submission, and arguably never again would an enemy come so close to achieving that goal. So critical did the food situation become that the state was forced to step in to regulate food supply and pricing, one of the many sweeping changes in British society forced upon it by the First World War. The crisis brought about many curtailments and restrictions on diet and eating habits, but these were borne by the British people mostly with stoicism, and in some cases even with humour. Although

Germany's U-boat fleet would be an increasing menace to British food supplies as the war went on. (Library of Congress)

before the war, Britain had appeared to be the nation with perhaps the most vulnerable food supply of all, in she was to prove herself to be one of the most robust.

Upon the eve of the First World War, British agriculture provided only a small fraction of the nation's food. Four out of every five slices of the bread the British ate before the war were made from wheat grown abroad, and three out of every five of these slices were spread with imported butter. In addition, the British imported four-fifths of their lard, two-thirds of their ham and bacon, and three-quarters of their cheese. This dependence on foreign food was due both to the decline of British agriculture in the nineteenth century, and Britain's unalloyed free-trade policy. Whilst other European countries put up tariff walls to protect their domestic food supplies, the British never perceived their reliance upon imported food to be a weakness, believing instead that the Royal Navy would always be strong enough to protect these food supplies in time of war. The power of the Royal Navy to guarantee the nation's supply of imports would be severely tested in the coming four years, as Germany mounted a concerted effort to force Britain into surrender by cutting off those supplies. Britain likewise attempted to starve her enemy into submission, and Sir Arthur (later Lord) Salter later pointed out:

> It was as much a war of competing blockades, the surface and the submarine, as of competing armies. Behind these two blockades the economic systems of the two opposing groups of countries were engaged in a deadly struggle for existence, and at several periods of the war the pressure of starvation seemed likely to achieve an issue beyond the settlement of the entrenched armies or the immobilized navies.[1]

Germany's submarine blockade of England started slowly. It was not until February 1915 that the Germans declared the waters around Britain a 'War Zone' which both enemy and neutral vessels would enter at their peril. But the threats and protests of neutrals, especially the United States, kept the Germans from continuing the unrestricted attacks on merchant vessels which were necessary to a successful submarine campaign. For at least eighteen months the British were, thanks mainly to the pressure of the neutrals, spared the rigors of unrestricted U-boat warfare. The Germans moreover had only a small number of submarines in the earlier part of the war, and probably could not have maintained an effective blockade anyway until they augmented their undersea fleet. Winston Churchill wrote afterwards that for most of the first two years of the war, the enemy submarines were of no appreciable inconvenience to Britain.

Winston Churchill, First Lord of the Admiralty, believed that the U-boats offered no real inconvenience to Britain during the first two years of the war. (Library of Congress)

Liberal Prime Minister H. H. Asquith was fundamentally opposed to government intervention in the free market, which food control and rationing would represent. (Library of Congress)

Because the U-boat campaign was not carried on effectively until later in the war, the British in the earlier part of the conflict had no difficulty in continuing to import a sufficient supply of food. Food imports were apparently so easy to come by that, despite the obvious potential problem posed by Germany's growing submarine fleet, the British government did virtually nothing in the first two years of the war to guard against a future food shortage. The administration of Prime Minister Herbert Asquith was Liberal to its core. Every fibre of that government recoiled against any measure which might interfere with free trade, or which might be considered an infringement of free market economics. Just as participation in the fighting was for the first eighteen months of the war to be a voluntary matter, dependent upon the conscience of the individual, so too food control and submission to government control of production were voluntary.

The earliest effects of the war upon domestic food supply manifested themselves in price rises; ironically the cause of this was largely the actions of the British government, rather than the German. With quantities of foodstuffs required for feeding the rapidly expanding armies, as well as government monopolisation of railways and rolling stock, the difficulties at first were ones of internal supply. However, trade unions and labour representatives argued that there was more to it than this, and that blatant profiteering was taking place. Albert Beveridge, an American journalist in London, reported:

> Leaflets and pamphlets were distributed, filled with astounding figures showing the rise of prices and demanding government intervention. A pamphlet entitled 'Why Starve?' showed that bread had risen since the outbreak of the war from five pence for a fourpound loaf to seven and one-half pence and was still going up; and while the price of all meat had risen sharply, that consumed by the common people had increased enormously. 'The best parts of British beef and mutton have gone up only an average of seven per cent., whereas the cheaper parts, which the poorer people buy, have risen twenty-two per cent,' declared this striking pamphlet.
>
> Similar soaring of prices was shown in other necessaries of life, the conclusion being, said this appeal, that: 'It is just as important that, in a state of war, the provisioning of the people should be undertaken as a national responsibility as that soldiers should be well looked after . . . National organization of agriculture and national control of the foodstuffs produced, together with the means of transit used in the interests of people in peace as it is now used for military purposes in war – these are the lines which must be followed.'[2]

In August 1915 the Parliamentary War Savings Committee issued a pamphlet outlining ways in which consumption could be reduced. The pamphlet was wide-ranging in its advice, advising economy not just in terms of foodstuffs but also clothing, education and travel. However, it was in the area of domestic consumables that its advice was most pertinent. It urged the importance of eating less meat, and pointed out that some much cheaper but nonetheless very palatable articles of food have the same if not superior nutritional value as animal flesh. Firmly in the pamphlet's sights, however, were alcoholic beverages. Alcohol had been a battleground for many years before the war, with the teetotalist movement periodically making inroads against the licensed trade, but it had been very much a case of two steps forward, one step back. However, the war would bring renewed focus to the national debate over alcohol, adding practical and economic arguments to what had previously been a debate centred largely on morality. The War Savings Committee pamphlet had this to say on the subject:

> It has been estimated that the average expenditure on alcoholic drinks in this country amounts to something over 6s 6d per family

A typical London pub around this time. One of the first steps in government control was in the area of alcoholic drinks and pub opening hours. (Author's collection)

per week. If every family in the land were to cut their drink bill down by, say, one half, and invest the saving on this one item in the War Loan, the amount would come to £80,000,000 per annum.[3]

Nevertheless, the official approach to the problem of alcohol control was that it was too important simply to be left on a voluntary basis. Concern over the treating of wounded soldiers to drinks in pubs, and over drunkenness among well-paid munitions workers, led to creeping state restrictions on the length of time that alcohol was on sale, and the strength at which alcoholic drinks could be sold. The pattern of opening times by which pubs opened their doors around midday, closed again after lunch, and then reopened in the evening was set during the First World War and remained largely in place until the reforms introduced by the Blair government in the twenty-first century. These infringements on the traditional pastime of the working man were deeply resented, for example, No 1 Branch of the National Union of Boot and Shoe Operatives met in Leicester in 1915, and resolved that:

This meeting, representing 9,000 members . . . protests against the action of the military authorities in closing licensed houses at so early an hour as 9pm, on the ground that that it is an uncalled for interference with the liberty of the subject, that it is unnecessary . . . and that it inflicts a hardship on many of the members of our trade who are working overtime in order to cope with Government orders.[4]

Asquith's successor David Lloyd George had a Welsh temperance background, and was strongly in favour of closing pubs down altogether during the duration of the war; however, he was persuaded that this would do more harm than good. King George V set an example to his people when he declared that he would not partake of alcohol, nor allow it an any of his households, until the war was won. The restrictions upon beers, wines and spirits remained one of the most unpopular aspects of wartime control, C. Sheridan Jones writing:

It has become impossible to get whisky after nine-thirty . . . Any publican found diluting his whisky insufficiently may lose his licence, and the man who dares to buy his wife a glass of wine is liable, as one is frequently reminded by conspicuous notices, to pay a fine of one hundred pounds and to serve six months in prison . . . Clubs are shut at half after midnight . . . And 'policewomen' have been put on to help us look after our morals. We have tried to persuade ourselves, that these things were necessary to defeat the enemy, and have become as patriotically miserable as possible, resigned, if necessary, to bear even prohibition, and consume cocoa rather than make trouble in war-time.[5]

However, that was by no means the whole story, and Sheridan Jones was surprised when, early in the war, he was told of nightclubs which continued to operate and serve alcohol late into the night, in defiance of the law. Eager to learn more, he was taken on a tour of these illicit drinking dens:

The first establishment we visited was not a mile away from Piccadilly Circus, and on our cicerone going bail for us we were all promptly admitted. It was being conducted with eminent propriety and some degree of dullness. Along the whole length of the room, with its bare, polished floors, its bright mirrors and its garish lights, were ranged a number of tables, at each of which sat a group of men and women, smoking, chatting and laughing. Except that the men seemed bored and the women tired, and that there was a certain depression and uniformity of aspect among them, we might have been in any restaurant or public-house you like to name. But there was less jollity and merriment, far less freedom and more restraint, and an indefinite sense, not of passion, but of a wickedness almost austere in its respectability, that conveyed something inexpressibly evil to my mind. The men spoke in whispers and the women answered with discretion. Ours was the noisiest party in the room, and the proprietor often looked our way with pained anxiety. I recollect also that we asked for 'coffee' and 'tea,' instead of whisky and brandy; why, I cannot think, but it was the etiquette of the establishment, which everyone observed, though, as I need hardly say, it would have availed nothing in the unlikely event of a raid. Also, our drinks cost us a good deal more than we should have paid for them under normal conditions, and were of rather inferior quality, though of no doubtful strength. After we had chatted awhile and drunk our fill, we had a look at the dancing saloon. There was a band, which played bright music not too brightly, and half-a-dozen couples going through complicated movements with a depressing correctitude that no suburban seminary could have approached . . . From our club near the Circus we went to one near Leicester Square, now closed, where we found much the same condition of affairs.

[Next our guide] took us, this time, not to a club but to a private hotel, the other side of the water, where we found some excellent champagne and some capital oysters. There were also three or four dancing girls and some soldiers, one of whom sang us some ripping songs, new to civilian ears. The party did not break up till 'early in the morning,' and we all had one of the jolliest times imaginable. How do the night clubs I have been describing manage to exist in the teeth of the law? Chiefly by being careful not to stay too long in one habitat. They disappear and re-emerge with startling suddenness. A little bird tells the proprietor that his establishment has been on his particular perch quite long enough, that the house is being watched, and that if he does not 'get a move on,' why, then, who knows ? – one fine evening the police may raid his beautiful premises. Promptly he packs up and goes and – opens within a night or two round the corner, with the same members and friends, the same band, the same everything. These denizens of the underworld keep a pretty close touch with each other, and 'a nod is as good as a wink to a blind horse.'[6]

Gradually, it became clear that life on the home front it could not simply be a case of 'business as usual' as the government had asserted. Yet necessity is the mother of invention, and shortages of certain items soon led to the development of substitutes. By late 1915, eggs were already in short supply and Bird's Egg Substitute (a form of powdered egg) was being widely advertised as a stop gap. Atora suet grew in popularity as a replacement for beef. In the case of Heinz Pork and Beans, it was no longer possible to continue to produce the product with a piece of cooked pork accompanying the haricot beans in each tin, and henceforth they were sold simply as Heinz Baked Beans. Margarine, though developed before 1914, was now promoted as an alternative to butter. As the war went on, newspapers published recipes containing ever more ingenious substitute foods, for example using beetroot as a replacement for sugar in making jam, or using Nasturtium seeds in pickles.

By the latter part of 1916, unease was growing in Britain over the food situation. There had been a poor harvest that year, and this combined with

As shortages began to bite, substitute foods became increasingly common. Bird's Egg Substitute was widely advertised. (Author's collection)

the slow but sure increase in British merchant shipping being sunk by U-boats, had led to steadily increasing prices. As with all areas of the British war effort, the voluntary approach was simply not up to the demands imposed by war, and the government was urged by many – Winston Churchill among them – to act quickly and decisively to put the food supply on a war footing. Despite the intensity of the opposition to these moves from some quarters, Churchill's calls were heeded. Before the war was over, Britain was to establish a Food Production Department with far-reaching powers over its agricultural economy, to ration and distribute a wide variety of foods, to control its entire merchant shipping industry in the interests of

Blackberry Jelly without Sugar

A FRENCH RECIPE.

Pick a large quantity of blackberries, for this fruit loses a great deal in the boiling. Put the blackberries in a pot, cover with water, and boil. Pass the fruit through a cloth to extract the juice, and add to the juice a lemon, a few carrots, and one or two ordinary, or, better still, sugar beetroots. Place on the fire, and when the liquid will solidify it is sufficiently cooked. Remove the lemon, carrots, and beet, which will not be required further, since the carrots and beet are used to take the place of sugar and the lemon for flavouring. The jelly is poured into jars and fastened down in the usual way.

Recipes like these were frequently published in the British press, using substitute ingredients. (Author's collection)

KITCHEN RECIPES IN WAR-TIME.

Nasturtium Pickle.—INGREDIENTS.—Nasturtium seeds, 2 shallots, teaspoonful salt, ½ teaspoonful bruised black pepper, 2 cloves, ½ oz. allspice, 1 pt. vinegar.

METHOD.—Pick the seeds on a dry day, before they are quite full grown, and spread them for 24 hours in a fairly warm, dry place. If dried in the sun the seeds are better. Put them into wide-mouthed bottles. Now prepare a spiced vinegar. Chop the shallots and put them with the spices and vinegar into a saucepan, heat gradually to boiling point. Draw the saucepan to the side of the stove so as to keep the contents warm, not hot, and leave for three hours; pour it into a jug and the next day strain on to the nasturtium seeds in the bottles, which should be covered down. The pickle should not be used for a month; it is a very good substitute for French capers, and the vinegar is useful for flavouring stews or gravies, and particularly for fish-sauce.

saving tonnage, and to dictate food prices on a grand scale. It is difficult to over-emphasise the enormity of such departures from the prevailing British standards of *laissez-faire* economic policy.

In September 1916, Charles Bathurst MP in a letter to *The Times* supported the demands for a clear public statement on food prices from the government. He stated that the atmosphere of suspicion that surrounded British farmers and millers – which held that they were manipulating the steady increase in food prices since the beginning of the war – was both grossly unfair and wholly without foundation. He believed that the government was fully aware that the prices of wheat, flour and bread in England were governed in Chicago and Winnipeg, the centres of grain production in the United States and Canada respectively. In November of that year, the Board of Trade published figures which showed that food prices had risen by 5 per cent in the previous month alone, and the estimated increase in the cost of living for the working classes, from July 1914 up to the present time, taking into account food, rent, clothing, fuel, lighting etc was around 55 per cent. Sheridan Jones observed conditions in a typical London market, and described the shopping habits of an average woman:

The purse is clutched and watched more closely. The price of food has risen too sharply for the purchaser to leave the business in hand for more than a moment. She must lay out her allowance with a particularity that gets value for every farthing, and despite the long articles in the papers that tell us of the budgets she can provide, she has no opportunity of practising that reckless extravagance that is supposed to characterise the soldier's wife. The stern, cold fact is that she is hard pressed to purchase the barest necessities, so precious have those necessities become. Yet she retains that priceless heritage of good spirits that marks out the Cockney. The reproach of extravagance against these women, the dependents of our soldiers, comes from those whose best excuse is their ignorance of the facts. For the truth is that our benevolent Government has seen to it that, when they have purchased the barest necessities, they have nothing left to be extravagant with. The prices of food, clothing and commodities of all kinds have risen at a bewildering pace, and the truth is that the soldier's wife is hard put to it to keep body and soul together.

Mrs John Smith finds now, when she goes out shopping, that a rabbit, for which she would pay ninepence or tenpence in pre-war days, now costs her one shilling and sixpence or two shillings, if not more; the onions, which go to make it appetising, are sixpence per pound instead of one penny or three halfpence. Potatoes, for which she used to pay twopence for four pounds, are seven pounds for a shilling, and not obtainable at that. Meat has become almost impossible, and foreign mutton, on which she was wont to economise, is now, for the cheapest portion, the neck (sixpence halfpenny before the war), one shilling, and even one and three, per pound, rising with the status of the butcher. It is the same meat, but the so-called 'English' butcher charges the same price for foreign mutton as for English, and it is useless to argue with him. Again, that 'little bit o' bacon' Mrs Smith got for Sunday breakfast has now become an extravagance she cannot entertain, and she purchases, instead, a few poor scraps for eightpence, which in pre-war days would have bought a pound of good streaky rashers that would have done service for a few days' dinner for the children.

But the price of bread is the greatest hardship that the war has inflicted on the poor. At elevenpence a quartern, with a number of hungry mouths to fill, the bread bill is enough to appal even the

A food queue outside a market in London, around 1917. (From *The Great War: I Was There*)

woman who is better off. The scarcity of sugar is another cruel deprivation that hits the poor hard. As one grocer said to me: 'I hate to refuse a poor woman half a pound of sugar, for a bit of bread and sugar keeps the young 'uns quiet while she gets her shoppin' in or does her washin'. But what can I do?' The alternative edibles that were urged upon our attention by an omniscient Government (which fondly thinks that it can feed us on anything or nothing) were, it will be remembered, lentils instead of meat, beans and oxtails for soup instead of bacon, margarine instead of butter, with 'substitutes for milk' – all these were offered us to make up for the deficiency of ordinary goods. We tried them, and immediately the prices galloped up. Lentils or split peas at twopence halfpenny a pint rose rapidly to fivepence, where they are trembling for the next rise. Oxtails from ninepence rose to one shilling and sixpence and two shillings, and at that price are useless to the poor. 'Milk substitutes' are unobtainable. Eggs, that stand-by of the woman worker and the busy mother, were, all through last year, impossible at fourpence each, and so they tried egg powder and found it decidedly wanting.

For, when all is said and done, we are a meat-eating people, and all the substitutes in the world will not make up for the loss of nutriment in beef, mutton or pork. What is the result? That the wife and mother is badly nourished and goes short, while the children are fed on 'substitutes' that all the figures in the world will not make nourishing. The reproach of extravagance under these circumstances becomes ludicrous. It is no wonder that the shadow of war hangs over the once cheery market-place, and that the old happy carelessness gladdens us no more.[7]

1917 would be a critical year on the British home front, as the U-boat blockade really began to bite. The reason for this was simple. Up to this point, the Germans had been fearful of unrestricted submarine warfare, on the wise grounds that this would very likely bring an enraged United States into the war on Britain's side. However, in January 1917 the German navy presented calculations which showed that if the U-boats were released from their constraints, the estimated tonnage of shipping which they could sink would curtail British food imports by such an extent that by the beginning of August of that year, Britain would have reached the point of starvation. The Kaiser and the German government accepted the proposal, on the basis that even if the United States did enter the war as a result, it would be too late for it to influence events and Britain would have succumbed already. At first, the total tonnages of shipping lost to unrestricted warfare exceeded even the German navy estimates of what was achievable. Furthermore, they had also underestimated their own ability to increase the number of U-boats at sea, and were building three new ones for every one lost to enemy action. By the end of 1917 the U-boat campaign against Allied shipping had almost succeeded in bringing Britain to her knees. Alice Foley was a working-class woman who worked in the cotton industry in Bolton, and was typical of those waiting for long periods of time to purchase food, often with no certainty of obtaining anything:

> I well remember trying to relieve mother from the strain of food queues, standing for long hours waiting for a few potatoes or a small packet of sugar or rice. We were usually a silent human coil, shuffling along the pavement, anxious but hopeful, yet often we reached the shop-door only to be told that all supplies had been sold for that day. We turned away empty-handed, some forlorn, others angry, and found it in our hearts to envy the more fortunate black marketeers.[8]

Women smile for the camera in this wartime queue, but it was no laughing matter if after several hours standing in line, supplies had run out. (Library of Congress: Bain collection)

So how, under these circumstances, did Britain avoid disaster? The answer to this question lies in a number of factors. Firstly, increasing numbers of British people were growing their own food, in their gardens if they had them, but for the many city dwellers who did not, on allotments. The trend towards allotment gardening was part of a wider back-to-the-land movement. Within a year after the movement had begun, 21,500 persons applied for allotments, but the local governmental authorities did not exert themselves to meet the need, and only 6,147 were provided with them. By the end of 1915, however, some 30,000 persons had been provided with land under the new plan and some 40,000 acres had been leased or purchased. In 1916 thousands more were added. While over half a million persons were already on allotments, in 1917 the demand for gardens and tillage spaces of small area was so great that Parliament passed an act known as the Allotments and Small Holdings Act. It created a body of commissioners, who, under the direction of the Board of Agriculture and Fisheries, had the duty of satisfying the clamour of workers for allotments. An American observer in Britain, Charles W. Holman, secretary of the US National Agricultural Organization Society, wrote later:

Alice Foley and her mother, seen around the end of the First World War. (From Foley, *A Bolton Childhood*)

About six hundred thousand allotments, as they are called, have been let to persons throughout the British Isles, and some thirty-five thousand persons now hold gardens by means of cooperative societies. The movement has taken firm root there, and is one of the subtle forces that are surely remaking the old into a new England. The movement is affording a new hope for the worker, a new hope for his wife and a new hope for his children. It is doubly attractive as it affords a way of going back to the land without leaving one's city job. It turns a splendid recreational trick and aids materially in splicing out one's allowance for food. Every evening in the tillage season one may see hundreds of workers hurrying from factory or mine or shop to the unhoused places which English county councils are consecrating to garden purposes. There they work during the long days until time for the late English meal.[9]

Next, resistance within the Royal Navy to the convoy system was finally overcome, and it was implemented initially on a trial basis. Merchant ships were now herded together and escorted across the Atlantic by destroyers, capable of sinking U-boats. Thirdly, the entry of the United States into the war in 1917 meant both an immediate increase in the number of warships available to guard convoys and destroy U-boats, and also in the quantity of foodstuffs available to Great Britain. Before the war the United States had exported on the average about 6.4 million tons of food and feed per year, but in 1917–18 it exported 15.1 million tons of food and feed, which went in considerable quantity to Great Britain. This was in part the policy of Herbert Hoover, the United States Food Administrator.

The final and perhaps the most important factor was the response of the British government, in beginning to tighten restrictions on food consumption. *The Times* in May 1917 reported that from now on evasion of the Food Controller's regulations would be taken very seriously. A case in point was the apparently widespread sale of potatoes at 3d per lb, under the pretence that they were to be used as seed potatoes when in fact they were intended for food use. This, the newspaper reported, was but one of many examples of the rules being flouted or avoided. Substitutes continued to be sought wherever possible. There were particular restrictions on fresh bread, and loaves were not allowed to be sold until twenty-four hours old, as people tend to eat more when bread is fresh. Other coarser types of flour were mixed with wheat flour (eventually to the ratio of 50:50) to produce so called 'war bread'. This was clearly not to everyone's taste, particularly those with a finer palate, but a Mr Slade wrote to his local newspaper in March 1917 on the subject of 'war bread' and its nutritional value:

POTATOES IN 1918.

Last year the
COUNTY OF BERKSHIRE
PRODUCED
11,100 Tons of Potatoes.
CONSUMED
26,100 Tons of Potatoes.

DEFICIT, 15,000 Tons.

LORD RHONDDA and Mr. PROTHERO appeal to every man who has a farm, a garden, or an allotment to plant more potatoes and make the County
SELF-SUPPORTING.

By the second half of the war, the British government was encouraging ever-greater land use, in order to increase the food supply. (Author's collection)

I have been greatly interested in certain letters which have appeared in various papers dealing with this subject . . . I think [these] writers overlook the fact that this is wartime, and that there is a most serious shortage, not only of wheat, but of other foodstuffs, and that, therefore, the nutritive qualities of bread in these times at least should be the primary consideration. I have always understood that with wheat, as with potatoes, the chief nourishment resides not in the centre, but just within the natural envelope of the foodstuff, and that it is therefore a crime to throw away potato peelings and to discard the whole of the branny cover of the wheat. Both these are too often wasted, or at best given to the pigs, whereas they should provide valuable nutriment for humans. In normal times a large proportion of the poor live chiefly upon bread, but today rich and poor alike should insist that the bread should be nutritious, even at the cost of any possible reduction in palatability and appearance.[10]

His point clearly was that even though war bread might look like a poor substitute for the pre-war white loaf, it was actually healthier. Around the same time there were restrictions on the use of flour for cakes and pastries and for a time these all but disappeared from restaurants and tea shops.

A 4lb Loaf of War Time Bread
(Eat half a pound a day)
Some Margarine, and
Butter Beans.
A'int Bad Grub anyway!

Postcards such as this made light of measures such as War Bread, baked with what today we would regard as wholemeal flour, but which some at the time regarded as coarse and unpalatable. (Author's collection)

There were other attempts at substitution; Arthur Knapp, a research chemist and food scientist at Cadbury Brothers Ltd of Birmingham, tells us that:

> When, during the war, the use of sugar for chocolate-making was restricted and little chocolate was produced, the cacao butter formerly used in this industry was freed for other purposes. Thus there was plenty of cacao butter available at a time when other fats were scarce. Cacao butter has a pleasant, bland taste resembling cocoa. The cocoa flavour is very persistent, as many experimenters found to their regret in their efforts to produce a tasteless cacao butter which could be used as margarine or for general purposes in cooking. The scarcity of edible fats during the war forced the confectioners to try cacao butter, which in normal times is too expensive for them to use, and as a result a very large amount was employed in making biscuits and confectionery.[11]

Knapp also described other uses to which the by-products of chocolate were put during the course of the war, with varying degrees of success:

> For years small quantities of cacao shell, under the name of 'miserables', have been used in Ireland and other countries for

This understated wartime advertisement for Bourneville Cocoa makes reference to the nutritional value of the product. (Author's collection)

PUNCH, OR THE LONDON CHARIVARI.—February 14, 1917.

VOLUNTARY FOOD ECONOMY

RATIONAL SERVICE.

John Bull. "SACRIFICE INDEED! WHY, I'M FEELING FITTER EVERY MINUTE, AND I'VE STILL PLENTY OF WEIGHT TO SPARE."

In this cartoon from Punch, *John Bull remarks that wartime food restrictions were actually making him feel fitter.* (From *Punch* magazine)

producing a dilute infusion for drinking. Although this 'cocoa tea' is not unpleasant, and has mild stimulating properties, it has never been popular, and even during the war, when it was widely advertised and sold in England under fancy names at fancy prices, it never had a large or enthusiastic body of consumers.[12]

Yet the government had still stopped short of compulsory restrictions, preferring instead to step up its campaign to reduce food consumption through voluntary rationing. This was run through the National War Savings

Committee. Around that time the *Win-The-War Cookery Book* was published for the Food Economy Campaign, with the approval of the Ministry of Food. It was aimed directly and explicitly at women, stating:

> The struggle is not only on land and sea; it is in your larder, your kitchen and your dining room. Every meal you serve is now literally a battle. Every well cooked meal that saves bread and wastes no food is a victory. Our soldiers are beating the Germans on land. Our sailors are beating the Germans on the sea. You can beat them in the larder and the kitchen.[13]

More specifically, the book was aimed at middle-class women. One paragraph read:

> The more expensive the foods you give your family, the more you are helping to win the war, for you are leaving the cheaper foods for the poor. Today the true patriot who can afford it will eat asparagus, not potatoes. Today you are called upon to save bread, not money. Spend the money you spend on food on the most expensive food your means permit; on the best joints and cuts of beef, mutton, and bacon, on the best kinds of fish, on poultry and eggs. Leave the cheaper foods to the poor; and above all, save bread . . . Bread is the chief food of the manual workers. It is cheap; it is already cooked. It saves money, work and coal. To the poor it is the chief necessity of life. They must, therefore, have it; and you who can afford to buy and cook other foods must, as far as you possibly can, leave the bread to them. If the poor could afford more gas and coal for more cooking, they would still lack the knowledge and experience of yourselves and your cooks. There would be needless waste – not only of actual materials, but also of nourishment.[14]

The book went on to encourage women to ensure that their servants to join in the battle against waste. The Lloyd George government also sought to stimulate the production of food as well as to economise in its consumption and created a new Food Production Department. The department was to direct an energetic campaign to increase food output. The Food Production Department decided that grasslands throughout the United Kingdom were to be ploughed and planted with crops with all possible speed; the acreage of wheat, oats, and potatoes was to be increased, however much this reduced the pasture available for meat production. Most farmers were still reluctant to plough up grass, but public and parliamentary opinion was swinging in favour of a more intensive, crop-oriented agriculture. Parliament debated the question in February 1917, just after the unrestricted submarine campaign had begun, and it was quite clear by then that the Unionists would abandon their defence of the farmers, and that the Liberals would put aside their economic dogma, in order to satisfy the urgent demand for food. The Food Production Department decided to try to achieve as large an increase as possible in the 1917 harvest of potatoes and oats only, and to concentrate much of its efforts on getting permanent grass ploughed during the summer and autumn of 1917 so as to make a larger 1918 wheat crop possible. The plan for 1918 called for an increase of nearly a fifth in the acreage under crops: the goal was an increase of 2.6 million acres in the area under corn and 170,000 acres more of potatoes. To ensure that any resistance by farmers would not prevent the realisation of these goals, the government assumed the power to require that pasture and meadows be ploughed through a Cultivation of Lands Order, under which the County Agricultural Executive committees were given the authority to specify what land should be ploughed by the farmer, and if necessary to undertake cultivation themselves or transfer the control of land from one farmer to another. The orders were rigorously enforced, though the majority of farmers co-operated patriotically.

As a concession to the farmers, in February 1917, Lloyd George announced the government's intention to guarantee the prices of wheat, oats and potatoes. These proposals were passed as the Corn Production Act of 1917; this act also restricted rents and allowed for the fixing of minimum agricultural wages. However, things were heavily stacked against farmers: eventually those in the United Kingdom lost one-third of their regular workers to the military or to other industries, and there were shortages of fertilisers and machinery. The Food Production Department partially compensated for the lack of regular labourers by providing women, boys, physically inferior men, and prisoners of war, and a limited number of agricultural deferments from military service were granted to farm workers. For the harvest of 1918 the Food Production Department was able to provide a force of 350,000 men, women, and boys. It also obtained more fertiliser and machinery. The department itself did some of the farm work. It acquired horses, tractors and steam traction units, and operated training schools for ploughmen. In fact, the greater part of the permanent grass broken up was ploughed by the Food Production Department. The ploughing goals were steadily met. Even in 1917 there was an increase of nearly a million acres in the area under the plough compared with the previous year. Potato production was increased by more than a third, and oats production by nearly a fifth over the previous year.

A middle-class woman from the Home Counties, who wrote under the pen name of Mrs Humphrey Ward, was convinced that the entry of the USA

This poster leaves one in no doubt that victory was inextricably linked to bread restrictions. (Library of Congress)

into the war could only help the food situation in Britain. Mrs Ward wrote an open letter to an American friend, outlining the dramatic improvement in the agricultural position as she saw it in 1918:

> . . . the country has been more and more generally covered with the National War Savings Committees which have been carrying into food-economy the energy they spent originally on the raising of the last great War Loan. The consumption of bread and flour throughout the country has gone down – not yet sufficiently – but enough to show that the idea has taken hold: – 'Save bread, and help victory!' And since your declaration of war it strengthens our own effort to know that America with her boundless food-supplies is standing by, and that her man-and sea-power are now to be combined with ours in defeating the last effort of Germany to secure by submarine piracy what she cannot win on the battle-field. Meanwhile changes which will have far-reaching consequences after the war are taking place in our own home food-supply. The long neglect of our home agriculture, the slow and painful dwindling of our country populations, are to come to an end. The Government calls for the

sowing of three million additional acres of wheat in Great Britain; and throughout the country the steam tractors are at work ploughing up land which has either never borne wheat, or which has ceased to bear it for nearly a century. Thirty-five thousand acres of corn land are to be added to the national store in this county of Hertfordshire alone. The wages of agricultural labourers have risen by more than one-third. The farmers are to be protected and encouraged as they never have been since the Cobdenite revolution; and the Corn Production Bill now passing through Parliament shows what the grim lesson of this war has done to change the old and easy optimism of our people. As to the energy that has been thrown into other means of food-supply, let the potatoes now growing in the flower-beds in front of Buckingham Palace stand for a symbol of it! The potato-crop of this year – barring accidents – will be enormous; and the whole life of our country villages has been quickened by the effort that has been made to increase the produce of the cottage gardens and allotments. The pride and pleasure of the women and the old men in what they have been able to do at home, while their sons and husbands are fighting at the front, is moving to see. Food prices are very high; life in spite of increased wages is hard. But the heart of England is set on winning this war.[15]

In the second half of the war, the British people also came to rely more heavily on fish. In the face of rising cost of other foodstuffs, it appeared to be an increasingly attractive option. In the Irish Sea, 1917 was a good year for herring in spite of the marauding U-boats which sank a number of fishing vessels in these waters. An Irish fisherman named Patrick Cadogan, in a letter dated 12 May 1917, tells us that but for the predations of U-boats, that year might well have been a bumper season:

I am sending you a few lines letting you know we are stopped of fishing [*sic*] since the 4th May we have our nets in the loft as we were afraid of the submarines that Thursday night he sunk seven boats but for the cruser [*sic*] meeting him he would have the most of them sunk before morning and gave them a poor chance of their lives he took four men of one small boat aboard the submarine he sunk the Sideward and put two of them into her punt with her own crew nine men in one boat and done the same to the Fastnet about 14 miles off the stags and all came safe and they would not leave more of them take the oars and they were making great money there was never anything like it iff [*sic*] we were home the day we left Peel we would have a great season the Ripple made 220 pounds

them two nights and the following Monday night some of the boats
had a season the Thomas Joseph made 392 pounds one night we had
only 10 shots and we had 13 pounds a man all the boats that was out
the week we left Peel have from 25 to 30 pounds a man the ripple
have about 35 pounds a man. John Cadogans boat have £56 and the
Glen Dawer have £71 a man . . . they would all make plenty money
this year but for the submarines . . .[16]

Some heavy losses undoubtedly were inflicted on the fishing fleets by
individual German commanders, who had at their disposal the most
destructive of naval weapons, and did not hesitate to employ them
ruthlessly. In one instance off the Isle of Man in February the following
year, a fishing boat called *Girl Emily*. was attacked by an enemy submarine.
The skipper later attempted to claim compensation for the damage to his
vessel and loss of his catch, describing the incident in a letter to the local
War Pensions Committee:

On Saturday 23rd February 1918, I being master of the fishing boat
'Girl Emily' of Peel put to sea with a crew of four men, about four
o'clock pm. Whilst about ten miles off Peel, fishing for cod, we
encountered a German submarine which came alongside of us.
They asked if I was fishing, I answered 'yes'. He then left us and
came around on our starboard quarter, and when about one hundred
yards away he fired at us, I was at the tiller and the shot struck a
stanchion not a yard away from my front. I was severely wounded
in the face with splinters. Some splinters entered beneath my right
eye, and have seriously affected my sight.
    The Germans then fired three times again the shots going through
the bulwarks and the sail. They came alongside and demanded our
fish which, as we were quite helpless we gave to them. There was
£20 worth of fish, and they took all. I was in the Doctor's care for
three weeks, and the experience has also shaken my nerve, so that as
a consequence I have not been able to prosecute my calling as a
fisherman as profitably as before the accident.[17]

The object of this German policy of piracy was twofold – first to instil fear
in the British fishermen through 'frightfulness', and second by removing
fishing vessels to lessen the supply of food. The first object was never
attained, even remotely; and the second was nullified by the persistence of
British fishermen in going to sea and their obstinate refusal to keep away
from it at the bidding of any enemy whatsoever.
    Though prices of fish fluctuated violently and it seemed impossible to

regulate them satisfactorily, and there can be no doubt that fish was dear – the 'profiteers' were said to be largely responsible for that – in its favour it must be said that at most times there was plenty of it, and any scarcity was generally due to bad weather and not to any fear of Germans. There was an inevitable falling off in the supplies compared with pre-war days, because the fishing areas were so greatly restricted and most of the fishing vessels and their crews were on Admiralty service; but large quantities of fish, of a high value, continued to be brought into port. In August 1917, for example, 10,414 tons of fish were delivered at Billingsgate, and large supplies were steadily brought into ports around the coast. These landings were proof of the courage of the men who made them and of the failure of the German methods of ruthlessness. So that the food supply might be further increased, on 18 August 1917 the naval authority for Ramsgate, Deal and district issued a proclamation relaxing the restrictions which governed fishing in the roadstead of the Downs. Previously the limit laid down since the war began allowed fishing for only half-a-mile from the shore. A much wider area was covered by the new Order, which permitted fishing to be carried on by any method up to approximately a mile and a quarter from the shore.

The concession enabled professional fishermen and anglers to get to the deeper waters of the outer Downs, where – probably due to the prevention of fishing in previous years – fish of many kinds abounded in great quantities, and were of unusually fine and large size. The new Order was to continue in force until the end of the following January, a period of nearly six months. The concession showed the readiness of the naval authorities to make allowances to enable fishermen to obtain supplies from the sea to augment the food resources of the country. Similar concessions were made in other places as circumstances arose, and the concessions greatly benefitted fishing communities. Soon it was obvious, however, that the prices of fish, like other food, would have to be fixed, and on 23 January 1918, the Food Controller issued an Order establishing maximum retail prices. These new prices varied from six pence a pound for such fish as pickled herrings (whole fish) to four shillings a pound for cuts of salmon. Under the Order, high prices were chargeable for various sorts of inferior fish which in pre-war days were ranked as 'offal'.

The British government deployed all the methods at its disposal to encourage citizens to consume less, and by this stage in the war its propaganda skills were considerable. Yet as with enlistment in the army, the voluntary system was increasingly found to be inadequate, and compulsion came ever nearer. The letters of another middle class English woman, a culinary expert named Mrs Burnett-Smith, to an American friend were published late in the war. There can be no doubt that Mrs Burnett-Smith's letters were written with the intention of being published, but they make interesting reading nonetheless. In one she wrote of that portion of the population which stubbornly refused to acquiesce in voluntary reduction of consumption, and came up with her own reasons why this might be so:

> Food is the question of the hour. The people who have read with uncomprehending eyes the imploring official appeals 'Eat less bread,' 'Save the Wheat,' 'Food will win the War,' are now face to face with real shortage. The psychology of this war, in so far as it operates in human consciousness, is a very remarkable thing. I had to sit down to think it over this morning after a very exhausting argument with a food waster and hoarder. These two words don't sort together, do they, but they are apt to the hour. He or she who hoards food at this moment of national stress, wastes it, because he is preserving it for his own wretched body, which is of no value to his country. A few minutes' silent contemplation brought me into a clearer light. The absolute refusal of those people to admit the need for conservation and self-denial, is a form of national pride. They simply can't admit the humiliating fact that Great Britain, proud mistress of the seas, is no longer self-supporting or sufficient to her own needs.[18]

In her mind, this could only lead to one conclusion:

> You cannot wax eloquent over it; the only dramatic moments are those when you flame red with indignation over the breaking down of the voluntary system. It has failed all along the line, and card rationing is bound to come.[19]

Mrs Burnett-Smith went on to describe some of the practical difficulties she faced in trying to convince ordinary people of the need to make food savings, and to employ substitute foods wherever possible:

> We have got to invent and concoct appetising dishes minus most of the ingredients we once thought necessary to them. This is going to be the testing fight. I am learning great new lessons every day. I only wish I could pass them on. A woman came up to me in the street the other day and said: 'Please, I've tried to do what you said wi them substitoots (oh, the scorn in her voice!). But 'Arry, 'e won't look at 'em. Calls 'em messes, 'e does; wants 'is 'onest beefsteak, 'e does, an' I don't blime 'im, either.' Neither do I, nevertheless it will be my mournful duty to try and impress on him and all the other Harrys who are making the lives of their helpmeets a burden over

this food conservation business, that the true patriot is the man who eats his imitation steak with a smile, assuring the woman who has laboured over its preparation that it is quite equal to the real thing. Nobody would be deceived, but life would be easier.[20]

Her frustration with people who stubbornly refused to subordinate their own needs to the national crisis could hardly be contained, and she continued:

When you speak to the average cottage woman about soup and explain how nourishing it is for the children and how cheaply it can be prepared out of bones, if only the necessary care is bestowed on it, she has a way of putting her hands on her hips and looking you very haughtily in the face with the air of a person receiving a personal insult. 'Feed me chillen on bones! Good Lord! 'as it come to that? Not me, thank you, ma'am. I'll get me bit o' meat and bread and butter as long as I can get 'em and wen they ain't to be got, will do without.' How are you to combat that sort of argument which is everywhere, like sorrow – 'not in single spies, but in battalions'! I shall have to think hard. These people have got to be educated. The whole process of teaching them the alphabet has to be entered on now, when we are in the thick of the testing fight. Oh, it is so very, very English, so tremendously, unutterably stupid, and maddening![21]

A queue outside a Leicester pork butchers is supervised by a policeman, 1918. (Courtesy of Record Office for Leicester, Leicestershire and Rutland)

In spite of the successes of 1917 in increasing supply, in the final months of that year reserves of some foods had run perilously low, and Mrs Burnett-Smith's predictions proved correct as 1918 opened with the introduction of compulsory rationing on dairy products and meat. Initially food control had been voluntary, and it was introduced locally rather than nationally, in a somewhat *ad hoc* fashion. Five months earlier, Leicester borough council had appointed a Food Control Committee, which first concerned itself with the distribution of sugar, and some 60,000 sugar ration cards were issued to Leicester families. Butter rationing began in Leicester, the first place in Britain to introduce it, on 7 January 1918, with each person allowed four ounces per week of either butter or margarine. By February, beef, mutton and pork were also rationed, and the amount available to each individual was reduced as the food crisis deepened. In addition, meatless days in hotels and restaurants were introduced. The same month, Leicester pork butchers met to discuss what could be done to alleviate the queues outside of their shops. One newspaper reported that:

> At the request of the Food Control Committee it was agreed to open to the public on two mornings of the week, viz on Tuesdays and Fridays at 6.30am to enable working men and working women to make their purchases before proceeding to business. On Mondays and Thursdays the pork butchers will close all day, and on Wednesdays and Saturdays the shops will open at 9am. On the four open days serving will go forward till stocks are exhausted; then the shops will close finally for the day. By this means queues waiting for the shops to reopen will disappear.[22]

With beef and pork now in exceedingly short supply, other sources of meat were sometimes substituted. Horseflesh was now offered for sale in Leicester from what were termed 'Belgian Butchers', and the town's medical officer Dr Killick Millard was strongly in favour of the use of horsemeat for public consumption, finding it every bit as good as beef. The only restriction placed on establishments selling substitute meat was an 1889 Act of Parliament, which stated that they must display a sign with clearly readable letters stating 'Horseflesh Sold Here'. Winnifred Taylor, a schoolgirl living on Upperton Road in Leicester, remembered many years afterwards:

> We were very short of food . . . and the bread was almost black. The meat was rationed, we had coupons of course, and I know that people with a lot of children did better, because they got quite a good ration for the children; I can remember our coupon falling or

blowing into the fire and my aunt grabbing it! Anyway it was passed by the butcher alright . . . but there were a lot of shortages really. We had to make potato dripping for instance, and my aunt was very good at contriving . . . she used to cook this bread in milk for our breakfast because cereals were difficult [to get] but we got through, and I had a friend whose father kept a fruiterers shop and green grocers, so I did well for fruit, but fruit was quite scarce . . .[23]

Another schoolgirl, Margot Cliff, remembered:

Some of my earliest memories were queuing with mother, before I went to school. I remember once queuing for what seemed like hours for butter at the 'Maypole', only enlivened by watching the assistant pat up slabs of butter into pounds with two wooden patters. Mother was lucky when we moved to Mere Road to find a helpful butcher, Mr Bamford, at the corner of Conduit Street and Sparkenhoe Street. She stuck with him all her life.[24]

However, rationing, with its underlying principle that all people, of whatever class, were equally deserving of the same basic portion of foodstuffs, was perhaps the most significant development to have occurred on the British home front during the First World War. It marked a seismic shift in attitudes in British society. For so long it had been rigidly stratified, and with a Victorian sense of moral certainty among the upper classes that this was God's way – as the hymn had it, the rich man in his castle, the poor man at his gate, God made them high and lowly, and ordered their estate – even if it meant that the poor were left to starve. The relationship between the individual and the state had been changed irrevocably.

A British woman apparently in fancy dress, representing food control. The hat carries the word 'sugar'. The British approached food hardship with a sense of humour, which to some extent defused social tensions. (Author's collection)

The chief distinction between the experience of food shortages of the British home front as opposed to its German counterpart, was the almost complete absence of serious protests in the former case. Such protest as there was in Britain was largely peaceful, for example in February 1918 Leicester members of the various railway unions met at the Bond Street Club in the town to discuss the food situation; the railwaymen had seen the ample supplies available in dining cars on trains, whilst the railway draymen had seen food supplies piled up at the rear of grocers' premises whilst queues formed at the front. The railwaymen believed that official incompetence rather than shortage was responsible for much of the inadequacy in food supply, and whilst they accepted that there must be some hardship, which had to be endured, they believed that it should be born fairly. A motion was moved – and accepted – that:

> . . . this conference, viewing with alarm the food shortage arising as the result of muddle and unequal distribution of supplies demands that the Government shall immediately ration the whole of the people with the supplies now available. We advise branches to stop work on Saturday of each week as a protest against the inactivity of the Government, and the scandalous conditions whereby our womenfolk have to stand in queues for hours to obtain food which they could not otherwise get owing to inadequate distribution arrangements. We are of the opinion that this is likely to have very serious after effects on the health of our wives and children and therefore recommend that the men should use the day off to take their places in the queues, and by so doing assist to bring this disgraceful state of affairs to an end.[25]

It could be argued that the most serious case of food-related disturbance in the British Isles occurred on the Isle of Man, in July 1918. In common with the United Kingdom, the price of bread there had been kept artificially low through government subsidies for most of the second half of the war. However, that summer the Lieutenant Governor of the island, Lord Raglan, announced suddenly and unilaterally that this would end. When the news of the coming increase in the price of the loaf was made public, the reaction of the by now well-organised Manx labour force was swift. The master bakers stated that they could not produce bread at ninepence a loaf without the subsidy, and it was clear that the workers were not going to accept the increase without a fight. At the instigation of the officials of the Isle of Man District of the Workers' Union, representatives of the various trade unions were summoned to meet at Douglas on Saturday 29 June, and it was decided unanimously that unless steps were taken to ensure the continuation of the ninepenny loaf, a general strike should result. The union men notified the government of the decision, and also decided that public meetings should be held in various parts of the Island with a view to enlisting public support for the demand for the subsidised loaf. The resulting total dislocation of ordinary life forced the Lieutenant Governor to back down, and the subsidy was restored. Commenting on the strike in an annual report, union organiser George Titt noted the fact that such a relatively small increase in a staple commodity upon which so many people relied could have disastrous consequences if left unchallenged:

> Perhaps the most important feature was the splendid fight put up in the form of a general strike by the whole of our members to retain the 9d loaf in July 1918. The feature of this fight was that the members of our Union were fighting not a sectional fight for their own personal benefit, because as members of the Workers' Union they could have used their organisation to increase their own wages to meet any increase in the cost of living, but as true citizens they recognised that thousands of other people were unable to increase their earnings to meet any increase in the price of bread, and therefore they took the social view, and decided that a fight must be put up on behalf of those who were less able to take care of themselves. This spirit is one that we hope will grow in volume among all sections of the working class in future . . .[26]

By the summer of 1918, however, the British food crisis was largely over. The potato harvest that year promised to be a good one, but more significantly, with the United States in the war, and Herbert Hoover as US Food Administrator, the supply of food available in the US, Britain, France and Italy was treated as a common pool. Hoover's assurances that there was enough to go round was welcome news in Britain, and made him a popular figure. One American commentator, William Edgar, noted a piece of verse which had recently appeared in an Ipswich newspaper:

> At breakfast, when we take our seat
> And find the morning rasher sweet,
> We ought to thank the British fleet
> And Hoover.
> When Huns in every German state
> Gaze sadly on an empty plate,
> Who makes them sing the Hymn of Hate?
> Why, Hoover.
> In tea or coffee, failing wines,

The Briton, every time he dines,
Should drink the health of Mr. Clynes
And Hoover.
And when, to our intense delight, –
The war-time bread again turns white,
Congratulations we should write
To Hoover.
To show our most profound respect,
A site we must at once select
On which a statue we'll erect
Of Hoover.[27]

The same writer, like many foreigners before him and since, was rather dismissive of British cooking, but his description of the situation he found in England in the summer of 1918 confirms that the United Kingdom had at last passed the worst point in the food crisis, at there was at least enough to go around:

By 1918, Britain was over the worst of its food crisis, as this advertisement from a Bath confectioner confirms. (Author's collection)

Of food in London there is no scarcity, except in a few items which are being conserved. There is a meat, a sugar and a fats ration, the last named covering butter, margarine and lard. Cream no longer appears, and skim milk takes its place . . . British cooking is not the most skillful in the world, and the result of the restrictions is to make eating rather a monotonous and uninteresting performance. There is plenty to eat, such as it is, and no doubt the nourishment is there. There is an abundance of good fish, and pork is plentiful; fruits are scarce and dear, and the vegetables are not prepared in an appetizing way; peas, for instance, being served half-cooked, and potatoes underdone and rather soggy. It is the fashion to eat sparingly, and avoid the things that are scarce.[28]

Edgar went on to denigrate the British policy at this time of using the whole of the wheat germ in making bread; ironically just the practice which nutritionists in the future would advocate for producing healthy bread:

As yet the bread of Britain shows no improvement in quality, and is unmistakably poor. Perhaps it is too soon to expect this amelioration, as the wheat harvest in the United Kingdom is not yet completed, but it is doubtful if British bread will be materially improved as long as the mistake continues to be made of milling on a high percentage basis. This fallacy, common to nearly all the belligerents, except the United States and Canada, is clung to here with true British pertinacity, notwithstanding that its evils have been manifest for months. The theory underlying it is that by grinding into flour a larger percentage of the wheat berry (eighty per cent in Britain, compared with seventy-four per cent in America) the supply 'goes further.' It probably does, but at the expense of the quality of the flour and its keeping properties, and the milk and meat supply. The bran and flinty particles of the wheat, that should go into dairy and other feeds to animals, provided by nature with the apparatus to digest them, are kept in the flour intended for man, thereby making it dark and coarse and, to a certain extent, indigestible, and, at the same time, greatly reducing the supply of animal feeds. Thus, by robbing the animals and deteriorating the human food, both man and beast are denied their rightful product. The system is economically unsound and wasteful, although highly favored by the world's food cranks.[29]

In conclusion, the successful outcome of the hunger war on the British home front was not easily predictable. A people so heavily dependent upon imports prior to 1914 left themselves hugely vulnerable to starvation in any conflict with a major foreign power. Overall, the British people narrowly avoided disaster on the Home Front in the First World War. There is no doubt that the German campaign to starve them into submission came perilously close to succeeding, though the Germans were aided and abetted in this by the *laissez-faire* attitude of British politicians in the early part of the war. That the U-boats were thwarted was due to a number of factors which worked together in the second half of the conflict to ensure Britain's survival against the odds: increased supplies from the USA (better protected by the convoy system), increased home production of goods both from the land and from the sea, and in addition a reduction in domestic consumption of foodstuffs. The state had also succeeded in changing the minds of its citizens and in redirecting the attitudes of its people. Yet this intervention of the state into the lives of individuals, although of vital necessity in a war of national survival, reached unprecedented levels. It would have far reaching consequences, and indeed the ripples of these wartime controls are still felt today, almost a hundred years later.

Chapter 5

On the German Home Front

In contrast with Britain, prior to the First World War Germany did not dare to depend on foreigners for her food. Instead, high tariffs on imports were used to protect domestic agriculture from cheaper foreign competition. Military arguments were often heard in German tariff debates before 1914, and some argued that she should let her 'grain grow and her cattle graze beneath the shelter of her guns'. Accordingly, while the British raised only 35 per cent of the calories they consumed, the Germans produced over 80 per cent of their caloric requirements themselves. Given this apparently favourable position, why was it that the German civilian was to suffer far greater privations of hunger than his British counterpart during the war? Why, when her initial successes on the battlefield had brought her control of large swathes of agricultural land in the east and west, was Germany not able to feed herself?

The answer to this question lies in large part with the blockade imposed by the Royal Navy on Germany in the First World War, which extended beyond prohibiting the import of munitions or the raw materials from which to make them. Britain, in the face of protests from neutral countries that she was in breach of international law, sought also to prevent the import of foodstuffs for the German civilian population. Indeed, not only did Britain disregard these protests, as the war drew on she tightened the noose around Germany's neck by restricting food supplies to neutral countries, thereby preventing them from re-exporting surplus food to Germany. When the United States entered the war in 1917, she also assisted in implementing this blockade against which, as a neutral, she had protested.

Prior to the outbreak of war, the standard of living for most people in Germany was high, and food was plentiful. An English girl, stranded in Germany by the sudden declaration of hostilities, made her way by train towards repatriation. Stopping at one station to change trains, she passed through the crowds of soldiers and civilians on the platform looking for a buffet, and was shown to the amply stocked station café:

A receipt card for a consignment of Maggi soup, from September 1914. The Maggi brand was one of the best known in Germany at the time. (Author's collection)

I sallied forth, and a boy scout showed the way into the refreshment-room where I bought some beautiful rolls, with enormous juicy slices of ham, and five huge sections of cake with nice damp icing. Drink I could not carry back after all, so gulped down a cup of coffee . . .[1]

Nevertheless, the impact of war on the German civilian population was felt immediately in certain parts of the country. Hamburg was a case in point; it was a city which depended upon the sea for its living, and with the oceans of the world effectively closed to the German merchant marine from the first declaration of war by Great Britain on 4 August 1914, there was great hardship here in particular. A German observer, Johanna Emmel, wrote of the situation:

Nowhere was the outbreak of war felt so forcefully and so suddenly as it was in Hamburg, in terms of the question of food supply for the population. With the entire shipping, navigation and other related businesses suddenly being forced to shut down, the city was struck at its core. The result was the greatest unemployment. It was necessary to take steps immediately to alleviate the plight of the unemployed, and the resulting destitute masses.

Obviously small means and measures could not resolve these problems. Therefore not only was there an extensive expansion of the already existing peacetime facilities of the 'Charitable Society for People's Coffee halls' [Gemeinnützigen Vereins für Volks-kaffeehallen], namely the 'people's dining halls' [Volks-speisehallen], which already existed in the workers' districts and which only covered their operating costs, but a number of new facilities were also established; in particular during the first days of the war, the city was covered by a network of large central dining places. Already after fourteen days about fifty-four such war kitchens were present. The performance of the individual kitchens ranged from 400 to 4,000 servings. All general supply companies that had existed before the war, were attached to the new facilities and were systematically merged into a single organic whole, under the control of the body known as 'Hamburg War Assistance' [Hamburgischen Kriegshilfe].

The entire operation is therefore standardised and centralised. The bills of fare are issued by the supply committee with details of ingredients. All kitchens cook according to this bill of fare and administer the food all over Hamburg at the same time and at the same prices. However, with the ever increasing cost of food prices, there came a point at which it was no longer possible to maintain the hitherto beheld principle of at least covering the outgoings.

The cost increased to 40 Pfennig for a litre of food, only 20 Pfennig of which was covered by the takings. The remaining 20 Pfennig was borne by the 'Hamburg War Assistance', which received significant subsidies from the state. Incidental costs were in Hamburg, however, at least initially very low as most paid no rent for the premises needed, and most of the directors and the auxiliary staff volunteered. The food was served, without a means test, to anyone, since one came to the legitimate conviction here that it was not as much shortage of money as shortage of food, which drove a large part of the population to participate in the mass feeding.[2]

Although the Hamburg model of communal kitchens would be followed in other parts of Germany as the war progressed, the situation elsewhere at least initially was not so serious. Albert Beveridge, an American journalist, visited Germany in early 1915 and discovered that although the Germans had already introduced *kriegsbrot* (war bread) – a mixture of wheat flour, rye and potato flour – food was still plentiful. He wrote:

Inside the Amol kitchen in Hamburg, 1915. The Amol pharmaceutical company was just one of many in the city to set up communal kitchens upon the outbreak of war. (Author's collection)

To the observer, food appears to be abundant and prices surprisingly low, considering that a state of war exists. On the dining car from Berlin to Posen, January twenty-second, large veal cutlets, with rice, asparagus and beans, cost two marks, or fifty cents. On January twenty-sixth, in a people's restaurant in Berlin, a very large pork steak, with sauerkraut and lentils, cost ninety pfennigs, about twenty-two cents; three shirred [baked] eggs cost sixty pfennigs, about fifteen cents, and half a young pheasant, with vegetables, was one and one-half marks, or thirty-seven cents. These examples are typical of a bill of fare containing more than one hundred and twenty dishes. With each order of meat went a generous slice of bread.

By taking meals at a large number of popular eating places, in various cities throughout Germany during several weeks, it was found that prices as well as quantity and quality of food did not vary perceptibly. The bread was noticeably darker in color, from five per cent. to ten per cent. of potato flour being used in its making. The Central Market in Berlin, during the latter part of January, displayed immense quantities of provisions of every variety, from newly-

This brand of biscuits, in English 'German Leader', features the image of Field Marshal Paul von Hindenburg. (Author's collection)

killed deer and other game yet undressed, and every other kind of meat, down to cabbages, cheese, butter and potatoes.

Soon after the outbreak of the war, a law was passed fixing a maximum price on basic necessities of life, a measure particularly advocated by the Socialists. The latter part of January and the early part of February, the government, by law, took over such foodstuffs. The large quantities of food served in restaurants, and seen in markets, shops and inns, made this law appear unnecessary. Careful inquiry suggested the conclusion that this government food monopoly is a precautionary measure, directed to next year and the year after, more than to the present. It would seem to be another of the many evidences which delving beneath the surface brings to light that Germany is preparing for a long war. And just this is the opinion of exceptionally cautious men. No one was found who feared that Germany can be starved.[3]

The first part of Beveridge's report might be taken with a pinch of salt, for there was a persistent rumour in Germany that some of the best food was served on the railways, in order to impress foreign travellers. Be that as it may, in contrast to the British government which initially adopted a *laissez-faire* attitude to food management, the Germans had acted swiftly to try to implement control of foodstuffs. The American ambassador to Germany, James Gerard, added further detail on this, writing later in his memoirs:

> On the fourth of August, 1914, a number of laws were passed, which had been evidently prepared long in advance, making various changes made necessary by war, such as alteration of the Coinage Law, the Bank Law, and the Law of Maximum Prices. Laws as to the high prices were made from time to time. For instance, the law of the twenty-eighth of October, 1914, provided in detail the maximum prices for rye in different parts of Germany. The maximum price at wholesale per German ton of native rye must not exceed 220 marks in Berlin, 236 marks in Cologne, 209 marks in Koenigsberg, 228 marks in Hamburg, 235 marks in Frankfort a/M. The maximum price for the German ton of native wheat was set at forty marks per ton higher than the above rates for rye. This maximum price was made with reference to deliveries without

Hamburg bread card. Germany was the first of the belligerent nations to issue ration cards, but this apparent efficiency masked muddle and confusion in other parts of the German food distribution system. (Author's collection)

sacks and for cash payments. The law as to the maximum prices applied to all objects of daily necessity, not only to food and fodder but to oil, coal and wood. Of course, these maximum prices were changed from time to time, but I think I can safely state that at no time in the war, while I was in Berlin, were the simple foods more expensive than in New York.[4]

In February 1915 the Germans also introduced bread ration cards, but this apparent act of teutonic efficiency masked confusion and muddle in the actual implementation. This and subsequent measures were introduced locally and in an *ad hoc* fashion, further adding to an already disorganised situation. The price controls did nothing to regulate or improve the supply of food, which is where the real difficulties in Germany originated. German agriculture was hit hard by the war. Not only were the great estates in the countryside left short-handed and short of animal power, but in the villages it was no better. Some six million men had by then been mobilised, and of this number 28 per cent came directly from the farms, and another 14 per cent had also formerly been engaged in food production and distribution. In order to fill the large orders of hay, oats, and straw for the army, the cattle had to be fed on grass instead and were kept on the meadows, which would lead to a shortage in stable manure, the most important factor in soil-fertilising.

There were other early examples of the muddle which characterised the German government's approach to food control. Early in the war, it had advised farmers to slaughter pigs because of a shortage of feed, but in 1915 the village butcher was in many cases busy at the front. Thus it came about that less expert men were put in charge of the conservation of pork products. The result could perhaps have been foreseen, but it was not. The farmers, eager not to lose an ounce of fat, and not especially keen to feed their home-raised grain to the animals, had their pigs butchered. That was all well and good, in a way. But the tons of sausages that were made, and the thousands of tons of pickled and smoked hams, shoulders, sides-of-bacon, and what not, had in many cases been improperly cured , and vast quantities of them began to spoil. The summer of that same year, the first signs of strain began to appear: James Gerard the American ambassador continued:

> While, of course, I cannot ascertain the exact amounts, I found . . .
> that great quantities of food and other supplies came into Germany
> from Holland and the Scandinavian countries, particularly from
> Sweden . . . Sweden is particularly active in this traffic . . .
> [Nevertheless] early in the summer of 1915, the first demonstration
> took place in Berlin. About five hundred women collected in front

of the Reichstag building. They were promptly suppressed by the police and no newspaper printed an account of the occurrence. These women were rather vague in their demands. They called von Buelow an old fat-head for his failure in Italy and complained that the whipped cream was not so good as before the war. There was some talk of high prices for food, and the women all said that they wanted their men back from the trenches.[5]

This demonstration would not be the last to be seen in Germany before the war was out (although as a general rule, the German hausfrau bore the hardships imposed upon her by the war with a stoicism which today is difficult to understand), but it was not yet about shortages of food, rather instead the cost of food. It was around the fourth month of the war that prices of food started to show a steady upward tendency. That this should be so was not difficult to understand, and the explanation of the authorities appeared very plausible indeed. Whenever the possibility of a shortage had at all to be intimated, the government took good care to balance its statement with the assertion that if everybody did what was fit and proper under the circumstances there would never be a shortage. If people ate war bread, a lack of breadstuffs was said to be out of the question. This was very

Germans queuing for food, 1915. (Library of Congress)

reassuring, of course. Not a little camouflage was also used by the merchants, and it was common for food-vendors to try to outdo one another in heaping their merchandise before the public gaze. Those who saw these displays generally gained from them the impression that food would never be scarce in Germany. Yet Gerard continued:

> In November, 1915, there were food disturbances and a serious agitation against a continuance of the war; and, in Leipzig, a Socialist paper was suppressed . . . In December, butter became very scarce and the women waiting in long lines before the shops often rushed the shops.[6]

In typically understated fashion, Berlin police commissioner Traugott von Jagow warned authorities in February 1915 that the 'economic war', as Germans referred to the British naval blockade, increasingly overshadowed Germany's military successes in the minds of the public. He added that unpleasant scenes were taking place more than ever in front of butchers' shops in the city. These scenes of crowds gathering for food, captivated public attention even when there was no protest associated with them. Officer Paul Rhein of the Berlin political police described one such incident in Berlin in February 1915:

> Thousands of women and children had gathered at the municipal market hall in Andreas Street to get a few pounds of potatoes. As the sale commenced, everyone stormed the market stands. The police . . . were powerless against the onslaught. A life-threatening press ensued at the stands . . . [those] women who got away from the crowds with some ten pounds of potatoes were bathed in sweat and dropped to their knees involuntarily before they could continue home.[7]

Queues were becoming an everyday fact of life for ordinary German people. An American woman in Germany, Ernesta Bullitt, kept a diary in 1915 which makes interesting reading, and which reveals that substitutes were already the order of the day:

> I had eggs and a glass of milk to-day, neither of which they say can be bought. Really, to the un-initiated, it looks as if Berlin could go on indefinitely with England's fleet strung around her neck but the eye of the paying guest is deceived. The bread, butter, and meat lines are long. Women stand hours to get their weekly allowance of a walnut size of butter for each one in their family; children are

This advertisement for Asbach Cognac shows a U-boat about to sink an enemy vessel, and was one of relatively few to make any visual reference to the war. (Author's collection)

happy, but thrive not, on jam and artificial honey . . . I dropped in for supper, unexpectedly, the other night at a friend's flat; they said they had all they could get to eat that day without paying half their yearly income for it. The fare was some large white balls which tasted like boiled dough, some little stewed prunes, and fried potatoes as a luxury. They scared me when they said the dough balls were a favourite German dish. You feel like saying: 'I'll come to dinner if you'll first tell me what I'll have to eat. If my food's worse than yours, you win!' Housekeepers are only allowed half a pound of meat per person a week, and cream may be got by a doctor's prescription only. Coffee is half something else, and tea is dried strawberry leaves. 'Did you ever imagine,' they ask one, 'that they would make so good a drink?'[8]

Interestingly, alcohol in Germany did not become the subject of state control to anything like the degree that occurred in many Allied nations, and there certainly does not appear to have been the same element of moral repugnance towards alcohol in Germany as was produced elsewhere by the war. An observer noted only that there were shortages, naturally caused by the scarcity of grain for brewing, but that, as with other deficiencies, Germans on the whole bore them stoically:

> When I left Germany they had no beer or tobacco cards, but there was talk about them. The beer restaurants receive only a certain amount of beer each day, and when this is gone the people must wait until the next day. Most beer halls serve only two glasses to each person. In Munich, because of the shortage of beer, some of the beer halls do not open until 6 o'clock at night, and at 4 o'clock the Müncheners gather at the doors with their mugs in their hands, patiently waiting. Sometimes they knock the mugs against the doors to a tune. Munich without beer is a very sad sight!
>
> In Berlin some of the restaurants will serve beer only to people who can get chairs, but this does not faze the clever Berliners, and when they want their beer they bring camp stools with them, and then they are sure to have a seat. It is forbidden to make certain kinds of fine beers because they take too much malt and sugar. None of the beer is as good as in times of peace, but the Germans have forgotten the delicacies of the past, and they live in the food ideals of the present, and they smack their lips and say, 'Isn't the beer fine tonight?'[9]

However, the inadequate nature of German food control during the First World War sapped morale and the will to fight on the home front, because it became a case of *sauve qui peut*. Those who had money were able to circumvent restrictions and live almost a normal existence, whilst those in the lowest rungs in society fared the worst. It was not that the German state was unresponsive to the needs of the working class – it was acutely concerned by the reports it was receiving of discontent on the home front, and reacted not with acts of suppression but attempts to ameliorate the problem. This succeeded in staving off revolution until November 1918, but by their nature these measures were reactive and *ad hoc*. There was also rising popular concern that, despite these official efforts on behalf of the interests of the working class, the state was helpless against a new set of 'inner enemies'. Berliners and other urban Germans now identified these enemies as deceptive merchants of foodstuffs and exploitative rural producers. Berliners believed merchants and farmers profited through the war, and by their actions fought against their 'fellow Germans', on the wrong side of the economic war. Such beliefs reinforced particular social divisions. One of those who it has to be said was least affected by this economic war was the aristocratic Evelyn, Countess Blücher, an Englishwoman married to a German

Evelyn, Countess Blücher, an Englishwoman married to a German nobleman.
(From Blücher, *An English Wife in Berlin*)

nobleman, who was nonetheless an astute observer of conditions in Germany. She wrote in her diary in 1915:

> In a quiet way the shortness of supplies is beginning to show. The price of milk was increased on October 1, and it is said that soon very little butter will be allowed to be used. It seems a funny thing to have run short, before bread, for instance, but it is said that milk will be scarce; firstly, because too many calves were killed in the spring, and also because the cows could not be fed properly.[10]

In fact one of the reasons why Germany failed to increase her food production sufficiently to counter the Allied blockade was her inability to force her farmers to comply with a food production policy. The farmers of Germany – probably mindful of the pork fiasco at the start of the war – refused to slaughter livestock in sufficient numbers which would allow pastureland to be turned over to arable production on any great scale. On 1 January 1913, there were 20,994,000 head of cattle in Germany; in 1916 there were 20,874,000; in 1917, still 20,095,000. Out of twenty-five million pigs before the war, seventeen million remained on 1 January 1916.[11] Furthermore, in spite of the – apparently – efficient system of ration cards in the towns, in rural areas farmers took whatever they wanted from their own produce before turning it over to the common good, further increasing internal divisions within Germany. The American journalist and traveller Thomas Curtin confirms this situation, adding:

> Cattle are, of course, not the only food supply. There is game. Venison is a much commoner food in Germany than in England, especially now there is much of it left. Hares, rabbits, partridges are in some parts of Germany much more numerous even than in England . . . Wherever I went in Germany, however, game was being netted . . . Before the war, pork, ham, and bacon were the most popular German food, but owing to the mistake of killing pigs in what I heard called the 'pork panic' the Germans are to-day facing a remarkable shortage of their favourite meat. I am convinced that they began 1917 with less than one-fourth as many pigs as they had before the war. The Berlin stockyards slaughtered over 25,000 pigs weekly before August, 1914. During the first 10 months of the war the figure actually rose to 50,000 pigs per week in that one city alone. In one week in September last the figure had fallen to 350 pigs! The great slaughter early in the war gave a false optimism . . . To-day the most tremendous efforts are being made to increase the number of pigs.[12]

This postcard from Dresden has the message 'Memories of the war year 1916' and features ration cards, as well as some of the staple German wartime foods: potatoes, fish and marmalade. The disgruntled dog appears above the caption 'a meatless day'! (Author's collection)

Countess Blücher wrote a prescient comment in her diary for 14 March 1916, already aware that the effect that food shortages were having upon German society might well have dire long-term consequences, even if in the short term the wealthy were insulated from the worst effects:

> Just as I write this, someone comes in from household shopping . . . She looks quite unhappy, and says that really England is succeeding, as food is getting so dreadfully scarce. Her butcher told her that he is seriously thinking of closing down. She could get no potatoes, no sugar even. The shopkeepers told her that the soldiers don't get meat more than three times a week now, and even vegetables are scarce! Then again one hears that so much is due to over-organization. The 'Magistrat' forbids the selling of butter, sugar, etc., until all has been bought up and distributed equally and justly. In the meantime masses of butter and other stuffs get spoilt. So, they say, the Bolle dairy gave their butter to a big soap factory for the making of soap, as the butter had got bad through lying by so long, and in this way it was not entirely wasted. And potatoes and such-like lie by waiting to be bought up, and the poor clamour for food. It is all terrible, and what it is going to lead to no one knows.[13]

It was widely believed that the best supplies were being sent to the army, but that theory is hardly borne out by a German soldier in training about this time, reporting that only the bread and *wurst* eaten by himself and his comrades were really superior to that available to civilians:

> The food was miserably insufficient for an active open-air life, and most of the men had to get supplies from home. Tea and coffee were dark slops scarcely to be distinguished from one another. On the other hand, the bread and sausage supplied were excellent – the best to be got in Germany at that time. We used to receive two loaves of bread a week, and when I took mine home the servant-girls all along the streets used to offer to buy them from me. We were paid about sixpence a day, but out of this we had to buy blacking, brushes, polishing materials, and several other odds and ends. We had two meals a day – dinner about twelve, and supper, a very light meal, at seven. Besides, coffee was supplied first thing in the morning.[14]

In fact, the German army in the field <u>was</u> receiving superior rations to those on the home front, or at least this was certainly true in the early part of the

Wounded soldiers with the bread supply at a depot in Germany. The original caption states that the loaves are dusted not with flour, but with chalk. (From *The Great War, I Was There*)

war. The German soldier on the Russian front in early 1915 was clearly well fed, the American journalist Beveridge writing:

> You make your lunch with the common soldiers, one of whom politely offers you his tin soup dish and another his spoon, the handle of which is a fork, apologizing that he has nothing better. The food is a thick soup made of navy beans, with slices and chunks of pork. Also, of course, there is plenty of brown bread. It is amazing the quantity of provisions the commissariat manages to get to the front. The soldier is never without abundant food, so far as you have been able to observe.[15]

However, further evidence that soldiers at home on leave or on garrison duty in barracks fared little better than the civilians around them comes from Madeleine Zabriskie Doty, an American peace activist who visited Germany in the summer of 1916. It was her second visit, the first taking place not long after the outbreak of war, and Doty was appalled by the changes she found upon her return. She wrote:

> As for the people, there is a somber grayness about them. They, too, are thin. I didn't see a big girth anywhere. Germany is stomachless. It isn't that people have nothing to eat, but they have too little. The food they have isn't the right kind. During the summer there seemed to be plenty of vegetables, fruit, and a fair supply of black bread, but this without grease, sugar, or meal does not satisfy digestion. It's like trying to run a wagon without oil. It begins to creak. The German race begins to creak. As a whole, it is pale, thin, and sunken-eyed. Sooner or later a crisis is inevitable . . . The soldiers as well as the civil population suffer. The front line trenches may be well fed, but the men home on leave or in barracks are noticeably thin. They are pale, weary, and without life. They also have no stomachs. There is a popular saying among them; it goes as follows:
>
> Dorrgemüse,
> Trocken Brot,
> Marmelade,
> Heldentod.
>
> which translated reads: Dried vegetables, dry bread, marmalade, and a hero's death.[16]

Doty had no doubts as to German efficiency, but observed that it generally worked <u>against</u> the mass of ordinary people, rather than in their favour. The German tendency to over-bureaucratise everything hindered rather than helped food supply. She gave an example:

> One Saturday evening I went to a big market in the poor quarter of Berlin. This market covers an entire block. In it are sold meat, groceries, and dairy products. I arrived at six. There was little meat visible. At one booth a butcher presided over a wholly empty counter. A little old woman stood before him weeping bitterly. Between sobs she let out a torrent of words. This is what she said: 'I must have some fat' – sob – 'I haven't had meat or fat for three weeks.' Sob, sob, sob. 'My stomach has turned against marmalade'

Eroberte russische Geschütze
werden in Berlin am Sedantag 1914
zum Schloß geführt.

A wartime postcard produced by the Oekter company, advertising marmalade. This was the product for which it was best known at the time, though the company still exists and has since diversified into a wide range of foods. (Author's collection)

– sob – 'I can't live on it any longer.' Sob, and indignantly: 'It's no use telling me to come earlier before the meat's gone. I can't come earlier. I have to work until six.' I pulled my companion's sleeve: 'Look!' I said, 'There's meat on that other counter; couldn't we buy some?' But no, of course not; the little old woman could only get meat with her meat card from her particular butcher. This time it was I who said: 'Curses on the military.' Conspicuously over many counters flapped the sign, 'Ersatz.' 'Ersatz' means substitute. Sausage Ersatz was a pale edition of the real article. One's speculations run riot. But there were few meat purchasers. The people were out for potatoes. The potato counter was as bad as a bargain day in a department store. At six o'clock there was a line stretching through the entire market and far out into the street. At least two thousand people were in line. I stood and watched for three hours, and the line never decreased. As fast as some left, others arrived. There were old men and women, mothers with babies and tiny children clinging to their skirts, and young children carrying huge baskets. The crowd swayed and muttered. It stood on one foot and then on the other. Women who had worked all day looked ready to drop with fatigue. At the counter three or four women employees were dealing out potatoes and punching cards as rapidly as possible. Occasionally little commotions broke the monotony. Once a baby cried. We hurried toward the sound. In a baby carriage a tiny creature sobbed drearily. Standing beside the carriage and clinging tight to the baby was a five-year-old, also weeping. Brother, twelve years old, had been standing in line three hours for his potatoes. Meanwhile, the babies had grown hungry. They had had nothing to eat since noon. Some kindly women gave them bread, which was devoured eagerly. Presently mother arrived, just released from the factory. She was tired and worn. She shook and scolded brother for being so slow. Then the little procession moved off, the babies, the little boy, all dirty, ragged, and barefooted, and the worn mother, with a bag of potatoes between them. All they had. Father was in the war.[17]

Doty remarked dryly that if the numerous clerks and pen-pushers who were employed creating card indexes for suppliers had been redeployed in actually <u>growing</u> food, the situation might not have been so serious. More details of how the German rationing system worked comes from the American Ambassador, Gerard. From his account we get some idea of the complexities of the administration, but also the fact that it was easy to circumvent in certain circumstances:

The so-called 'war bread', the staple food of the population, which was made soon after the commencement of the war, was composed partially of rye and potato flour. It was not at all unpalatable, especially when toasted; and when it was seen that the war would not be as short as the Germans had expected, the bread cards were issued. That is, every Monday morning each person was given a card which had annexed to it a number of little perforated sections about the size of a quarter of a postage stamp, each marked with twenty-five, fifty or one hundred. The total of these figures constituted the allowance of each person in grammes per week. The person desiring to buy bread either at a baker's or in a restaurant must turn in these little stamped sections for an amount equivalent to the weight of bread purchased. Each baker was given a certain amount of meal at the commencement of each week, and he had to account for this meal at the end of the week by turning in its equivalent in bread cards. As food became scarce, the card system

Zu schnell nur warst Du aufgegessen,
Du bleibst im Magen unvergessen.

Trauer~Anzeige.

Allen Freunden, Verwandten und Bekann~
ten die traurige Mitteilung, daß unser letzter

Laib Brot

im Alter von 5 Tagen

und unsere hoffnungsvollen

5 kleine Brötchen
im Alter von 3 Tagen

ins bessere Jenseits unseres Magens einge~
gangen sind. Ein unheilbares chronisches Lei~
den, die **Verzehrungssucht** (Fresseritis emi~
nentis) hat ihrem kurzen Dasein ein leider zu
frühes Ende bereitet. Wer ihn gekannt, den
guten **Laib** selig, der weiß, wie uneigennützig
er uns seine **besten Stücke** sowie letzten
Bissen gab. Er ließ sich von Jedem **an~
schmieren**, mit Butter, Honig und Marmelade
und sagte nichts. Er war der **Ernährer** der
Familie, in jeder Gesellschaft beliebt und ge~
achtet, Sein Andenken wird unvergesslich sein.
Nach dem letzten Willen des Dahingegange~
nen, bitten wir bei **Kondolenzbesuchen** um
Abgabe von **Butter~, Mehl~ und Brotmar~
ken.** Blumenspenden dankend verbeten.

Die trauernden Hinterbliebenen:

Moritz Roggenmehl, z. Z. im Felde
Carl Weizenmehl, z. Z. ausgegangen
Commerzienrat Kuchen, vermißt
Clara Fettmilch, Schweden
Geh. S.~R. Hunger,
Direktor Zucker, in Gefangenschaft
Familie Weiß~ und Schwarzbrot
Moses Fromm, Mazzebäcker unter Aufsicht.

Nachdruck wird gerichtlich verfolgt.

A humorous spoof obituary for a loaf of bread and five small rolls, which are sadly missed; produced in Germany in 1917. (Author's collection)

was applied to meat, potatoes, milk, sugar, butter and soap. Green vegetables and fruits were exempt from the card system, as were for a long time chickens, ducks, geese, turkeys and game. Because of these exemptions the rich usually managed to live well, although the price of a goose rose to ridiculous heights. There was, of course, much underground traffic in cards and sales of illicit or smuggled butter, etc. The police were very stern in their enforcement of the law and the manager of one of the largest hotels in Berlin was taken to prison because he had made the servants give him their allowance of butter, which he in turn sold to the rich guests of the hotel. No one over six years of age at the time I left could get milk without a doctor's certificate. One result of this was that the children of the poor were surer of obtaining milk than before the war, as the women of the Frauendienst [Women's Service] and social workers saw to it that each child had its share.[18]

For a Socialist deputy in the Reichstag, Dr Sudukum, the rationing system which was now in force in Germany represented the achievement of a long-held ambition, of equality and social justice for poorer Germans:

I have worked hard in the development of the 'People's Kitchens' in Berlin. We started in the suburbs early in 1916, in some great central kitchens in which we cook a nourishing meat and vegetable stew. From these kitchens distributing vehicles – Gulasch-kanonen (stew cannons) as they are jocularly called – are sent through the city, and from them one may purchase enough for a meal at less than the cost of production. We have added a new central kitchen each

A travelling soup kitchen, Berlin 1917. By this stage the difference in living standards between 'haves' and 'have nots' in Germany was apparent. (Author's collection)

week until we now have 30, each of which supplies 10,000 people
a day with a meal, or, more correctly, a meal and a half. In July,
however, the work assumed greater proportions, for the municipal
authorities also created great central kitchens. Most of the dinners
are taken to the homes and eaten there. The People's Kitchen idea
is now spreading throughout Germany. But I believe in going
further. I believe in putting every German – I make no exception –
upon rations. That is what is done in a besieged city, and our
position is sufficiently analogous to a besieged city to warrant the
same measures. All our food would then be available for equal
distribution, and each person would get his allowance.[19]

Clearly, however, Dr Sudukum's aspirations were a million miles from what
was actually happening on the streets, where those with money and
influence were able to buy their way around the restrictions and controls
on food. Countess Blücher gives another example of the social tensions
which were rising day by day in Germany, in her diary for April 1916:

My sister-in-law in Bonn gives a description of disturbances [there].
She says: 'Yesterday there was a fearful mob and a fight in the
Rathausstrasse for lard. It was the day for waiting outside the stores
for this article; the town provides it for the people on certain days,
and who arrives first is first served, a carriage with rich people in it
drove up, and the inmates were served before the others, which
caused a riot. The policemen had to use their swords, for the crowd
nearly lynched them. The mob broke the windows of the police
station.'[20]

Admittedly, this was a second-hand account, and Countess Blücher had not
witnessed these events herself, but in Berlin, in May 1916, the situation
grew even more serious. Several riots had already occurred there in the early
part of the year, and soldiers had been used to restore order. Now Countess
Blücher wrote:

On returning to Berlin after a peaceful Easter spent with Princess
Munster in Demeburg, we were horrified to find the streets
surrounding our hotel in a great state of excitement. The hotel even
seemed to be in a state of siege, being surrounded by a cordon of
police and a rather threatening-looking mob, who, it seemed, had
already stolen the bread supplies for the hotel, evidently supposing
that we were living in a superabundance of luxuries, whilst they
were wanting in everything. As a matter of fact, our supply of bread

is limited to the same allowance as everyone else's in Germany, 1900 grms. a week, including 400 grms. of flour . . . The barest necessaries of life were wanting, and many people kept Easter in the face of an empty larder. The unexpected duration of the war has led to unforeseen complications in the economic administration, so that all sorts of changes are taking place in the Board of Provisions; added to which the keeping back of food supplies by speculators for the purpose of demanding exorbitant prices reached such a climax, that it almost seemed as if a revolution on a small scale were threatening in Berlin. The butchers' shops were closed for two to three weeks on set prices being denominated by Government for meat; vegetables were not to be had; butter almost unknown; whilst soap had become so scarce that regulations were enforced forbidding white dresses to be worn in some parts of Germany. Everyone is now allowed 1 lb. of soap for washing purposes a month, and 100 grms. of toilet soap extra. Long processions of women waiting for hours before the butchers', grocers', and bakers' shops were to be seen everywhere, and gave rise to the name of the 'butter-polonaise.' These women often got up in the middle of the night, to be first on the scene, and took camp-stools with them, working or knitting, and seemed rather to enjoy this opportunity of unlimited gossiping, evil tongues said. One industrious woman was even said to have taken her sewing machine with her!

. . . Our daily rations are at present: 1/2 lb. of sugar, 1/2 lb. of meat or lard, 1 lb. of potatoes, with 100 grms. of butter per head weekly. Eggs are hardly to be had, two companies having bought them all up in the province of Brandenburg, and they cost 32 to 30 Pf. apiece, if available at all. We can hardly complain of starvation, but the whole population is being under-fed, which of course, in the long run, means a deterioration of physical and mental forces in all classes.[21]

By June 1916 the situation had deteriorated further still, but Countess Blücher was especially concerned with the plight of her fellow countrymen being held prisoner in Germany. Although she seemed reassured that these men were well provided for with supplies from home and elsewhere, in fact pilfering from food parcels by guards was a perennial problem:

. . . the present depression reigning here is in part owing to the worry over the food question, which is increasing daily. We were told the other day that the authorities intend closing the schools for three months, as they want to keep as many women and children as possible out of the towns on account of the food-supply. A great difficulty is the scarcity of fodder for the cattle, which means less milk and butter. One would expect that all this shortage would prove a very serious question in regard to the [British] prisoners, but as a matter of fact they are really better off than we are, as 'The Prisoners' Aid Society' sends 58,000 packages from England weekly to the prisoners, and 10,000 loaves of bread from Switzerland. Each prisoner receives his package and loaf, and I must give the German authorities their due as to the proper delivery of these parcels.[22]

Around the same time, June 1916, the American woman, Mrs Bullitt, wrote amusingly in her diary of a disastrous outing to a restaurant. In this account the deterioration in the standard of living of all classes is apparent:

Dinner at the Esplanade tonight was really too awful. We had neither meat nor bread cards, so were reduced to a dish called: 'lost eggs', and asparagus. The eggs were lost in some dreadful vegetable and the asparagus was that fat white and tasteless stuff they grow here. Billy remarked that the sauce hollandaise must have been difficult to make without either butter, eggs, or olive oil, and his tea, he said, reminded him of when his nurse used to stick her finger in a cup of hot water and tell him to 'drink his tea, Dearie.' I had apricots for dessert and ate a great number; that they had begun to ferment was no longer a drawback at least they tasted of something.[23]

A German farm cart, around the time of the First World War. The workers may be POWs. (Author's collection)

In fact the really serious shortages were being felt only by those in the urban centres, for those in the rural areas who grew their own food as a general rule took what they needed first, before turning their produce over to the state for the rationing system. There was even a story about a farmer in the east of the country who, at a point when most in Berlin had not seen butter for over a year, was using his to lubricate the axles of his cart, because he had so much of it and could not get hold of grease! The effect on the political situation of food shortages in the urban areas continued to be the main concern of Countess Blücher in September 1916, who refers once again to the incompetence of the authorities in storing food effectively:

> The great topic of interest which is hypnotizing the mental powers of all Germany, and putting great strain on the national sagacity, is the best way of preserving human life on a minimum of albumen and farinaceous foods. Letters received from friends reveal the desperate plight they are in to cope with the necessities of the day. We hear too of food-riots in Berlin and other big towns, but in order to prevent a panic they have all been hushed up. Prince Friedrich Wilhelm, a nephew of the Emperor, and the Landrat not very far from here, was shot at last week, the people blaming him for the shortness of food, etc.; and an official in the Board of Provisions here told my husband, a month ago, that if the war lasted another six months it would be impossible to keep the people in hand at all, the disquietude is increasing so alarmingly. There has been food enough during the last year, but it seems that so much has been stored up that whole cart-loads have had to be thrown into the Rhine, as it has all gone bad. This is what enrages the people so fearfully.[24]

Around the same time, an American student, Josephine Therese, arrived in Berlin to study music. What shocked her most was the corruption of the German rationing system. She observed that her neighbour had a present for the grocer, and noted:

> . . . a 'present' has but one significance in Berlin now, and that is 'something to eat.' Frau Schmidt has a package under her arm, and passes it over to him surreptitiously, with an ingratiating smile. We notice that she received a much more generous allowance than we did, and we determine to follow her example next Monday. Bribery? Don't look shocked. We are in Berlin and it is the common and accepted thing here now especially at the illicit 'speak-easies' so much sought after by the police and hungry population alike, and

Typical German shops, the one on the right selling fruit and vegetables. Many sources record the fact that shopkeepers would go to great efforts to keep up their window displays, even if they had nothing to sell and the 'produce' in the window was artificial. (Author's collection)

which Mr. Miller has told us about. There, by means of a well-filled purse, the favoured few can still get food smuggled in from the country, through underground channels, for there are plenty of farmers and food dealers who, lured by gold, are willing to take their chance of incurring a heavy punishment, and who have already amassed fortunes, for they charge every bit that the traffic will bear. Even many of the public storekeepers dare official wrath, sometimes most brazenly, to supply their old or particularly favored customers, going so far as to tip them off by telephone, as did Frau Schmidt's grocer this morning, when a lot of something new has come in unexpectedly. Nor in that manner only. We have just had a demonstration of another, for, when the grocer quoted us a price of five marks for the last lot of parsnip, and Frau Schmidt said. 'I'll give you ten for it', he sold it to her. The government may close his shop some day for such outrageous practices, but most of his fellows do the same.[25]

She continued her shopping trip, discovering that substitutes and fish were staple parts of the diet:

To our delight we now discover that we can actually get some butter this week; a whole quarter of a pound, but we surmise that, when

we get it home, our enthusiasm will wane somewhat, for it is sure
to be a white, greasy, evil-smelling mass that is certainly not more
than half real butter. We are frugal, and will probably still further
mix it with a much-advertised preparation, guaranteed to make two
pounds where only one was before. More German efficiency! On
our way to the butcher's we pass the fish store, where no cards are
as yet required, and lay in a stock of 'Ausland' smoked fish at one
mark fifteen pfennig a pound. Now to the meat market; but do we
order the third cut of the rump and a tender, thick slice of veal?
Well, hardly. We take what is given us and are again thankful. Today
it is hamburger steak, a half a pound of it, and this will make us one
fairly good meal – if we mix it with dry breadcrumbs.[26]

Her only positive comment was that prices were not excessively high, for
the government kept them down, but the amounts obtainable now were
barely enough to keep body and soul together. The substitute butter which
Therese encountered was but one of many artificial foods which German
food scientists developed during the war, with varying degrees of success.
'Ersatz' coffee was reputedly as good as the real thing, as were artificial
strawberries made from potatoes. Curtin tells us:

*This poster encourages Germans to collect acorns and chestnuts, for use in
substitute food products.* (German Federal Archives)

Since the war, food exhibitions in various cities, but more especially in Berlin, have had as one of their most prominent features booths where you could sample substitutes for coffee, yeast, eggs, butter, olive oil, and the like. Undoubtedly many of these substitutes are destined to take their place in the future alongside some of the products for which they are rendering vicarious service. In fact, in a 'Proclamation touching the Protection of Inventions, Designs, and Trade Marks in the Exhibition of Substitute-Materials in Berlin-Charlottenburg, 1916', it is provided that the substitutes to be exhibited shall enjoy the protection of the Law. Even before the war, substitutes like Kathreiner's malt coffee were household words, whilst the roasting of acorns for admixture with coffee was not only a usual practice on the part of some families in the lower middle class, but was so generally recognised among the humbler folk that the children of poor families were given special printed permissions by the police to gather acorns for the purpose on the sacred grass of the public parks . . .

Thus, when wider circles of the population were driven to resort to substitutes, there was already in existence a State-organised system to control the output. Since the war began, sausage has served as a German stand-by from the time that beef and pork became difficult to obtain. In the late spring, however, the increased demand for sausage made that also more difficult to procure, and we often got a substitute full of breadcrumbs, which made the food-value of this particular Wurst considerably less than its size would indicate. It was frequently so soft that it was practically impossible to cut, and we had to spread it on our bread like butter.

The substitute of which the world has read the most is war bread. This differs in various localities, but it consists chiefly of a mixture of rye and potato with a little wheat flour . . . Imitation tea is made of plum and other leaves boiled in real tea and dried.[27]

With the harvests of both 1916 and 1917 being exceptionally poor, grain production fell from 21.8 million tons to 14.9 million tons in those two years, and the winter of 1916/17 was known in Germany as 'the turnip winter' due to the exclusive, unnourishing and monotonous diet of these glebes which the population was forced to endure. Official food rations in 1917 were 1,000 calories per day, while the health ministry considered 2,280 calories to be a subsistence minimum. Whilst it is estimated that 750,000 people died directly of starvation in Germany between 1914 and 1918, many more than this succumbed to disease, through lack of adequate

Another German poster, calling for civilians to collect beech nuts from which oil could be extracted. (Library of Congress)

nourishment in their diet. An American girl in Germany at this time, Mary Ethel McAuley, had first hand experience of the turnip diet:

> . . . when I say turnips I mean what they call Kohlruben – we sometimes call it rutabaga. We ate this vegetable constantly during the spring of 1917. Most people hated it, but it was fine for filling up space. Dogs were fed almost entirely on it. When I was in Dresden I went to the Zoo, and there they had packages of carrots and Kohlruben for sale for feeding the monkeys. The monkeys were hungry and they gobbled up the carrots, but they absolutely refused

to eat the Kohlruben, and when they were handed a piece they threw it down in disgust.[28]

In fact the zoo was to play a further, somewhat unexpected part in McAuley's diet whilst in Germany, and she tells us that:

> When I was in Dresden in May, 1917, I ate elephant meat. An elephant got hurt in the Zoo and had to be killed. A beer restaurant bought his meat for 7000 marks, and it was served with sauerkraut to the public without a card at 1.30 marks. It tasted like the finest kind of chopped meat, and the restaurant was packed as long as the elephant lasted.[29]

It is an extraordinary testament to the state of affairs in Germany by the second half of the war, that citizens were willing (indeed eager) to eat the flesh of an injured zoo animal, and it is clear that it was more than the mere novelty of tasting the meat which motivated most of the customers at the restaurant which purchased the carcass. Desperate times call for desperate measures, and by this stage in the war, any notion of doing the 'right' thing because it was patriotic seems to have vanished. Countess Blücher wrote in February 1917:

> On the whole, all the conscientious scruples which really did hinder many people from storing up underhand supplies of food some six months ago have disappeared before the pangs of hunger, and the feeling prevalent in all classes is: every man for himself and the devil for us all![30]

George Schreiner, meanwhile, was an American writer who travelled extensively through Germany and Austria-Hungary during the war. Although during one of his visits to Berlin he had lunch with a well-to-do woman who was reduced to serving war bread without butter, and who he reported bore this situation stoically, later that evening he dined at another house, and was struck by the contrast which he found there:

> I had accepted an invitation to dinner. It was a good dinner – war or peace. Its pièce de résistance was a whole broiled ham, which, as my hostess admitted, had cost in the clandestine market some one hundred and forty marks, roughly twenty-five dollars at the rate of exchange then in force. There was bread enough and side dishes galore. It was also a meatless day. The ham was one of several which had found the household in question through the channels of

illicit trade, which even the strenuous efforts of the Prussian government had not been able to close as yet. The family had the necessary cash, and in order to indulge in former habits as fully as possible, it was using that cash freely.[31]

This was probably a more typical meal for someone of this social class, and the ability of those with money to circumvent the food crisis in Germany was causing increasing social unrest. Government meddling and incompetence also aroused the ire of the average citizen. The summer of 1917 was exceptionally warm in Germany, and as a result the crop of fruit and berries was large. Yet, even so, the amount to be had in the cities was limited, because the government, as usual, stepped in and established a maximum price above which the farmers could not sell, and many refused to ship for that amount. As a result, the city people wherever possible went to the farms themselves to collect the fruit, or sent an errand boy there to fetch some. In response, the food authorities established a rule that no one could buy more than a pound of any one kind, and even went as far as to place policemen on the farms to see that the regulation was obeyed. In certain cases the police actually arrested children for attempting to take away more than a pound of fruit! Countess Blücher tells us of another incident in July 1917:

One consequence of all the blundering is that there is murmuring everywhere, in the army as well as amongst the civilians. For example, when on the advice of Michaelis the bread allowance was cut down, there was great grumbling amongst the people and a revolt seemed threatening. The food controllers in a panic promised them extra meat at a cheap price, to make up for the curtailed bread rations, and ordered all the milk cows in certain districts to be slaughtered. This promptly took place, to the great rage of the agriculturists, who indignantly opposed the 'madness of the order'. But it was too late, the order had been carried out, and for a week or two there was such a surplus of meat that it actually had to be given or thrown away, to prevent its spoiling in the hot weather. The result is now that milk is running short, and there is renewed grumbling, although the extra supply of cheap meat proved a great boon to the populations in the towns and helped them to tide over hard times. As an accompaniment to the incessant murmuring and increasing incredulity of the people, there is a decided inclination to a milder form of revolt, and riots and disturbances do now and then take place, though they are hushed up. The Germans are such a patient and long-suffering race that they do not as yet realize their own power, and the Prussian precept, 'Es ist verboten,' has been so drummed into them that they accept all regulations and orders without any further demur. I do believe that if they were bidden to go out and eat grass, they would obey in herds, without any further question.[32]

After having sampled the food and living standards of the upper classes, Thomas Curtin decided to inspect those of the working classes in Germany. The poor of Berlin inhabited the northern and eastern districts, and in 1917 Curtin paid a visit to the east end of Berlin to observe the condition of the working-class families which lived here. He wrote:

Late in the morning I left the Stettiner Bahnhof in the north and walked eastward through the Invalidenstrasse. There was practically no meat in the butchers' shops, just the customary lines of empty hooks. A long queue farther on attracted my attention and I crossed the street to see what the people were waiting for. A glance at the dark red carcases in the shop told me that this was

Thomas Curtin, who observed the conditions among the poor of Berlin in 1917. (From Curtin, The Land of Deepening Shadow)

horse-meat day for that district. The number of vacant shops of all descriptions was increasing. The small shoemaker and tailor were closing up. The centralisation of food distribution is greater here than in the better-class districts, with the result that many small shopkeepers have been driven out of business. In parts of Lothringerstrasse a quarter of the shops were vacant, in other parts one-half.

The bakers' shops are nearly empty except at morning and evening . . . Shortly before noon I reached the Zentral ViehundSchlachthof (the slaughter-houses). Through a great gateway poured women and children, each carrying some sort of a tin or dish full of stew. Some of the children were scarcely beyond the age of babyhood, and their faces showed unmistakable traces of toil. The poor little things drudged hard enough in peace time, and in war they are merely part of the big machine. The diminishing supply of cattle and pigs for killing has afforded an opportunity to convert a section of the slaughter-houses into one of the great People's Kitchens. Few eat there, however. Just before noon and at

Poor Germans being fed at a communal soup kitchen, 1917. (Author's collection)

noon the people come in thousands for the stew, which costs forty pfennigs (about 5d.) a quart, and a quart is supposed to be enough for a meal and a half.

I have been in the great Schlachthof kitchen, where I have eaten the stew, and I have nothing but praise for the work being done. This kitchen, like the others I have visited, is the last word in neatness. The labour-saving devices, such as electric potato-parers, are of the most modern type . . . Among the women who prepare the food and wait upon the people there is a noticeable spirit of co-operation and a pride in the part they are playing to help the Fatherland durchhalten (hold out).

Should any of the stew remain unsold it is taken by a well-known restaurant in the Potsdamer Platz, which has a contract with the municipal authorities. Little was wasted in Germany before the war; nothing, absolutely nothing, is wasted to-day.

As at the central slaughter-house, so in other districts the poor are served in thousands with standard stew. The immense Alexander Market has been cleared of its booths and tables and serves more than 30,000 people. One director of this work told me that the Berlin authorities would supply nearly 400,000 people before the end of the winter . . . When I once more resumed my walk I saw the lines of people waiting for food in every street. Each time I turned a corner great black masses dominated the scene. I paused at a line of more than three hundred waiting for potatoes. Ten yards away not a sound could be heard. The very silence added to the depression. With faces anxious and drawn they stood four abreast, and moved with the orderliness of soldiers. Not a sign of disturbance, and not a policeman in sight.[33]

Lilo Linke was a German girl brought up in Berlin's poor east end. Aged just eleven in the winter of 1917, she remembered queuing for hours in the bitter cold, the winter wind slicing through the crowds of women standing silently on the pavement, four abreast. For many of these women, undernourished as they were, standing for so long in these conditions was too much:

This moment the butcher's shop was opened, and suddenly a flicker of life reappeared in the crowd as it pushed forward two or three steps. I pulled myself together. In half an hour I would be in the shop myself. But slowly a fear began to rise in me, right from my feet through my whole body, a fear of nothing special, just a general feeling of anxiety which seemed to

Berlin girl Lilo Linke, aged 11. In the winter of 1917, she queued for hours for food. (From The Great War, I was There)

empty me and hindered me from breathing. I was so lonely. I must sit down. Or try to go home. But I had to wait. I felt sick. Nobody there to hold me. I touched the woman on my left: 'I must sit down . . . Oh, I am dying . . .'

She looked at me in surprise. Other women turned round, there was a murmuring and unrest; I tried to stand straight and look alright, I even grinned reassuringly: but suddenly my head made a funny jerk, everything around me swam away, my strength left me. Oh, heaven, heaven, I was dying! But I only fainted . . .[34]

Linke tells us more about the diet upon which her family existed, and it is scarcely creditable that growing children could survive on such unappetising substitute foods:

> Sugar was absolutely necessary to make 'Ersatz-Kaffee' – dishwater, as we called it – at all drinkable. To dream of a drop of milk with it was simply ridiculous in its extravagance. For days we nourished ourselves on a sweet, greenish pulp: indigestible ruins of frozen potatoes. Or was it only a bad imitation of them, as all the rest of our food was only imitating real stuff? To overcome the foul taste we poured 'Ersatz-Sauce' over them, but the only similarity with gravy was its dark brown colour . . . Turnips [were] useful in many ways. Not only could they be eaten simply as a vegetable – and they were delicious cooked with bones or a slice of horsemeat, of which I was especially fond – but they could be turned into almost anything from salad to marmalade.[35]

The contrast between the war experiences of Lilo Linke and Countess Blücher could scarcely have been wider and provides further graphic illustration of the widening gap in living standards between rich and poor in Germany by the war's end. The Countess held a lavish reception for about 150 members of the nobility and other distinguished guests at her home in Berlin in March 1918 and wrote:

> As for the food question, which is generally a vexed one, the supper-table certainly looked very opulent with its dainty dishes and masses of blood-red tulips; but everything was raised on our own estate, and the geese, ducks, pheasants, ham, fowls, salads, etc., could all be offered with a good conscience, and there was nothing 'forbidden' on the menu. The Spanish Ambassador whispered in my ear that he only regretted one particular guest not being present at the scene. On my asking whom he meant, he replied: 'Lloyd George; for if he could see that supper-table he would know how nonsensical it is to talk of Germany being starved out.'[36]

The Countess divided her time between Berlin and her estate in the country at Krieblowitz in Silesia (now part of Poland). In an echo of the elephant incident of the previous year, in May 1918 some of the exotic animals from the estate menagerie were eaten:

Food is growing scarcer from day to day, and we have been reduced to killing and eating our kangaroos. They have been kept here as a great curiosity and rarity for years past. Yesterday my husband received a letter from one of the provision-dealers in Breslau, saying he would give any price my husband liked to mention if he would sell him a kangaroo.[37]

The mood of the ordinary people, even in the countryside, now was growing uglier:

I notice a great change in the people here from what they were last year. They are all 'tired of suffering,' as they express it. 'We want our sons and husbands back, and we want food,' is all they say. And the priests and clergymen too say how difficult it is to hold them in now. Any moment they fear them breaking all control . . .[38]

A poor German woman: her seven sons were all in the army, and she and her three grandchildren were surviving on potatoes. (From Doty, Behind the Battle Line*)*

By June 1918 the Countess tells us that the food situation was becoming critical:

> The food question is always the most important topic of the day. The less there is of it, the more do we talk of it. The Austrians have already eaten up their stores, and are grumbling and turning to Germany for fresh supplies. It is rather like turning from a sandy desert to a rocky mountain for nourishment. And there is unfortunately no Moses to show us the way to a promising future. We ourselves have little to eat but smoked meat and dried peas and beans, but in the towns they are considerably worse off. The potatoes have come to a premature end, and in Berlin the population have now a portion of 1 lb. per head a week, and these even are bad. The cold winds of this wintry June have retarded the growth of vegetables, and there is almost nothing to be had. We are all waiting hungrily for the harvest and the prospect of at least more bread and flour.[39]

Remaining at Krieblowitz until August, later she was able to report that there was an improvement in the weather later in the summer, which brought with it some good news:

> The cold dry weeks of June and the despondent outlook for the harvest gave place to rainy weeks in July, which came in time to repair the damage done, so that the promise of a good harvest cheered the hearts of the hungry watching people; and August has fulfilled these expectations, and the crops have proved to be abundant everywhere. Only the late corn and oats are suffering under the cold rainy weather of the last two weeks, and the precious cut corn is beginning to sprout, too damp to be brought in. In these lean years the eyes of all Germany follow anxiously the news of the harvest in the newspapers. The late potatoes are a success; one can hear the universal sigh of relief at these tidings. Meatless weeks have been ordered, as too many milk-cows are being slaughtered. If the war continues much longer there will be no live stock left at all.[40]

However, for the hard-pressed German people this was too little, too late. The Allied stranglehold on Germany's food supply had proved decisive, indeed the German commander Erich Ludendorff was in no doubt that the blockade had sapped Germany's moral fibre and fighting spirit, to the point at which she could no longer continue, stating in his war memoirs that:

Humour in a desperate situation: in this German postcard, the young man is surrounded by female admirers. The caption leaves no doubt as to their motives, and translates as '[They are] only after a ration card'. (Author's collection)

The waning morale at home was intimately connected with the food situation. In wide quarters a certain decay of bodily and mental powers of resistance was noticeable, resulting in an unmanly and hysterical state of mind which under the spell of enemy propaganda encouraged the pacifist leanings of many Germans . . . This state of mind was a tremendous element of weakness. It could be eliminated to some extent by strong patriotic feeling, but in the long run could only be overcome by better nourishment. Our enemies' starvation blockade triumphed, and caused us both physical and spiritual distress.[41]

The most controversial aspect of the Allied blockade of Germany, however, was the fact that it was continued after the Armistice, up until the signing of the Treaty of Versailles in July 1919, thus inflicting further hardship on the civilian population. Back in Berlin in November 1918, Countess Blücher was a witness to the revolution which took Germany out of the war, and also made the connection between poor food, low morale and social unrest explicitly clear:

The few people I have already spoken to were depressed and horrified at the terms of the armistice, especially that the blockade is not to be raised, which means for so many people a gradual death from exhaustion. As one English-woman said to me, the idea of

German schoolchildren are fed from large vats of soup, 1919. (From *The Great War, I was There*)

continuing to exist and work on the minimum of food still possible under the circumstances was so dreadful, that she thought it would be the most sensible thing to go with her child and try to get shot in one of the numerous street-fights; whilst another lady whose husband is at the front, and from whom she has heard nothing for a long time, is contemplating turning on the gas on herself and her two small children, and putting an end to the horrors of living. A diet of heavy vegetables, cooked without fat of any kind, with dry bread and potatoes, is not in the long-run consistent with the nerve-power necessary under the circumstances.[42]

Having finally got their boot on their enemy's throat, the Allies were in no hurry to remove it again, certainly not whilst negotiations over the actual peace terms were taking place – even if the continuation of the blockade into 1919 was regarded by many in Germany as practically a war crime. One observer noted:

As you go through the schools, stand in the class-rooms, watch the children at work, you have the sense of a whole generation stricken by a blight. It is revealed in the puckered brows, the lustreless, uncertain eye, the anaemic faces, the bandy legs, the dry, cracked, flabby skins, the swollen abdomens, the universal air of exhaustion. It is a generation who have never known what a sufficiency of food means. For five years – that is, for almost the whole of the life they remember – they have been starved. They were never worse starved than during the nine months' blockade that followed the war. They are still starving – a whole nation of children. The fortunate ones die (50 per cent, more infants died in Berlin alone during 1919, a year of 'peace,' than in 1913); the rest are starting their life with a physical and mental inefficiency that will make life a burden. The 'English sickness' alone (rickets), the result mainly of the post-war blockade, has claimed hundreds of thousands. Tuberculosis in all its variations has swept the child life like a plague. In Leipzig there are 8,000 tuberculous children; in Cologne, 10,000; Berlin, 30,000. The mortality among small children has reached 25 per cent. The mortality of older children has gone up 85 per cent – nearly double. In the 115th public school of Berlin, out of 650 children examined, 305 had no proper sleeping space, 370 had no heating in their homes, 341 had not a drop of milk from week-end to week-end. The number of children who have died of tuberculosis and hunger in Germany had reached a million in April last.[43]

This post-Armistice blockade continues to cause controversy among historians today. Was it justified? Given Germany's wholehearted – if ultimately less successful – use of blockade tactics herself, there can be little doubt that she too would have continued with it in this fashion had circumstances been reversed.

Thus whilst Ludendorff (and others) were accurate in linking Germany's decline and eventual defeat on the battlefield with the steadily worsening food situation at home, it was an oversimplification of the matter simply to lay the blame for Germany's food crisis entirely at the door of the Allied blockade. Far more complex factors were at work here; on the one hand the difficulties which Germany faced were exacerbated by the government's generally inept handling of food control, and more particularly its failure to gain control over food production. On another level, what really sapped civilian morale was not shortages as such, for the majority of people in Germany faced these with truly remarkable stoicism, at least initially. Rather, what destroyed civilian morale were the insidious methods which some sections of society used to circumvent these shortages. This had the effect of turning Germans against Germans, and class against class. In the end, many Germans no longer felt that they were 'all in the same boat', or that all classes were pulling together, and so Germany's war ended with revolution on the streets and with the red flag being brandished in Berlin.

Chapter 6

Italy and France

Italy entered the First World War on 24 May 1915, some nine months after the beginning of the general conflict between the European powers. Even when she did join the war, her commitment to it was characterised by hesitance and uncertainty. There was no widespread support for intervention, nor any obvious outpouring of national sentiment as a result (in contrast with most other belligerents). Her declaration of war was initially only against Austria-Hungary, and remained so until 1916 when she was persuaded to extend hostilities to Germany. As a nation, Italy had existed only since the Risorgimento of 1870, and one of the reasons for her entry into the war was the feeling among some in the Italian establishment that she lacked a sense of national identity; these people hoped that a hard but hopefully short war would fuse together her many regional groups, each speaking their own distinctive dialect. However, as well as being politically weak she was also economically underdeveloped; indeed, Italy in 1914 was also one of the poorest countries in Europe, and her food supply was not strong enough to withstand the rigours of protracted warfare. By contrast, France was well developed economically and was probably the country which suffered the least food hardship during the First World War, certainly amongst the combatant nations. Although her agricultural output during the war dropped, partly as a result of loss of territory to Germany in 1914, and she came to rely more on imports as the war went on, France saw far less social strain as a result than her neighbour across the Alps.

Although the cities of northern Italy were industrialised, much of the south was rural and underdeveloped. Italy's history in the nineteenth century had been strongly defined by emigration, rather than development and social progress at home, with the rural areas in particular experiencing large scale de-population; Italians were among the largest ethnic groups entering the United States in these years. Industrial workers in the north, and poor agricultural workers in the south, would bear the brunt of wartime hardships in Italy. Even before her entry into the conflict, war conditions had produced an acute economic crisis in the country. From the autumn of 1914, naval operations in the Adriatic destroyed the Italian fishing industry, whilst the

The narrow streets of Naples, around 1914. (Library of Congress)

exodus of foreign guests from hotels threw many of their employees out of work, and in addition about 500,000 migrant Italian workers from Germany, Austria and France returned home. Conditions were aggravated by the rise in the cost of food, and the tendency of employers, with a glut on the labour market, to reduce wages and increase the hours of work. The hope of many workers for industrial and economic reforms had already been frustrated by the war, and a resolution adopted by the Italian Socialist Party in February 1915 called for the workers to resist calls for any greater involvement in it, stating: '. . .the condition of the Italian workers is aggravated by unemployment and by the increase in the price of bread and food, due to the state of war in the greater part of Europe . . .'[1] After Italy's eventual declaration of hostilities against Austria-Hungary, the Socialists sought to mitigate the continuing hardships being experienced by the working classes, another resolution in June 1915 stating:

> . . . the directorate requires all branches to establish in every locality aid, advisory, and defensive committees of the economic organizations; to maintain contact with the workers and their families in greater measure than in the past; to defend in the most suitable manner the principles of socialism; and to combat the inane dissemination of race and national hatred . . . Italian socialists should . . . establish committees for the relief of war victims and see to it that they function properly in providing food supplies, requisitioning grain, reducing rents, preventing profiteering, establishing employment offices, taking more effective measures for the care of widows and orphans, etc., but in performing this work should not renounce any of the principles of the party and merely demonstrate the solidarity of humanity.[2]

The initial approach of the Italian government towards the supply of goods on the home front was along *laissez-faire* lines, and therefore it was not long before prices began to rise to previously unknown levels. This sudden inflation came as a considerable shock to Italian consumers, who were used to price stability over a long period of time. To begin with, however, there was little in the way of shortages; indeed Italy had the opposite problem in the early months of the war. Development of the economy due to government spending, together with inflation, created a new sense of luxuriousness in the shops and department stores in the cities behind the front. To soldiers coming home on leave from the battlefield, this contrast between the high life at home and the grim reality of war at the sharp end could not go unnoticed. An optimistic report on the situation in Italy was published by an American visitor, Charles Truitt, who wrote:

Poor Italian women, in the village of Amalfi, southern Italy. (Library of Congress: Bain collection)

So far, there has been little apprehension regarding the food supply. Women always have done most of the work in fields and gardens, so the absence of men will have but little effect upon the cultivating and gathering of crops. Much of the grain, however, has to be imported and because of the scarcity of ships the price of wheat has advanced. Accordingly, 'war' bread is in order. It is not good to look at, this mixture of potato, rice and wheat flours, but we are assured by the food experts that it is more wholesome than bread made from white flour only. It is a dirty gray in color and strong teeth are needed to masticate it, but the taste is delicious.[3]

Truitt was wide of the mark, however. The diversion of agricultural labourers to the army did indeed affect farm production, and this was becoming a major problem. As a result of it, food prices rose, and inflation became a serious concern. It was a situation made worse by the fact that in many cases men <u>were</u> the primary family breadwinners. When the government expanded conscription, and called up these men, this left many families without incomes. To make matters worse, if the husband or father was killed or badly injured, then the family was left impoverished.

Allowances paid to soldiers and their families were low, and if middle- and upper-class families could generally make do, then poor families certainly could not. Those which barely survived in the best of times now found themselves in very difficult circumstances indeed. Truitt himself goes some way to acknowledging this when he writes of the charitable foundations and groups which stepped in to try to assist:

> Each district in the city has its public kitchen, where cooked food is sold at low prices. In addition, there are places where dinners are served free of charge to wives and children of the poorer soldiers. The food is donated by daughters of prosperous families and is cooked and served by them. The people of means are doing everything they can, both through money and personal service, to lighten the burden of the families whose men are absent at the front. All class barriers are down and the whole spirit of Italy seems to be one of eager service.[4]

Five soup kitchens were opened in Palermo, and in October 1915 the committee for Civil Defence in the city provided for eight more to be opened by the Princess di Valdina in the suburbs. A Committee for Gratuitous Soups was formed in Turin by the Federation of Women's Activities. This committee collected offerings of small change in order to distribute completely free soup. The same federation, realising the necessity of providing food not only to the poorer classes but also to the middle class which had been economically stricken by the war, instituted the *Pranzi di Guerra*, or war dinners. A good meal consisting of soup, a dish of meat and vegetables, two loaves of bread and a glass of wine, could be purchased for fourteen cents. Young mothers received special attention in Naples at the Casa di Previdenza ed Assistenza per la Maternita, and in Rome at the home of Signora Mina Ramponi who was assisted by many other ladies. This latter committee furnished the mother at the birth of the child with baby-linen and a schedule book to get milk and food daily at the war kitchens.

However, as food shortages began to grow, the Italian government now stepped in to control supplies. The long queues which formed outside the shops after the first price control and quota restriction measures were a new experience for city dwellers, and these had unexpected repercussions for productivity. An official from the Ministry for Arms and Munitions warned:

> There is serious discontent among the working class who are absenting themselves from work . . . in a manner exceedingly

> dangerous for the industrial economy and the battle on the Home Front. Too often workers are . . . excusing themselves with having to spend long hours at the shops in order to provide basic necessities.[5]

Sidney Sonnino: '[Italians] have given their sons and even their livestock to the country, but they will not give up their wheat.' (Library of Congress)

As the war went on, the Italian state assumed more and more control over food supplies and food prices. Initially there was fear in some quarters of the establishment that this would provoke a backlash, and Sidney Sonnino, a conservative leader in the Italian parliament, warned:

> You do not know the countryside of Italy and the psychology of the peasants. They have given their sons and even their livestock to the country, but they will not give up their wheat. You are worried that there may be riots in the cities because of bread shortages; there will be even more serious ones in the countryside.[6]

In the event, however Sonnino's fears proved unfounded, as the control of prices which accompanied requisition actually helped the producers.

For the Italian army, fighting in the high Alpine plains, food supply was considerably more challenging than on the Western Front. Nonetheless, strenuous efforts were made to ensure that the Italian soldier was adequately fed. One might expect officers to live well, and this was generally true. One observer wrote of a visit to a brigade or divisional headquarters near the front line, and of sharing a table with a general and some of his staff officers (the latter being noted as particularly abstemious):

> The building where the headquarters is situated is a small chalet. In one corner there is a hole, covered with sandbags. 'In war, we must make do', says the general, indicating for us to sit at the table. He need not have made any such excuse on behalf of the lunch. After one of those great Italian antipastis, we are served pasta, fish, chicken and ice cream. The bread we eat is the same as the soldiers' bread, toasted and tasty. Although the table abounds with Chianti

bottles and Marsala, there is a significant number of diners who drink nothing but water.[7]

Another writer who dined in an Italian mess commented upon an even more lavish spread, comprising no less than four courses:

> So far as the officers are concerned . . . mess arrangements, when up in the fighting line, of course, depend largely on circumstances, though these do not seem to be always governed by the difficulty of access to the position or its remoteness from the base. I had a pleasant proof of this at Pal Grande. The officers hospitably insisted on our taking 'pot luck' with them, as they were just going to have lunch, and it turned out one of the best al fresco repasts I have ever sat down to. The 'mess-room' was a well-protected dug-out which had been fitted up in somewhat similar fashion to a settler's hut in the Far West; it was quite snug, in fact, and we were a merry party crowded round the table that occupied nearly the whole of the interior, in spite of the continuous booming of the guns and the screech of the shells overhead. I had quite expected to get the roughest of meals in the circumstances; imagine, therefore, my surprise when we started with a fine macaroni soup; this was followed by beef steaks and fried potatoes; then came a jam omelette, and we finished up with cheese and fruit, the whole being washed down with excellent Verona wine. Black coffee was then brought in, and one of our hosts produced a bottle of cognac and a box of cigars. You could not have wished for a more delightful meal: it made one feel that even life in an entrenchment 8,000 feet up has its compensations at times. Of course it would not do to infer that in all positions the officers were able to indulge in so sumptuous a 'pot luck' repast, but I gathered that whenever it is possible a mess is formed, a cook found from amongst the men, and meals served comfortably.[8]

Even other ranks seem to have lived fairly well in the Italian army most of the time, although the food was sometimes monotonous and uninspiring. The same correspondent wrote:

> Napoleon's well known aphorism that an army fights on its belly is well borne out in the Italian Army; and even on these lofty peaks the soldier, whatever he may have to endure in the shape of inevitable hardship, never suffers from want of food and well-cooked meals. The food convoys make their journeys with unfailing regularity, for

there must be no hitch in the commissariat arrangements – and it is safe to assert that there is not a single soldier, no matter how isolated he may be, who does not receive every day his regulation allowance of 400 grammes of meat (about half a pound), a kilo and a half of bread, macaroni or polenta, coffee, tobacco, and half a litre of wine. Of course the menu is not very varied, but neither is the national Italian cuisine at any time. Rancio, a soup-like stew, made of meat and macaroni or some similar pasta, with a sufficiency of good, wholesome bread and a drink of red wine, should be

This wartime advertisement for Florio Marsala wine shows a consignment reaching cheering Italian troops in the Alps. Transport by mule was common on this front. (Author's collection)

sufficient to satisfy the appetite of any soldier. I made a meal of rancio on many occasions after a long and cold motor run, and always found it so appetising and comforting that I wished I could have got it every day. This stew is the usual plat du jour of the Italian soldier as is the stchi in the Russian Army, and is always served out steaming hot. In advanced trenches, outposts or similar exposed positions, where culinary operations are, of course, impossible, the rancio is taken to the men after dark in special receptacles for keeping it hot, known as Cassette di Cottura, which are constructed on the Thermos principle. The men would indeed begin to think things were going badly if the 'food party' could not succeed in reaching them.[9]

The observation that Italian cuisine was not particularly varied at this time is an interesting one, because some historians have argued that modern Italian cookery was actually born during the First World War, when for the first time recruits from different areas mixed together, and new dishes were born of the fusion of ideas and recipes which resulted. Some sources even assert that Italy's national dessert, tiramisu, was invented during the First World War as a dish which could easily be packed and shipped by families to relatives at the front. These sources also state that the meaning of the name in Italian, 'pick me up', refers to the morale-boosting effect of the cake, but the claims appear to be unsupported by any contemporary accounts. In 1917, another element was added to this culinary mix when British troops arrived in Italy to support the Italian army, and a certain amount of 'cross-fertilisation' occurred between the rations of the two nations. Charles Carrington, an officer in the Royal Warwickshire Regiment in a letter dated 22 December 1917 told his parents that: 'To the staple food of bully beef and biscuits we now add sour red wine and polenta, a sort of pudding of maize flour and water which the peasants chiefly live on.' [10] Other evidence for the standard of living of the Italian army at this time, and of this cross-fertilisation, comes from a British gunner officer writing in the summer of 1917, who tells us:

Our rations at this time were a special Anglo-Italian blend; less meat, bacon, cheese and tea than in the British ration, but macaroni, rice, coffee, wine and lemons from the Italian. It was a good ration and no one suffered from eating a little less meat than at home. In order to check the spread of dysentery, it was ordered by the medical authorities that no meat was to be eaten at midday.[11]

The following year, this same officer was still with the Italians and added:

For a week or two in May an Italian Engineer officer messed with us. He had a sleeping hut on the hill just behind us, and was in charge of a party of men who were working on British Field Artillery positions. His men were on British rations and did not altogether like them. They would have preferred more bread and less meat and jam, and they missed their coffee. Our tea they did not fancy. The first time it was issued to them, they thought it was medicine. 'Why do the English give us "camomile"?' they asked their officer, 'we are not ill!'[12]

Turning to the home front in Italy during the First World War, it is apparent that the diet of the poor was heavily dominated by bread and flour products and vegetables. In 1917 Prime Minister Salandra told his successor:

[the peasants and city workers in the south] live on bread and flour and nothing else . . . But as much bread as necessary is considered a natural right, on which no authority in the world can impose limits. If the opinion were to form that bread is in short supply because of the war, the war would be hated and condemned.[13]

Prime Minister Salandra: '[Italians in the south] live on bread and flour and nothing else . . . ' (Library of Congress)

A more detailed account of typical fare on the Italian home front comes from an American civilian travelling in the country in the latter part of the war. His description reinforces the view that for the peasant class at least in Italy at this time, their food was basic, and some of the 'traditional' dishes which today we take for granted as being Italian (for example pizza) were simply not known in Italy then:

Cooking with them is a matter of great simplicity. They rarely eat meat, save on Sundays or holidays, and their principal diet is soup, spaghetti, or macaroni in one form or another, vegetables, not cooked simply, but with soup, rice, cheese or salt fish, and fruit. The only food that they take that is not mixed with some other food is bread. Vegetables which grow in abundance in Italy are never to be found on the table . . . plainly cooked and not mixed with another vegetable or sauce. Frying is the favorite method of cooking, and oil, when it is to be obtained, is the sole medium. The tomato plays a role in the dietary of the Italian which isn't approached by any other country, for it is the invariable sauce with which pasta of various forms is eaten, more particularly during war-time, when it has been impossible to have butter. The morning meal of the contadini and of the laborer is the same as that of all Italians, a few mouthfuls of coffee, nowadays usually without milk, but ordinarily two-thirds milk, and a piece of bread. Naturally, he comes to the midday meal with a ravenous appetite, and it is a gorge of anything that he can lay his hands to. Usually it is followed by mental torpor which requires a certain amount of sleep for its satisfaction, the evening meal is rather simpler and consists in many peasants' households of a plate of soup, a loaf of bread, and some raw vegetable, such as finocchio, fave, or onion, occasionally prepared with oil and a little vinegar, but often taken without preparation.[14]

Food shortages had not yet seriously begun to bite in Italy. A diplomat visiting Venice in March 1917 commented upon the wide variety of foodstuffs still available, adding:

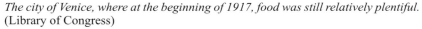

The city of Venice, where at the beginning of 1917, food was still relatively plentiful. (Library of Congress)

This morning in Venice's market-place, crowded with women buying things for their Sunday dinner, half a dozen aeroplanes swirling a few hundred feet over our heads, keeping a look-out for enemy planes that so often fly from Trieste in thirty minutes, I noted the following food prices:

Lemons, each	Lire 0.05 centessimi.
Oranges, each	.10
Bread, per kilo	.50
Cheese (similar to Swiss) per kilo,	Lire 3.80 centessimi.
Chickens, each	5.00
Lamb, bones included, per kilo	4.00
Eggs, each	.13
Potatoes, per kilo, from 60 & 70 cmi. to	1.20
String beans, per kilo	1.40
Radishes, per dozen	.15
Salami (dried sausage) per kilo,	8.00
(Before the war the same Salami cost only lire 5.00)	
Apples, first grade, per kilo	2.50
' second ' ' '	1.50
Cauliflower, per head	.20 and .25
Fish, flat like a flounder, per kilo,	4.50
' round, about 10 inches long, kilo,	2.50
' large, about two feet long, per kilo,	6.50
Eels, per kilo	2.50
Sardines, fresh, per kilo	2.40
1 hard boiled egg, ready to eat	.20[15]

However, later in 1917 southern Italy suffered a severe drought, seriously reducing the region's ability to produce wheat. Ordinarily this might not have been a problem, because before the war enormous quantities of wheat had come to Italy from the shores of the Black Sea. Now however, the Black Sea was closed. After walking through the parched landscape with a local guide, one reporter wrote:

Here and there Antonio pointed out the bare bottoms of streams that always before, in his memory, had run bank full. The weather last spring and summer played us all a villainous trick. It has been many years since grain crops fell so far below the average. Lack of fertiliser and of labor accounted for something; a mistake of the food control – all European food controllers made their initial mistakes – accounted for still more. But the drought was the main trouble . . . the Italians are and always have been a bread-eating people. Julius Caesar's unconquerable legions of Italian peasants lived and conquered the world on wheat and barley bread, eating meat only occasionally, when a raid on the barbarians threw cattle into their hands. For the fatty element necessary to human nutriment they relied mostly on oil – the olive oil of Italy and Southern Gaul. That characteristic has persisted. Your Italian of common occupation can live from year's end to year's end on bread and oil.

It is a mistake to suppose that macaroni is, for the average Italian, a regular, necessary dish. Macaroni is a luxury of the rich and well-to-do – a pleasant though expensive way of dishing up breadstuffs. The Italian peasant is more likely to take his bread in the form of polenta – cornmeal mush kept long in the pot, and cut out and warmed over as needed. To no people of the world is bread so much the staff of life. Just now, when in the natural course of things Italy is depending a great deal on fruit and fresh vegetables – perishable commodities – the food situation appears a little spotted; some districts are doing better than others. In general the country seems to eat sparingly but sufficiently. Let me begin with my own hotel and restaurant experiences, admitting in the beginning that hotels and restaurants are only an imperfect guide to the general conditions of any country.

Restaurant prices generally have gone up from seventy-five to one hundred per cent. You can get no butter, and there is far less oil in Italian cookery than formerly. With breakfast or tea you get a little measured teaspoonful of government sugar – the real stuff mixed with saccharin. This mixture tends to leave a greasy aftertaste in the mouth. You find beside your plate one chunk of war bread about as big as a man's fist. That is all you get unless you specially ask the waiter for more – and pay for it.[16]

To add to Italy's problems, in 1917 for a variety of reasons she also, began to run short of coal and this in turn impacted upon the supply of bread. The lack of coal necessitated a considerable reduction in railway traffic, and the temporary collapse of railway transport immediately interfered with the supply of necessities for the urban populations and of military necessities to the army. The soldiers' rations were greatly reduced, a circumstance which produced much discontent amongst them, and the population of northern Italy was brought to the verge of starvation. The consequences of these shortages manifested themselves very quickly. The summer of 1917 saw increasing unrest. Serious hunger riots broke out in

Civilians in northern Italy, late 1917. By the end of the year, serious food hardship had begun to affect this part of the country. (Author's collection)

the northern towns, and the propaganda of the extreme socialists, hitherto heeded by a comparative few, spread rapidly among the mass of the population, discontented as they were by food shortages. Representatives of the Russian Soviets took the opportunity to visit Italy and conferred with all groups from the moderate socialist Leonida Bissolati to the most revolutionary of the Syndicalists. Major bread riots occurred first in Milan, and later in Turin. These were suppressed by troops with the loss of forty lives. The propaganda also invaded the army with one result being the defeat at Caporetto. Italy was saved from national disaster only by the assistance of the other Allies, who sent her guns and munitions, but what was of far greater and more instant value were the bread, coal and meat which was also supplied. This intervention by the Allies with supplies of food and fuel was the most effective kind of military aid, though nobody referred to it as such at the time. If this sort of intervention had reached Russia, then the outcome of events in that country might have been different.

Units of the American Red Cross also started to arrive in Italy in December 1917, and began distributing food aid to the civilian population. A report from this time outlined the invaluable work which this organisation performed:

It was the uniform policy of the Red Cross in its activities to fall in line with Italian usage. One of the most widespread means of poor relief in Italy has long been the economic kitchen. This is a place where deserving poor can procure prepared food at or slightly below cost. Social reformers have questioned the wisdom of this method of dealing with the problem of the poor, but no one could question its value and effectiveness in times of war in an impoverished nation when abnormally high prices and reduced earning capacity meant that for a large number of people the wolf was always looking in at the door. So the Red Cross contributed to this form of relief so far as it affected the refugees and families of soldiers both by aiding existing Italian institutions and by starting independent kitchens where need was greatest. Every case was investigated, generally in cooperation with Italian authorities and a ticket (*tessera*) given to those entitled to receive food indicating the number of rations which the holder could procure. At the noon hour at each of these kitchens the line would form of old men, women, and children, carrying all manner of bizarre receptacles to receive the midday meal, which consists of the thick and savory and nourishing 'soup,' or *minestra*, concocted on scientific dietary principles, containing beans or peas or rice, with tomato sauce and greens and fat and usually meat. The barreled beef and particularly the lard and clear-belly bacon sent in such large quantities from America proved a godsend to the people for whom these foods had become all but unobtainable. Fifty soup kitchens in all came under the care of the Red Cross, dispensing most of the time an average of approximately thirty thousand rations a day. Two cents were paid for a generous portion. In cases of special poverty it was given free. Uncooked food was also distributed to a limited number of investigated families in certain regions where special conditions prevailed, but this was not done to any large extent until after the armistice, and in the liberated territories.[17]

The American Red Cross also provided 'rolling canteens' behind the lines, which distributed food and comforts to Italian soldiers. An account of one of these canteens, written by an Italian infantryman, was published in the *Corriere della Sera* newspaper, and subsequently an English translation was included in the history of the American Red Cross in Italy:

The heat is merciless. On the roadside under the shade of a cluster of trees stands a hut with an Italian flag and a flag showing a field of blue with stars and red and white stripes. The soldiers crowd the place. This is a rest house of the American Red Cross. You can find many of these close to the lines, at points of heavy traffic and where it is most difficult to obtain cool drinks or to find anything to eat. Here our great American Ally brings a lot of good things. Here they place a table, fix an awning, spread the Stars and Stripes and the Italian flag, and here they stand themselves, smooth-shaven, khaki-clad, and with their round caps, offering every good thing in God's grace to the passing soldiers, coffee, cool drinks, bread, chocolate as we once knew it, and crackers that we no longer are accustomed to. A real providence, and the offering is made with such good, with such cordial fraternity. The soldiers have already baptized these Rest Houses. They call them in a jocular way American Bars and when from afar they see on the road the tri-color and the Stars and Stripes, they cry 'Let us go visit America.'[18]

However, the Italians were not totally reliant upon outside assistance, and took what steps they could themselves to alleviate the crisis. In the early part of the war, charitable institutions had done much work to distribute free food to those most in need in the main Italian cities. By 1917, however, this was no longer adequate and in that year ration cards were introduced in the urban areas. This actually improved morale on the Italian home front; the public firmly believed that access to basic food requirements at prices compatible with their earnings was an inalienable right. As in Britain, the subsuming of this function by the state had far-reaching implications, in that it inferred a reduction in privilege and an equalising tendency for all classes when confronted with a national emergency. Other Italians did what they could to help themselves; a post-war report on the Italian co-operative movement makes interesting reading, and it remarks upon:

A very interesting development [which] has taken place all over Italy by which the municipal authorities undertake a considerable amount of the work of supplying the necessities of life to their people. Over 200 Italian cities and towns have undertaken this work and most of them began it between the years 1917 and 1919, though there are some traces of it as early as 1912. The system adopted is to form a committee consisting of representatives from the cooperative societies and charitable institutions. This committee gets funds from the municipality and from the associated societies, which it uses for organizing a supply of foodstuffs, clothing, etc., which are sold either through the co-operative societies or through stores specially set up for the purpose. The city of Milan, though not the first town to organize a municipal supply, has developed it more than any other town in Italy. The Azienda Consorziale dei Consumi de Milano did not actually begin work until September, 1918, though there had been a previous society of the same nature but more limited scope.[19]

In 1918, in spite of the hardship being experienced on the Italian home front, there was still entertainment to be found in Rome. An American, Joseph Collins, wrote of a visit to the theatre in the Eternal City around this time:

There was not a vacant seat. High up in the galleries they were standing three and four deep. The boxes were full and I, coming at the eleventh hour, got one of the last orchestra seats. Were it not that there were many men in uniform, soldiers and officers, no one could have surmised that we were in the most critical hour of our existence. Here there was no echo of Lloyd George's statement, that it depends upon the next few weeks whether we shall be practically obliterated, no reverberation of Field-Marshal Haig, that we are standing with our backs to the wall. It was difficult to convince oneself that you had to go but a stone's throw from where you sat, to see long lines of women and children waiting to buy oil or bread or sugar by means of an official ticket, and that the best minds of

A ration card issued by the Commune of Bologna during the First World War.
(Author's collection)

the nation were concerning themselves with how they could apportion their declining stores of food to make them last until the seas were again safe to bring succour to the countries unable to provide for their population. There was an air of cheerfulness, of comfort, of self-indulgence throughout the entire place.[20]

Rationing that year was severe, and Italians probably faced the smallest food portions of any of the Allied peoples. By 1918 in Milan, the ration for meat was less than two pounds per person a month, and there were practically no fats, oils, butter or milk. The new scale of rations allowed little more than thirteen pounds of rationed food per month, in addition to nine ounces of bread per day. This meant that the people of Italy were living on about seven ounces of food per day – little less than half a pound – in addition to their nine ounces of bread, and whatever fruit and vegetables they could get. The allotment of all kinds of meat, in addition to being extremely small, was often hard to obtain. On meat days long lines of persons awaiting their turn to receive their share formed outside the meat shops. Beef was particularly scarce in Italy, and its sale was strictly regulated. No butcher was supposed to sell it to anyone without a meat card. A sausage maker in Turin, accused of using beef meat in his sausages, was fined and imprisoned for five days. The sausage maker, however, had purchased large quantities of beef from a butcher in the same street, although he did not have meat cards. The butcher was also fined, and imprisoned for six days.

There were now three meatless days a week. Restaurants were required send to the authorities a list of food furnished, with prices for each portion, or for the whole meal, or for the week, indicating also any extra that for any reason might be charged to the restaurant diners. The authorities would approve the list if it corresponded to normal or prescribed prices, and a copy stamped and signed by the competent authority had to be displayed to the public. One method by which the Italian government attempted to increase the supply of foodstuffs in 1918 was the mechanisation of agriculture, in order to improve productivity. The Fiat motor company in particular undertook production of tractors for supply to Italian farmers. One report on this aspect of the Italian war effort states that:

An advertisement from the Fiat motor company in 1918 extols the advantages of its new motor tractor over traditional ploughing. (Author's collection)

Motor ploughing is certainly one of the most splendid undertakings attempted somewhat more than a year ago by the Italian Government, which has already organized it so well that today it has reached full development and is destined to have a tremendously beneficial influence on the agricultural year 1918-1919. Ever since the first months of 1917, because of the difficulties presented by the food situation for the period of the war, effective plans were devised to augment the food production, and among these the most important and most urgent seemed to be that of ploughing by mechanical means. It was well understood from the very beginning that it would be impossible to count solely on private initiative, as all good intentions could not have surmounted the enormous difficulties in the way, such as securing financial aid, the creation of the proper personnel, the acquisition of the machines, etc., hence the Government undertook to provide the organization and practical realization of so highly utilitarian an enterprise. And while up to the middle of 1917 motor ploughing was little known, its use began to increase; today we have almost reached such a vast organization as to be able to put more than 8,000 motor ploughs in the field, thus adding to the potentiality of labor and to the results of 1917-1918 a ten times greater sum. The special schools established at Cremona and Piacenza in 1917 under the auspices of the Minister of Arms and Munitions, have, by means of intensive instruction lasting more than twenty days for drivers and about two months for mechanicians, prepared a personnel of over 3,000 individuals who, in 1917, operated the 800 machines then available. Today the schools have naturally been enlarged and this in turn has greatly augmented the number of the instructed personnel, which has succeeded in ploughing, and continues ploughing, thousands and thousands of acres in Sicily, Puglia, Calabria, Basilicata, Sardinia, etc.[21]

Another move by the Italian government was the encouragement of war gardens in urban areas. Some 2,500 of these were to be found in Milan alone. They were a familiar sight and every spare foot of land, even in the heart of the city, was carefully cultivated, not by farmers, but by the townspeople. Office workers and industrial labourers spent their spare hours in the evening tending these plots. In addition, large tracts of land outside the city of Milan which for years before the war lay uncultivated, were transformed into carefully planned, profit-yielding gardens. At Monza, maize was planted on the broad stretches of ground which bordered the main avenues, and the Royal Park was transformed into a vegetable garden.

The yield from these war gardens provided practical help for several thousand families hard-pressed by the war.

Thus the Italian state was one whose people suffered some of the harshest food shortage during the war, sparking popular protest and unrest. Yet through a mixture of its own countermeasures and the assistance of associate powers such as the US, Italy fended off disaster on the home front. By contrast, amongst the combatant nations, France was probably the country which suffered the least food hardship during the First World War. France did not rely heavily upon imports before the war, being more or less agriculturally self-sufficient. Although her agricultural output during the conflict declined (in part due to the German occupation of her territory), and she came to rely more on imports during the course of the war, as a general rule her transport systems were efficient enough in most cases to be able to get the food produced in the countryside to the major urban areas. Nevertheless, in Paris, there was panic buying when war broke out. This was quite understandable when one considers that the city had been besieged in the Franco-Prussian War of 1871, and that this would have been fresh in the minds of many people living there. A correspondent described the scenes in Paris on 4 August 1914, as one grocer introduced his own impromptu rationing in an attempt to impose order on incipient pandemonium:

> Felix Potin is the largest grocery establishment in Paris. Early in the morning, before the hour of opening, several thousand purchasers, holding big baskets and potato-sacks, were waiting like depositors making a run on a bank. When I tried, half an hour later, to force my way through the crowd towards breakfast, it was a solid but by no means passive mass. A hurry-up call had been sent in for the police, who were having difficulty in getting through the crowd themselves to protect the doors of the grocery. Generally, Felix Potin puts out on the sidewalk a most delightful variety of fruits, vegetables and meats to tempt the housewives. But not this morning! The establishment was tightly shut, and customers were being admitted in Noah fashion at one side-door.
>
> From the conversation, I gathered that the Germans were on the way to Paris, that the railways would soon be cut off, and that it was now or never to get some food in. Everyone had come prepared to carry off as much as possible of sugar, tea, coffee, and dried and canned vegetables. When I reached the corner there was a big sign, stating that Mr. Felix Potin desired to inform his honorable customers that he had in his storehouses enough food to feed Paris for six months, but that horses and truckmen were lacking for

A well-stocked Parisian market in 1914. Supplies were quickly consumed in the panic of the first days of war. (From Gibbons, *Paris Reborn*)

providing immediately in his retail shops all that customers might desire to buy and for delivering purchases. So, to Mr. Potin's infinite regret, he was compelled to limit the amount of purchase to what one could carry out of the shop.

This statement, instead of reassuring 'the honorable customers', made them feel more strongly that they had been justified in rising and girding up their loins early that morning to fight for a few weeks' food supply. Many believed that they could get ahead of Potin by retaining an auto-taxi or cab, to which they could stagger with a heavy load when they left the shop.[22]

It was, however, a curious fact that, as soon as Paris began to be relieved of its initial apprehension and it became clear that the Germans were not after all about to immediately capture the city, its people began to eat up what they had laid in. For two weeks rice and beans and dried fish formed the menu of every meal, amidst much good-natured joking, while the fish and vegetable markets were filled with stocks that spoiled. Out in the countryside, an American lady named Mary Waddington was merely playing at food preservation, her diary for 19 August 1914 noting:

> Mr. Herrick and Austin Lee dined this evening. Both men are most interesting. Our repast was frugal – war rations, a soup, piece of beef, salad, a vegetable and a compote – not exactly an ambassadorial banquet. Fruit is plentiful and cheap.[23]

Later in 1914, at a place called L'aigle, she noted that steps to control the bread supply were gradually being introduced:

> . . . the announcement was not tragic, though significant: 'Defense de porter le pain dans la ville.' ('Carrying bread in the city forbidden.') It tells that one is put upon war rations and everybody must go and get his bread, which, in the big cities, means standing for hours in the crowd at the baker's door . . .[24]

Back in Paris, crowds again began to form at grocery shops in September 1914 as the city was now directly threatened by the nearby German army approaching the Marne. An English resident, Nevil Hopkins, remarks upon scenes similar to those witnessed upon the outbreak of war, with the same grocer again under siege from his customers:

> On my way uptown again from the Gare St. Nazare, I passed by the well-known grocery store of Felix Potin, where as a boy at school

Early morning shoppers buying game at a Parisian market. (Library of Congress)

my parents used to buy the most delicious marrons glaces with which they lured me to be good. Here, in fact, was a great crowd of persons who intended to stay in Paris, come what might. A great line 'en queue' was making a run upon this famous provision market and many had waiting cabs retained at fabulous prices to haul away their stores.[25]

Yet Paris had more than enough supplies to enable her to withstand a siege, should one have developed. Even with the German armies menacing the eastern outskirts of the city, food supplies could of course still reach the inhabitants without interruption from the west and south. One observer wrote of the high degree of preparation in Paris to ensure the food supply for its citizens:

If the Germans besiege Paris, we have sufficient food supplies to last us for many months, before we need to take a census of the horses and dogs and cats and rats. I doubt if there is any city in the world more abundantly provisioned than is Paris to-day. Not only are the great warehouses filled to overflowing with dry groceries and canned-goods, but the Government has taken special pains to see that there is fresh meat and fresh milk for invalids and children. The Bois de Boulogne is full of cattle. The city has organized a brigade of dairy workers. Every invalid and baby in this great city has been registered. More than that, late summer and autumn vegetables are being planted in the vacant spaces within the line of the forts.[26]

Hopkins concurred, fearing only a shortage of sugar and salt. He added:

Thousands of cows were grazing in the Bois de Bolougne and enormous trainloads and wagon-loads of foods and other supplies were coming into Paris every hour. I saw enormous two-wheeled carts which must have dated back to the days of Noah, mended and patched, braced and repaired in at least a score of places, creaking under loads of potatoes, the drivers walking along-side. What won my hearty admiration was the fact that there had been no rise in food prices!![27]

The Battle of the Marne and the advancing German army drove many refugees from eastern France into Paris. Here they were fed in soup kitchens, run by charities and well-wishers. One of these kitchens was at the old Seminary of Saint Sulpice, where, according to one eyewitness:

. . . refugees find a haven. The mother, footsore and desperate from the baby's continual cry for milk and the other children's cry for bread, is met with outstretched arms, and greeted with brimming eyes, brave smile and a kiss. The kiss does more to renew her courage than food. But there is food, too. And do you know . . . how that food has been cooked? Across from the Seminary is the Mairie of the Sixth Arrondissement. The policemen, attached to the poste there, are giving up in turns their rest and meal hour to do the cooking. When the influx was greatest, and the soup portion would have given out, the policemen contributed, more than their meal hour. Their meal, too, was slipped into the pot, and none knew but God.[28]

Mary Waddington, in *My War Diary*, recounts life at La Ferté-sous-Jouarre on the Marne. During the battle, in September 1914, her gardens had been despoiled by German cavalry horses billeted there. It was for this reason, as much as for reasons of national emergency, that afterwards she decided to go further and turn the lawns over entirely for vegetable use. Writing during the following winter she adds:

The queue for a Paris soup canteen, 1914. The city had to accommodate large numbers of refugees fleeing before the German army. (From Gibbons, *Paris Reborn*)

Mardi Gras, February 16th. It has been a bright, beautiful day. One could hardly believe it after the cold rain and hail of yesterday. We walked about the garden in the morning – if garden it can be called. All the lawns and flower-beds have been dug up. The house stands

Refugees queue for food, Paris 1914. (Library of Congress: Bain collection)

in the middle of ploughed fields. We are debating what we shall plant – potatoes and beans, I think, so that we can have our vegetables in winter, as well as improve the earth. They say potatoes purify the soil, and perhaps next year, if the war is over, we can have new lawns, but we shan't do anything to the house and garden until the Germans are out of France.[29]

For those French people now living under German occupation, the food situation was far more critical and uncertain. From the earliest days of the invasion, they were at the whim of the occupying German forces. Isabelle Rimbaud, in occupied northern France, wrote:

Women and children are standing in a queue at the closed doors of a bakery; the cabarets are packed with civilians who neither drink nor smoke as there is no drink or tobacco, nor food either but content themselves with lively conversation . . . Food is becoming scarcer and scarcer, and the farms on the southern outskirts of the town which the Germans did not pillage are now our only source of supplies . . . Tréloup did not suffer greatly from the passing through of the Germans. Its inhabited houses were not broken into. The

Germans arrived at noon in clouds, like a whirlwind, and spread through the streets, a hunger-stricken crowd, and entered houses where people were just sitting down to dinner. They laid hands on all food on the table or being prepared, on the contents of the sideboards, and on eatables of every kind. They clamorously demanded bread; and as for drink, the number of empty bottles scattered in the streets and gardens proves better than any words that it was not paid for. The victuals gobbled up and the great afternoon heat over, the storm passed on towards Chateau-Thierry and Paris, while the village folk, expecting the arrival of other German columns and ignorant of what was going on all round them, got under cover, terror-stricken by the roar of the guns.[30]

This carefully-staged propaganda photograph shows civilians in the occupied part of France being fed from a German army field kitchen. (Library of Congress)

The reality was somewhat different: these French civilians harvest turnips under the watchful eye of German soldiers, February 1917. (Author's collection)

By contrast, for those French people not directly behind the fighting lines, the war seems to have had little impact on standards of living. One English lady visiting the French capital, Maud Fortescue Sutton-Pickhard, was disappointed by the standard of fare which she found in restaurants there, declaring haughtily:

> The food was execrable. Real war-time food; although we were dining at Voisin's, one of the best cafés in Paris. The champagne was excellent and plentiful, owing to the happy fact that Paris is not yet in the hands of the Germans! All over France the cooking is infinitely below the usual standard, so much so that one wonders if all the cooks have gone off to the war, leaving nothing but kitchen scullions to take their place. Prices, however, are high enough. The dinner for nine people cost our host 480 francs, exclusive of the tip.[31]

Maud Fortescue Sutton-Pickhard, an Englishwoman in Paris. (From Sutton-Pickhard, *France in Wartime*)

Yet her experience was by all accounts rather exceptional. Another writer tells us that:

> Paris at the end of August, 1915, seems three times as animated as it was a year ago. General business is fairly active. The big department shops like the Galeries Lafayette, the Printemps and the Louvre are crowded with Parisian women shoppers. Food prices have advanced only in rare cases, the increase being principally on meat, which costs about 50 per cent, more, although, strange to say, there is a plentiful supply of cattle at the abattoir.[32]

Further evidence that the high standard of dining so beloved of the French people was maintained apparently untouched by the war (certainly well into 1916) comes from Mary Waddington. On one occasion she invited some of the young French officers billeted with her to dinner:

> We invited all the gentlemen to dine tonight. We had brought down chickens and ham, vegetables and fruit from Paris, and they accepted with pleasure, sending us word by Mme. G. that they had a filet de boeuf, which they begged we would accept.[33]

An even better account comes from the pen of the American diplomat, Lee

Meriwether, writing home to his wife in the USA on 8 October 1916, who states:

> Although the war is more than two years old, food conditions in France seem no worse than in the United States. The other day when Mr. and Mrs. Dodge, of the Embassy, dined with me at a café on the Boulevard des Italiens dinner for the three of us, including a bottle of Saumur Mousseux, cost 27 francs – about $4.64. We had hors d'oeuvres (sardines, anchovies, olives, radishes, etc.), roast chicken, fried potatoes, lettuce with egg and French dressing, cheese, coffee and wine. I know of no first-class restaurant in New York where so good a dinner may be had at so reasonable a price.[34]

Perhaps the most significant wartime change observable in the cafés and bars of Paris was the disappearance of absinthe, which was banned by the French government in 1915. The so called 'green fairy', as the drink was known after its verdant colour, had been deeply controversial and its history was a chequered one. It originated in Switzerland, but by the end of the nineteenth century Paris had become the city with the highest rate of

Inside a French café or bar, around 1914. Such establishments, though an important part of French culture, would be heavily restricted during the war. (Library of Congress)

absinthe consumption in the world. However, the drink, which was highly alcoholic at 60–70 per cent proof, was widely believed to have toxic properties, as it was derived from the poisonous shrub wormwood. Some attributed effects such as addiction, paranoia and psychosis to drinking it. Although it was consumed by all classes, it was particularly popular with the poor as it was a cheap, industrial alcohol. For this reason, it has also become associated with the artistic scene in Paris in the late nineteenth century. France's wartime restriction on absinthe lasted for almost a hundred years, and as a result of the ban, pastis became a popular drink in that country, due to its similar taste. Journalist Philip Gibbs wrote at the time:

Orders and regulations were issued in a rapid volley fire which left Paris without any of its old life or liberty. The terrasses were withdrawn from the cafés. No longer could the philosophic Parisian sip his petit verre and watch the drama of the boulevards from the shady side of a marble-topped table. He must sit indoors like an Englishman, in the darkness of his public-house, as though ashamed of drinking in the open. Absinthe was banned by a thunderstroke from the Invalides, where the military governor had established his headquarters, and Parisians who had acquired the absinthe habit trembled in every limb at this judgment which would reduce them to physical and moral wrecks, as creatures of the drug habit suddenly robbed of their nerve-controlling tabloids. It was an edict welcomed by all men of self-control who knew that France had been

A pre-war French poster advertising absinthe, the so-called 'Green Fairy'. (Author's collection)

poisoned by this filthy liquid, but they too became a little pale when all the cafes of Paris were closed at eight o'clock. 'Sapristi! Qu'est qu'on peut faire les soirs? On ne peut pas dormir tout le temps! Et la guerre durera peut-etre trois mois!' To close the cafés at eight o'clock seemed a tragic infliction to the true Parisian, for whom life only begins after that hour, when the stupidity of the day's toil is finished and the mind is awakened to the intellectual interests of the world, in friendly conversation, in philosophical discussions, in heated arguments, in wit and satire. How then could they follow the

RÉPUBLIQUE FRANÇAISE — PRÉFECTURE DU DOUBS

LOI

relative à l'interdiction de la fabrication, de la vente en gros et au détail, ainsi que la circulation de l'Absinthe et des liqueurs similaires.

Le Sénat et la Chambre des députés ont adopté,

Le Président de la République promulgue la loi dont la teneur suit :

Article premier. — Sont interdites la fabrication, la vente en gros et au détail, ainsi que la circulation de l'absinthe et des liqueurs similaires visées par l'article 15 de la loi du 30 janvier 1907 et l'article 17 de la loi du 26 décembre 1908.

Les contraventions au § 1" du présent article seront punies de la fermeture de l'établissement et, en outre, à la requête de l'administration des contributions indirectes, des peines fiscales prévues à l'article 1" de la loi du 28 février 1872 et à l'article 19 de celle du 30 janvier 1907.

Art. 2. — La présente loi est applicable à l'Algérie et aux colonies.

La présente loi, délibérée et adoptée par le Sénat et par la Chambre des députés sera exécutée comme loi de l'Etat.

Fait à Paris le 16 mars 1915.

R. POINCARÉ.

Par le Président de la République :

Le Président du Conseil,	*Le Ministre de l'Intérieur,*	*Le Garde des Sceaux, Ministre de la Justice,*
René VIVIANI.	**L. MALVY.**	**Aristide BRIAND.**
Le Ministre des Colonies,	*Le Ministre des Finances,*	*Pour copie conforme : Le Secrétaire général,*
Gaston DOUMERGUE.	**A. RIBOT.**	CHABBERT.

La SOLIDARITE, imprimerie coopérative, Besançon.

The proclamation issued by the French government in 1915, announcing the prohibition of absinthe. The drink was not available again in France until the early 2000s. (Author's collection)

war and understand its progress if the cafés were closed at eight o'clock? But the edict was given and Paris obeyed, loyally and with resignation.[35]

This was not the only wartime restriction which France imposed upon alcohol. Every other sort of drink was freely available, except to women and soldiers who were not officially allowed to buy it. In most places they got their liqueurs served in coffee-cups, and cocktails did not rank as alcoholic drinks. The restriction on women had come about because female munition workers in France, as in England, finding themselves suddenly well paid and without domestic duties, in some cases followed the example shown them by their men and turned to wines and spirits for amusement. Of course, the men were deeply shocked by this. The common labourer, who had never accustomed his wife to seeing him sober on Saturdays, was appalled to discover that she had tried for herself how much fun might be got out of what he had always claimed as an amusement to which he had a divine right. More was done to check French women from drinking during the war, than had ever been attempted to prevent drunkenness among men in the preceding hundred years of legislation. An order came into force in France by which no boy under eighteen and no woman might be served in cafés, restaurants or wine-shops, and pastry-cooks were prevented from buying anything alcoholic above a certain very low degree. One of the effects of this rule was that no woman could have a lemon squash with a little Angostura in it, which was one of the most popular and refreshing drinks in hot weather. Another effect was that any woman accompanied by a man could drink as much alcohol as she liked so long as he ordered it for his own consumption, and she had the tact to drink it at a moment when not too many people were looking at her!

Whilst absinthe passed out of French popular culture as a result of the First World War, another iconic French product became firmly entrenched because of it. Banania, a chocolate-flavoured breakfast porridge made with banana flour, was invented in 1912 initially as a food for babies. However in 1915 it became associated through advertising with a depiction of a grinning French *tirailleur Senegalaise*, a black colonial soldier. The association was further strengthened with the slogan: *Pour nos soldats la nourriture abondante qui se conserve sous le moindre volume possible* ('For our soldiers an abundant food which keeps, using the least possible space'). Around this time, troops from French West African colonies had begun to arrive on the Western front and had made a name for their bravery, as well as their heavy losses. The association has continued ever since, although the imagery has come in for considerable criticism in modern times. The product's other slogan *Y'a Bon* was a parody of the dialect French spoken by the Senegalese, and has not been used since 1977 because of cultural sensitivities.

The principle which was first applied by French leaders to food control was that, by leaving every foodstuff unrestricted in its sale, excessive consumption would, by force of circumstance, become impossible, due the rapidly rising price of food. Unfortunately, however, salaries and wages

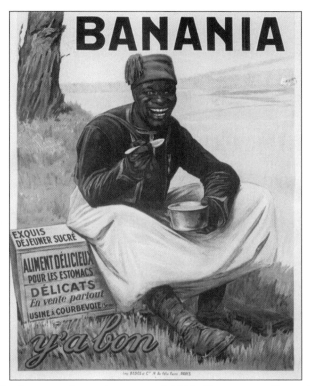

A poster for Banania, dating from around 1915. The grinning Senegalese soldier has represented this popular French brand in various guises ever since. (Author's collection)

rose almost as rapidly as did the price of food. Only in 1917 did France begin to introduce general restrictions and controls on food consumption, and the story of rationing in France is one which may surprise British readers. The British press, for reasons of propaganda, tended to exaggerate the alimentary dangers faced by France. Even in the final year of the war, Madeleine Doty was able to write:

> In the countries through which I had traveled, except England, there had been but three topics of conversation, food, clothes and heat; how to live without freezing or starving. But here it was different. The battle field was a few miles away. Hospital trains moved back and forth. The newspapers had flaring headlines. Women in black filled the land. Yet curiously enough in this land of conflict the civil population throve. Physically France was better off than any of the other countries. Paris had plenty of food.[36]

A busy street market in Paris, around the time of the First World War. (Library of Congress)

The only real trouble people in Paris had, from a food point of view, throughout the war arose from the fact that one could not persuade anybody in the country to obey the spirit of any of the elaborate regulations drawn up for the general benefit of the community. Food Minister succeeded Food Minister, system followed upon system, and still there remained the fact that on meatless days one could always, if one were determined enough, obtain meat, or find a lump of sugar in the coffee-cup when sugar was officially supposed to be unobtainable. The French, from the point of view of discipline, were extraordinary; their sons went out without a moment's questioning at the call of mobilisation, and then the civilian population settled down to disobey all sorts of edicts and decrees the observance of which was declared to be of national importance!

The French were never at any time during the war able to appreciate how far Great Britain restricted herself in the matter of food. They were constitutionally unable to see in any regulation anything but a rule to be broken, either by slipping a five-franc note into the hand of a *maître d'hôtel,* or on some larger scale of more-or-less innocent corruption. Food ministers everywhere had an uncomfortable job, but in France their function was especially difficult. The French were (and indeed still are) deeply conservative in all ways connected with the table and their food, and they quietly and mulishly refused to consider that any restriction or regulation need apply to them. One observer noted that:

> When asked to eat less bread or less meat, [French people] reply, 'But we like eating it!' and seem to think that that settles the question. When we had three meatless days a week, they bought large quantities on the day preceding them; and, if the weather turned hot and some of the meat went bad, they openly lamented the fact, without seeming conscious that they had committed an unpatriotic action in buying it. They wanted meat, they were used to meat, and meat they would have. Hermann-Paul published a mordant picture of a woman in deep black, crying: 'They've killed my husband and taken my son prisoner, but they won't make me do without meat!' That attitude was general. It was astounding to live among a people who every day gave proof of the highest qualities of patriotism and endurance and heroism, whose fighting men one loved and admired more every day, and to see with what obstinacy they held out against even the lightest restriction. When bread was rationed, the very people who proclaimed the most loudly that they could not possibly manage on ten ounces a day would break up their bread at table, instead of cutting it, take far more than they needed, and display not only selfishness in the matter but wanton carelessness.[37]

In addition, the way this food control was imposed was *ad hoc* and chaotic, and made it difficult even for those who wished to, to adhere to the rules. They were constantly changing. One observer spoke of having eaten a meal in a restaurant which was legal while it was being cooked, and illegal before it was served. People were utterly bewildered by the clouds of new rules which buzzed about like gnats. 'Two meatless days no, one; no, let's try three; or, what about six meatless evenings? Oh well, let's go back to two meatless days.' Six meatless evenings a week was the rule for a while, and this was particularly absurd. No meat could be sold in any restaurant in the evening; that was all the rule amounted to, so the Parisian lunched out, and dined at home! Three consecutive meatless days turned many a hair grey. The price of fish soared as a result, vegetables followed suit, and the bread chose that particular moment to turn greyer and sourer even than usual. The two-day restriction would have been easier, except for the fact that the days

This French poster, from the second half of the war, advises people to eat fish instead of meat. (Library of Congress)

were fixed for Monday and Tuesday. On Monday the Paris fish-market was closed. The result was that on Sunday, fish and meat doubled their prices. The government tried to meet the situation by ordering the fish-market to open on Mondays, but the men employed there immediately threatened to go on strike, as they had no other free time in the week. In the meantime, fish left over from Sunday's sales was left to rot on Monday, and on Tuesday citizens were told that the high price of this commodity was due to difficulties of transport!

Elizabeth Putnam, an American woman, travelled to France to work as a clerk in a military hospital. She spent some time in Paris before taking up her duties, and her published diaries from this period make for revealing reading about the food situation in France. Putnam had refined tastes, and regularly refers to her meals and places in which she ate. At no point does she make any reference to rationing impacting upon her lifestyle, and the only mention of a possible shortage of bread was an instance in which winter weather prevented trains carrying wheat from reaching Paris. In that city in July 1917, she wrote to a friend:

> I enjoyed a solitary meal at Henriette's, a restaurant close by – the first meal I have had alone (with a book) in years and years. The room has frescoed walls of the Queen of Hearts and the Tarts and the Knave, in soft, fady colors, life-size, all round, done by an English art student who couldn't pay her bills in the ordinary way. Want to know what I had? I tell you food gets to be an event these days! Omelet, peas, – both piping hot, – tomato salad, wild strawberries with a little brown jug of that marvellous thick, slightly sour cream, and sugar. Doesn't that sound good?[38]

Some observers remarked upon how curious it was to go from French restaurants to English ones. In the latter, as in the private household, a regulation was a thing to be kept. In the former, it was always a breakable object, which public spirit required one to attack. This was so much the odder, when one considers that the restrictions were so much less severe in Paris than in London. Whilst French menus were regulated, so that diners should not eat too much, they were still allowed to have oysters, soup, or hors-d'oeuvres; two other courses at pleasure; sweet, fruit, and three ounces of bread. Until quite late in the war butter could be served in restaurants, also cream.

After a long time, in March 1917 official restrictions were imposed on sugar. However, householders had had trouble in getting any at all even before sugar-cards were thought of. The rationing of sugar was one of the few areas in which Parisians found themselves worse off than Londoners, and sugar was a particularly contentious issue for the French. Its control was accompanied by a great deal of muddle, and indeed profiteering. Confectioners, during all the time they were allowed to bake cakes and sweet things, seemed to have no trouble in getting enough sugar for their wares. It is true that for a time they were not allowed to make any sweets or cakes, but long before the prohibition the private household was sugarless, while the confectioners' windows were brimming with good things. One eyewitness counted over 120 different kinds of expensive sweetmeat and cake in one fashionable window on one afternoon, at a time when mothers of young families were finding it impossible to get sugar for their children. This particular shop was reported as being full of people, mostly women, but also a few soldiers, eating cakes coated with chocolate and filled with cream, cakes powdered with sugar, and cakes covered with crystallised fruits. Marrons glacé and expensive crystallised fruit from the south were still on sale at Christmas 1917. The prohibition of sweets made from chocolate came long after the rations of the ordinary household had been reduced. These things naturally made the French public feel that it was being messed about with. First of all, there were cakeless days. On Tuesdays and Wednesdays confectioners did not open their shops, but on Mondays, of course, they were besieged!

The restriction did away with the five o'clock *goûter* (afternoon snack), but not with the private consumption of cakes. Then came a decree abolishing fresh pastry and biscuits, though dry ones could still be baked. Here for a while London again had the advantage. Then came another extraordinary regulation. Whilst customers might buy all the cakes they could afford, and more (though the prices were eye-watering), they could not eat them on the premises on which they were bought! One of two things, therefore, happened: one went into another shop and ate the cake while making a purchase; or one simply took them home. In any case, those who

The title of this French illustration might well translate as 'the new table manners'. The first line reads 'Eat less bread and more potatoes'. (Library of Congress)

were determined to have cake, had it; while those who interpreted rationing in the light of national interest had for many months given up all such frivolous feeding. At last the manufacture of biscuits, gingerbread and the like was absolutely forbidden, but since there were large stocks in hand grocers were given a certain length of time in which to sell them. That extension was renewed time and time again; as late as August 1918 these things were still on sale, and, after being told that it was unpatriotic to buy them, French people were being implored to do so, in order to finish up the stocks! Public official sales of biscuits were made in different districts of Paris. Perhaps it is hardly to be wondered at that regulations of this kind failed to command the obedience of the public.

William Greg, who visited Paris in the first months of 1918. (From Greg, *Three Months in France*)

New arrivals in France frequently commented upon the food situation there as they saw it. Another American visitor to Paris was William Greg, who was a member of the YMCA and who went there in the first months of 1918. He observed:

> I kept a sharp lookout for conditions in France and found a reasonable quantity of food everywhere, although milk, sugar, and butter seemed to be scarce. I did not see many fat people – slimness was characteristic of the women, except the foreigners living in Paris, of whom, it must be remembered, there are many thousands.[39]

The same observer noted that food in the hotels and restaurants, while not abundant, was sufficient. He also had difficulty at first in obtaining bread without a bread card. When he had eventually been issued with some, he reported that:

> [We] waited an hour until the baker finished her morning batch. (I did not see any men around the place.) Perhaps twenty-five women were waiting there for their loaves, each having a proper permit for a limited quantity. The French loaves, at least in war time, weigh three pounds more or less, and are made like a big doughnut with a hole large enough to put your hand through. When the batch was

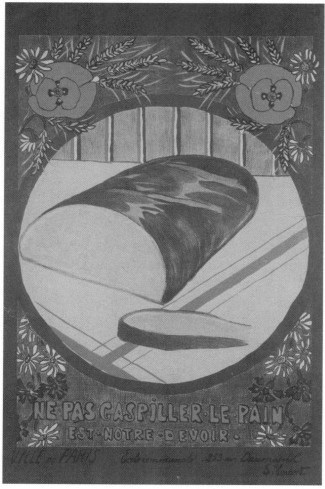

'It is our duty not to waste bread' says this French poster. (Library of Congress)

completed our twenty-five women customers slipped the loaves over their arms and went about their business.[40]

French war bread fluctuated greatly in terms of quality. As early as 1914 the famous rolls of France had been forbidden in Paris, although one could still get them at Versailles. The bread went through numerous colour-changes, from a sour, damp grey, mostly holes and extremely indigestible, to an unhealthy brown. Sometimes it was sour and sometimes it was bitter, and sometimes it was both. It was made with successive mixtures of different flours. Whilst English bread did much the same thing, it was reported by those who had sampled both that it never came within miles of the French product in terms of unpalatability. When it was toasted, all the edges round its air-holes burned, and the insides of them became damp! The flabby crust was just eatable, if loaded with butter or jam or chutney, or something else which would take away the taste; but the crumb could only be swallowed by those of a heroic nature, with a noble disregard of the horrid sensations which followed. Most French people were forced to give up their habit of eating bread between every two mouthfuls of their meal. The end result was great waste of flour, because enormous quantities were left on tables by people who had naturally begun a slice, but could not finish it. Serious restrictions on bread were only introduced by the French in March and April 1918. The American diplomat Lee Meriwether wrote at this time:

> . . . the new rule . . . yesterday went into effect, forbidding bread being served in hotels and restaurants except upon presenting a ticket. Everybody has the right to a monthly ration card permitting the purchase of stipulated quantities of food, 500 grams of sugar per month, 300 grams of bread per day, etc., but until yesterday cards were not required in hotels and restaurants. Being the first day, also being April first, a lot of people who hadn't heard of the new law, thought it an April fool joke. But when they had to eat their dinner without any bread the idea of a joke vanished; in a few days we shall have adjusted ourselves to the situation and then, so far as I can see, it will work no particular hardship, while it will tend to secure an even distribution of the staff of life. For no matter how much money you may have, you cannot have an ounce more bread than the poorest workman in France. You may have your 300 grams per day – quite enough, 300 grams make six good-sized rolls, or one long piece of French bread – but you cannot have any more, even though you save up your tickets. For the tickets are not 'cumulative,' the ticket dated April 1 must be used on that day or not at all. Yesterday my ticket enabled me to buy six rolls, at a cost of 12 cents, and although my appetite is not a small one, bedtime found me with one roll still on hand . . .[41]

Whilst France had sugar cards and bread cards, rationing never went as far as it did in England, and the French stopped short of issuing a meat card. The French also were never rationed for fats. Butter vanished from the market every time its price was fixed, or rather it was said that it vanished from the counter to recesses <u>under</u> the counter, from which it emerged if it heard the clink of much money. Wealthy French city dwellers paid large sums for butter, mainly because the bread was so unpalatable on its own. Margarine was a poor substitute, because it was not of the same quality as margarine in England, and tended to be watery and unsuitable for cooking with. Dripping, an English staple often eaten with bread, was hardly known in France. French butchers instead would generally melt it down and spice it, adding garlic and other things, thus making it somewhat removed from the plain dripping of England. These generalisations of course did not apply uniformly across France, and butter was more readily available in country areas. It was even said that British Prime Minister David Lloyd George, returning from an inter-Allied conference in France, had his driver stop at a country market in order to buy two pounds of butter which he duly presented to his wife at 10 Downing Street!

This illustrates just one of many inconsistencies of experience across a country as large as France. The situation was also complicated by the fact that many of her provinces were for so long overrun by the enemy. It was obviously impossible, when those provinces became freed towards the end of the war, in the first moment of their joy to impose upon them any drastic system of deprivation. The army, too, had naturally to be fed upon a scale capable of maintaining its physical health and its pugnacious spirit. It was equally impossible that the civilian populations in the zone of the armies should be subjected to the same regulations as those living on the sunny shores of the Mediterranean.

Thus whilst it would be wrong to say that France did not experience food hardship at all in the First World War, for those French people not under German occupation the effects of the war on diet and food habits were as nothing compared to the effects experienced in the central empires, or even in Great Britain. As a great culinary nation, in which fine food and fine dining were an integral part of the cultural DNA, the French were perhaps less predisposed than for example the British or Germans to accept rationing and shortages, yet France also presents something of a conundrum; she was apparently among the least organised of the Allied nations in terms of her food supply, yet at the same time one of the best in ensuring that the standard of living of her citizens never fell to unacceptable levels. There were no food riots in France in the First World War. Italy, by contrast, soon began to struggle with her food supply. Deprived of her supplies normally obtained from the Black Sea, she was forced to rely on what she could produce herself. In a parallel with the situation in Russia, food shortage quickly translated into political protest, and only timely intervention by the other Allies was to keep Italy in the war. In short, the country's food supply was ill-equipped for a long war, and the pressures which shortages produced threatened to force apart rather than cement the fractures in Italian society.

Chapter 7

Austria-Hungary and the Ottoman Empire

As the First World War progressed, Germany's two main allies became increasingly ramshackle and disorganised. The German alliance with Austria-Hungary was likened at the time to being chained to a corpse, so ineffective was the latter and such a burden was it upon the former. Likewise the sprawling Turkish Ottoman Empire, barely competent at governing itself before 1914 and notoriously corrupt, was ill-equipped to withstand the rigours of a long modern war. Whereas the Allied food situation became increasingly cohesive as the war progressed, with the food supply of the US, Great Britain, France and Italy being pooled for maximum effectiveness, there was no such co-ordination among the Central Powers, and indeed Germany wantonly plundered the supplies of her allies whenever she was able to do so. Within Austria-Hungary and Ottoman Turkey, official incompetence, indifference and greed concerning food supplies all conspired to undermine the war efforts of both empires.

Austria-Hungary, as the name suggests, was in fact two separate entities, the 'dual monarchy' of the Empire of Austria and the Kingdom of Hungary, apparently unified but in reality administered separately. This was a situation which would only add to the difficulties of waging a major conflict. Before the First World War, Austria-Hungary had been self-sufficient in terms of its food supply, and Austrian government officials were highly optimistic at the start of the fighting that attempts by France, Britain and Russia to starve out Austria and Hungary would come to naught. Indeed, it took some time for food shortages to become apparent in the Austro-Hungarian Empire. American journalist George Schreiner, visiting the country in late 1914, noted that:

> The Vienna restaurants and cafés were serving wheat bread, butter, and cream as before. In a single place I identified as many as thirty-seven different varieties of cakes and pastry. Everybody was

A street trader selling bread and sausage in Vienna, around 1914. (Library of Congress: Bain collection)

drinking coffee with whipped cream – 'Kaffee mit Obers' – and nobody gave food conservation a thought. While the Berlin bills of fare had been generous, to say the least, those of Vienna were nothing short of wasteful. Even that of the well-known Hardman emporium on the Kärntner Ring, not an extravagant place by any means, enumerated no less than one hundred and forty-seven separate items 'à la carte'.[1]

The views of the government officials seemed to be confirmed when two weeks later, Schreiner took a trip to the Galician front in the east:

Going there I passed through northern Hungary. The barns of that district were bursting. The crops had been good, I was told. Every siding was crowded with cars loaded with sugar-beets and potatoes, and out in the fields the sturdy women of the race, short-skirted and high-booted, were taking from the soil more beets and more potatoes. The harvesting of these crops had been delayed by the absence of the men, due to the mobilizations. By the time I reached Neu-Sandez in Galicia, then seat of the Austro-Hungarian general headquarters, I had fully convinced myself that the Entente's program of starvation was very much out of the question. I found that the soldiers were well fed. The wheeled field kitchens were spreading appetizing smells over the countryside, and that their output was good was shown by the fine physical condition of the men. Having established this much, and the Russians coming altogether too close, I had occasion a week later to visit Budapest. In that city everybody was eating without a thought of the future, and that eating was good, as will be attested by anybody who has ever sat down to a Budapestian lamb 'pörkölt' . . . [2]

A bridge across the Danube in Budapest, capital of Hungary. (Library of Congress)

A street market in Debrecen, Hungary, around the time of the First World War.
(Library of Congress)

Also in Hungary at this time was another American, Karl Kitchen, who confirms that the buoyant atmosphere in Budapest was so far unaffected by the war, and it was still possible to eat there as handsomely as at any time prior to the war. He wrote:

> My first war meal in the Hungarian capital consisted of czardas, excellent fogosh, more czardas with string beans and chocolate pudding. It was called luncheon, and cost five crowns. A crown is only 15 cents at the present rate of exchange, so the price was not excessive as both the czardas and the fogosh were very good. The sauce with the latter will long be remembered.[3]

Traders selling food at a street market in Hungary. (Library of Congress)

However, warning signs were soon beginning to show themselves. Bread ration cards were introduced around the end of 1914, but it must be borne in mind that regulation of this type of food thus far consisted only of attempts by the Austrian government to provide bread for the multitude at a reasonable price, without distribution also being placed under efficient control. The activities of food speculators were largely responsible for forcing up the price of breadstuffs, but the Austrian government seemed reluctant to interfere in order to check the avarice of the dealers. Nevertheless, the population had to have cheap bread, and attention also had to be given the paucity of the supply. In Austrian minds, fixed prices were to make possible the former, and a limitation in consumption by means of the ticket was to overcome the latter. The changed circumstances in Vienna in March 1915 were reported by British secret agent Marc Hélys, who travelled extensively in the enemy nations posing as a sales representative for a chocolate company:

> In Vienna they do not grumble so much as in Berlin about the shortage of butter; but they bitterly resent the absence of cream. One of the chief delights of the city is the famous Vienna coffee, with its foaming crest of whipped cream extending half way down the glass. During my previous visit this had been easily obtainable, but eight months of war had resulted in the prohibition of the sale of milk and cream save for infants, all the rest being used in the manufacture of explosives. When I learned that I should be forced to drink black coffee, I felt a momentary grievance against the Allies . . . Lard and other fatty substances used in the preparation of food are of a very inferior quality. I have good cause to remember this as, for four days, I was extremely ill on account of the odious stuff used in the cooking of some food I had eaten. Curiously enough, I found the bread of a much better quality than during my previous visit; but there was very little of it, for the reign of the bread-ticket was not yet over. Meat was scarce and very expensive. As a rule, I dined at the Restaurant Hartmann, in peace time a well-known place for good dinners. I found, however, that it had greatly deteriorated, that the food was far from good and ridiculously expensive. For a meal consisting of soup, meat and vegetables, with some fruit, I had to pay eight kronen (a kronen being 10d.), double the peace price. Some idea of the scarcity of meat may be obtained from the fact that a single portion of roast beef costs about four kronen (3s. 4d.). I should explain that Hartmann's is not a place like the Ritz Hotel, but a middle-class restaurant where in time of peace the prices are extremely moderate.[4]

A market scene in Vienna, capital of the Austro-Hungarian Empire. (Library of Congress)

This procedure of issuing bread tickets left the food speculators with a free hand. They could buy as before, and sell when and to whom they pleased. Thus it came about that, while the masses of Austria-Hungary had to eat war-bread in prescribed quantities, those better off materially still had their wheat-flour products. The authorities were not ignorant of this, but had good reason not to interfere. The time was coming when all the financial resources of the country had to be 'mobilised', and this was to be done by extracting from the population all the spare coin possible, and concentrating it in the hands of the food speculators. These people could then either be taxed, or enabled to buy war loans. These were men that were easy for the government to deal with. Very often they were bankers, and kings of industry and commerce. To provide the government with funds for the war was to them a just question of profit. The bread ticket did not favour an equitable distribution of wheat products in Austria, nor was it ever really intended to do that. Its sole purpose at first was to tax food in such a manner that those who were willing to buy more food than the bread ticket prescribed had to pay heavily for this privilege. That this was a social injustice was plain to see to those who reasoned far enough, but the mass of the Austrian people accepted the system at its face value, prone as it was to accepting the word and the stamp of authority.

George Schreiner, back in Austria once again in 1915, also found that the situation was changing for the worse, largely because of the lack of foresight and planning by the government in Vienna:

> I had no difficulty anywhere in getting all the wheat bread and farinaceous dishes I wanted. It was not even necessary to ask for them. It was taken for granted that I belonged to the class that did not have to eat war-bread and do without pudding and cake, and that was enough. While I was supposed to have a bread ticket, few ever asked for it. In the restaurants which I frequented I generally found a dinner roll hidden under the napkin, which for that purpose was as a rule folded in the manner known as the 'bishop's mitre'. But gone for the many was the era of enough food. The bread ration in Berlin was three hundred grams (ten and a half ounces) per day, and in Vienna it was two hundred and ten grams (seven and two-fifths ounces). Together with a normal supply of other eatables, flour for cooking, for instance, these rations were not really short, and in my case they were generous. But with most it was now a question of paying abnormally high prices for meat and the like, so that enough bread was more of a necessity than ever. It was rather odd that in Austria the bread ration should be smaller than in Germany. That country had in the past produced more breadstuff per capita than her ally, and would have been able to import from Hungary had conditions been different. Hungary had in the past exported wheat flour to many parts, due largely to the fine quality of her grain. Now, of a sudden, it, too, faced a shortage. The fact is that Austria-Hungary had mobilized a large part of her male population and had for that reason been extremely short of farm labor during the season of 1915. The large reserve stores had been exhausted by improvidence, and, to make things worse, the crops of that year were not favored by the weather. Meanwhile, much of the wheat had passed into the hands of the speculators, who were releasing it only when their price was paid. In Austria the bread ticket was the convenient answer to all complaints, and in Hungary, where the bread ticket was not generally introduced as yet, the food shark had the support of the government to such an extent that criticism of his methods was futile. Now and then an enterprising editor would be heard from – as far as his press-room, where the censor caused such hardihoods to be routed from the plate. The food outlook in Austria-Hungary was no pleasant one. Drastic regulation would be needed to alleviate conditions.[5]

The Austro-Hungarian government, however, was slow to take action, and control of food was introduced much later than in Germany, in spite of the widespread view of ordinary people that it was urgently needed. An American girl, Mary Ethel McAuley, visited Vienna and reported what she found:

I had never realized the wonderfulness of the German food card system until I went to Vienna. In Germany you can buy at a reasonable price your allotted ration of food, and the poor people are just as well off as the rich, but in Vienna the rich people have everything and the poor people are in great need because of the lack of food regulations, and while there is an abundance of food it is so dear that the poor cannot afford to buy. And Vienna is not like Berlin, there are a great many poor people in Vienna.

For some time there has been a bread card in Vienna, and at the time of my visit, November 1916, the government was just beginning to take the food question in hand, and a few weeks before Christmas a coffee and a sugar card were issued. But the Austrians have not the gift for organization which the Germans have . . . I talked to many Austrians, and they all told me that they were anxious to have the entire German food card system established in Austria.

Austria is a great agricultural and wheat-raising country, and yet when I was there, there was very little bread in Vienna. The beautiful white Viennese bread had entirely disappeared, and a soggy brown stuff had taken its place. There was one kind called 'Anker Bread' that was still very good, and the people stood in line to get it. And all this was not because flour was scarce but because of its poor distribution.

None of the restaurants are allowed to serve bread, even if you have a bread card you cannot get it, and the only place a stranger can get bread in Vienna is for breakfast at his hotel. People who eat in restaurants carry their bread with them, and generals and all sorts of high officials have little packages of bread concealed in their pockets which they slyly pull out at the table.

All the white flour is baked into cakes, and the Viennese cakes are as white and as wonderful as in their palmiest days. But the price! In a cafe a piece of cake of two thin layers costs one crown twenty-five hellers, about a quarter in our money.[6]

Austria-Hungary suffered in much the same way as Germany, in that so much of her rural population had been taken into the army that production

Bread for sale in Krakow, the ancient capital of Poland, but at this time in the Austro-Hungarian Empire. (Author's collection)

of wheat had been severely curtailed. The Russian prisoners of war who had appeared on many farms to replace the conscripted labourers were interested mainly in shirking, and many landowners found them to be useless. Not only that, on the large estates the owners found that their managers and superintendents had also been taken as junior officers, so even discounting the loss of their labour force in the form of men and draught animals, what was also missing was the expertise both to get the most out of what little labour was available, and to get the best out of the land. Although women were utilised as workers on farms in some instances in Austria, it was never on the same scale or organised as efficiently as the British Womens' Land Army. Meanwhile, the Austrian and Hungarian governments, taking now many a leaf from the book of the Germans, were urging a greater production of food next season. Highly technical books were being digested into the everyday language of the farmer. It was pointed out what sorts of ploughing would be most useful, and what might be omitted in case it could not be done. How and when to fertilise under prevailing conditions was also explained. Schreiner recounts a conversation with an Austrian farmer in the summer of 1915:

'It is all right for the government to expect that we are to raise the same, if not better, crops during the war,' said one of them. 'For the fine gentlemen who sit in the Ministerial offices that does not mean much. Out here it is different. Their circulars are very interesting, but the fact is that we cannot carry out the suggestions they make. They have left me my youngest son. He is a mere boy – just eighteen. The other boys – three of them – who helped me run this place, I have lost. One of them was killed in Galicia, and the other two have been taken prisoners. I may never see them again. They say my two boys are prisoners. But I have heard nothing of them. My crops would have been better if I hadn't tried to follow some of the advice in the government circulars. It was my duty to raise all I could on my land, they said. I doubted the wisdom of putting out too much, with nobody to help me. It would have been better had I followed my own judgment and plowed half the land and let the other lie fallow, in which case it would have been better for the crops next year. Instead of that I planted all the fields, used a great deal of seed, wasted much of my labor, first in plowing, then in cultivating, and later in harvesting, and now I have actually less return than usually I had from half the land.'[7]

Much of the profiteering on food supplies in Austria-Hungary was carried out by bankers. It should not be forgotten that the governments of the Central Powers were dependent upon bankers for war loans, so not only were the governments anxious not to upset them, but actually colluded with them in seeing food prices rise. On one occasion the same group of food speculators permitted two million eggs to spoil in a railway yard at Vienna because the price was not good enough. The profiteers were then agitating for a better price for eggs and hoped that the maximum would be raised. But the government was a little slow on this occasion, and before the price went up, 'according to regulation', the eggs were an unpleasant memory to the yard-hands. Naturally, nobody was prosecuted in this case. Food hoarding was also a problem, for aside from the moral issues, food which is improperly stored is apt to spoil, leading to waste. Schreiner tells us:

An acquaintance of mine in Vienna had hoarded diligently and amply. The man had on hand wheat flour, large quantities of potatoes, butter in salt, and eggs in lime-water, and conserved fruits

A village scene in rural Hungary. (Author's collection)

and vegetables which represented an excess consumption in sugar. He had also laid in great quantities of honey, coffee, and other groceries. There was food enough to last his family two years, so long as a little could be had in the legal market each day . . . The storage methods employed were wrong, of course, and facilities were very limited. The potatoes froze in the cellar and sprouted in the warm rooms. Weevils took birth in the flour, because it was stored in a wardrobe only some four feet away from a stove. The canned goods stood on every shelf in the place, littered the floors and filled the corners. Faulty preserving methods or the constant changes of temperature caused most of them to ferment and spoil. Every now and then something about the apartment would explode. The man had bought up almost the last of olive-oil that could be had in Central Europe. That, too, turned rancid. As I remember it now, he told me that of all the food he had bought – that he had hoarded it he never admitted – he had been able to use about one-third, and the annoyance he had from the spoiled two-thirds killed all the joy there was in having saved one-third. Hoarding in this case was an utter failure.[8]

To preserve food is almost a science, and suitable storage facilities play an important rôle in this. The private hoarder had no proper facilities. That it was unlawful to hoard food caused them to press ahead in storing it without asking advice of people familiar with the requirements; and the possibility that agents of the food authorities might come to inspect the quarters of the hoarder made hiding imperative. Often the servants would become informers, so that the food had to be hidden from them in barrels, trunks and locked chests. The result of this can be easily imagined. There was a time when more food was spoiled in Central Europe by hoarding than there was consumed.

Just as in Germany, ingenious substitute foods were developed in Austria-Hungary in an attempt to fool the palate, and George Schreiner was in most cases impressed with the results:

> They used to sell in the cafés of Vienna, and other large cities, a cake made mostly of ground clover meal, to which was added the flour of horse-chestnuts, a little rice, some glucose, a little sugar and honey, and chopped prunes when raisins could not be had. The thing was very palatable, and nutritious, as an analysis would show. There were enough food units in it to make the vehicle, which here was clover meal, really worthwhile . . . There was the rice 'lamb' chop, for instance. The rice was boiled and then formed into lumps resembling a chop. Into the lump a skewer of wood was stuck to serve as a bone, and to make the illusion more complete a little paper rosette was used to top off the 'bone'. All of it was very 'comme il faut'. Then the things were fried in real mutton tallow, and when they came on the table its looks and aroma, now reinforced by green peas and a sprig of watercress, would satisfy the most exacting. Nor could fault be found with the taste. The vegetable beefsteak was another thing that gave great satisfaction, once you had become used to the color of the thing's interior, which was pale green – a signal in a real steak that it should not be eaten. The steak in question was a synthetic affair, composed of cornmeal, spinach, potatoes, and ground nuts. An egg was used to bind the mass together.[9]

Just as in Germany, the time which Austrian women had to spend queuing for food often left them little opportunity for anything else. Schreiner tells us of an encounter which he had with a woman in a potato queue in Vienna:

> She had arrived at the store at about seven o'clock. There were three children she had to take care of. She had given them a breakfast of

coffee and bread for the oldest, and milk for the two others. 'I have nobody with whom I could leave the children,' she said. 'My neighbors also have to stand in the food-line. So I keep them from the stove by placing the table on its side in front of it. Against one end of the table I move the couch. The children can't move that, and against the other end I push my dresser.' It appears that the woman had come home once from the food-line and had found her rooms on the verge of going up in a blaze. One of the children had opened the door of the stove and the live coals had fallen out. They had set fire to some kindlings and a chair. The children thought that great fun . . . 'During the summer I worked in an ammunition factory near here,' she said. 'I earned about twenty-six crowns a week, and some of the money I was able to save. I am using that now. I really don't know what I am going to do when it is gone. There is work enough to be had. But what is to become of the children? To get food for them I must stand in line here and waste half of my time every day.'[10]

In many cases the desperate situation many women found themselves in led to a moral and sexual degeneracy. Schreiner describes many such cases in Vienna and Budapest, where a certain class of war profiteer had as he describes it nothing but money, and at the same time many young women were in a desperate financial position, with the price of foodstuffs and other essentials rising around them daily. For a few weeks, some would become the plaything of a wealthy industrialist and – before they were cast off in favour of a prettier face – be able to feed themselves and their families. After that,

. . . they would for a while frequent cafés where they would meet the officers on leave and small fry of civilians, and not long after that they did business on the street with a government license and certificate showing that they were being inspected by the authorities in the interest of public health.[11]

It was ironic that the first of the Central Powers to experience serious food shortage in the Great War was the Ottoman Empire, an overwhelmingly agricultural state, covering modern Turkey and most of the present countries of the Middle East. Misery and starvation soon began to afflict the poorest people in this sprawling entity. Out of an adult male population of about four million, more than 1,500,000 were enlisted in the ranks of the Ottoman army during the war, and so about a million families were left without breadwinners, almost all of these in a condition of extreme destitution. The Turkish Government paid its soldiers the equivalent of a paltry twenty-five US cents a month, and gave their families a separation allowance equating to $1.20 a month. As a result, soon thousands of poor people with a father or husband in the Ottoman army were suffering from lack of food, and many were enfeebled by malnutrition; the lower classes of the civilian population across Anatolia were hit hard in this way. However, in July 1915, Constantinople witnessed the first bread queues formed by those who had the means to buy it on the black market, had there been any available to buy. To put this into context, those now forming the Constantinople bread-lines ate only a modest diet, even in normal times. The Turkish and Levantine populations of the city lived mainly on bread and olives, with a little 'pilaff' – a rice dish – and the addition of a small piece of meat, usually mutton, once a day. The Turks generally drank coffee, and the Levantine a glass of red wine. A British observer in the city around this time noted:

> The condition of affairs in the city approached famine; the electric tramway service, as far as the public is concerned, has practically come to a standstill. I took careful note of the prices of necessaries; sugar is 5s. a pound, coffee 6s. a pound, and cigarettes have been advanced by 40 per cent. Anyone who knows Turkey will understand what this means for a people that smokes practically all day long. Matches are 8d. a box. The stock of paraffin oil has been exhausted, likewise that of chocolate, and all cheese, save the horrible Turkish variety, is no longer procurable. Mutton has advanced 40 per cent in price and beef is not to be had. The small Turkish eggs, which used to cost one farthing each eight months ago, are now twopence each. Soap is ridiculously expensive, but the Turk does not suffer much in consequence! There is very little rice, but fish, of course, is as plentiful as ever, thanks to the unique situation of Constantinople.[12]

The Ottoman capital normally obtained its food supplies via the waterways that gave access to the city – the Bosphorus from the north, and the Black Sea and the Dardanelles from the south and the Mediterranean. Both of these avenues of trade and traffic were closed early in the war. The Russians kept the entrance to the Bosphorus well patrolled, and the French and British saw to it that nothing entered the Dardanelles, even if they themselves could not navigate the strait very far, as the Gallipoli campaign proved. The Anatolian Railway, together with a few unimportant branch lines, was now the only means of reaching the agricultural districts of Asia Minor – the Konia Vilayet and the Cilician Plain, for instance. However the

A scene in Constantinople, around 1914. (Author's collection)

line was single-tracked, and was heavily overloaded with military transports
as a result of the war. The consequence of this was that – in a situation which
closely paralleled that of Petrograd in Russia – Constantinople ate up what
stores there were to hand, and then waited vainly for more. There was more
available, of course, if only it could be transported. The Ottoman Empire
consisted predominantly of arable farming, the only livestock husbanded
in the main were the goat and the fat-tailed sheep. That its capital and only
large city should be without breadstuff as early as July 1915 was hard to
believe, yet it was a fact. In May of that year George Schreiner made a trip
through Anatolia, Syria, and Arabia, and recorded what he saw there:

> By that time the crops in Asia Minor are well advanced and wheat
> is almost ripe. These crops were good, but, like the crops of the
> preceding season, which had not yet been moved, owing to the war,
> they were of little value to the people of Constantinople. They could
> not be had. I hate estimates, and for that reason will not indulge in
> them here. But the fact is that from Eregli, in the Cappadocian
> Plain, to Eski-Shehir, on the Anatolian high plateau, I saw enough

wheat rotting at the railroad stations to supply the Central Powers for two years. Not only was every shed filled with the grain, but the farmers who had come later were obliged to store theirs out in the open, where it lay without shelter of any sort. Rain and warmth had caused the grain on top to sprout lustily, while the inside of the heap was rotting.

It was totally beyond the capacity of the government controlled railway to move the grain because of the priority given to military freight. Thus it was that the shops of the 'ekmekdjis' in Constantinople were besieged by hungry thousands, only a few of whom ever got the loaf which the ticket, issued by the police, promised.[13]

That was not all, however. Speculators and profiteers soon sensed a chance of making some money and were not slow in availing themselves of it. Prices rose until the poor could buy nothing but corn meal. Speculation in olives added further to the distress of the multitude, and the government, with that ineptness which was typical of authority in Turkey, failed to do anything that had practical value. Though the Young Turks had at first set their faces against corruption, many of the party leaders had relapsed, with the result that little was done to check the activities of the middle men who hoarded food for purposes of speculation and price-boosting. Harry Stuermer spent two years in Constantinople during the First World War, and observed:

> . . . now let us see what the Government did in connection with the food problem. At a comparatively early stage they followed Germany's example and introduced bread tickets, which were quite successful so long as the flour lasted. In the autumn of 1915 they took the organisation of the bread supply for large towns out of the hands of the municipalities, and gave it over to the War Office. They got Parliament to vote a large fund to buy up all available supplies of flour, and in view of the immense importance of bread as the chief means of nourishment of the masses, they decided to sell it at a very considerable loss to themselves, so that the price of the daily ration (though not of the supplementary ration) remained very much as it had been in peace time. The Government always favoured the purely Mohammedan quarters of the town so far as bread supply was concerned, and the people living in Fatih and other parts of Stamboul were very much better off than the inhabitants of Graeco-European Pera. Then Talaat [Minister of the Interior] made speeches in the House on the food question in which he did all in

A street scene in the Ottoman capital, early twentieth century. (Author's collection)

his power to throw dust in the eyes of the starving population, but he did not really succeed in blinding anyone as to the true state of affairs. In February 1916, when there was practically a famine in the land, he even went so far as to declare in Parliament that the food supplies for the whole of Turkey had been so increased by enormous purchases in Rumania, that they were now fully assured for two years.[14]

In fact, corruption among the Young Turk leadership was more widespread even than this. In imitation of German war-time methods, either wrongly understood or willfully misapplied through greed, the Turkish Government requisitioned pretty well everything in the food line, or in the shape of articles of daily use that might soon become scarce and thus might rise in price. However, whilst in Germany the supplies so requisitioned were usually applied to the general good, in Turkey the members of the 'Committee of Union and Progress' looked with indifference bordering upon contempt at the privations and sufferings of the ordinary people, and used the supplies they had requisitioned for the personal enrichment of their clique.

During the periods of the very acute bread crises, which occurred more than once, but notably at the beginning of 1916, some dozen men literally died of hunger every day in Constantinople alone. It was not uncommon to see women collapsing from exhaustion in the streets. In Constantinople there was not only a shortage of skilled labour, but also of coal required for milling purposes. The result was that when the townspeople did receive a daily ration of just a quarter of a kilogramme of bread, it was mostly of an indigestible quality – said to be utterly uneatable by Europeans – although occasionally it was quite good if somewhat coarse. If the unfortunate people in Constantinople wanted to supplement this insufficient allowance, they could do so when things were in a flourishing condition at the price of about two or three piastres, and later four or five piastres. Even this was for the most part only obtainable by clandestine means from soldiers, who were usually willing to turn part of their bread ration into money. Bread was the most important food in Constantinople, but the prices of the other foodstuffs soon reached exorbitant heights. The poor had once had the option of rice, but this too was soon beyond them, as were beans, meat, and the cheapest sheep's cheese and olives, hitherto the most common Turkish condiment to eat with bread.

From many parts of the interior, particularly Syria, there were reliable reports of a still worse state of affairs. Even in more normal times there was sometimes a difficulty in obtaining bread, for the means of communication in this vast and primitive land were precarious at best, and it was often no easy matter to get the grain transported to the centres of consumption. If the situation was bad in the capital, then it was worse in remoter corners of the ramshackle empire. A Jewish writer in present-day Lebanon, Alexander Aaronsohn, wrote of the situation there in 1916:

> . . . even the Mohammedan population were hoping that the Allies
> would push their victory and land troops in Syria and Palestine; for
> though they hated the infidel, they loved the Turk not at all, and the

A vegetable market at Konya, central Anatolia, around the time of the First World War. This was one of Turkey's main agricultural areas. (Author's collection)

country was exhausted and the blockade of the Mediterranean by the Allies prevented the import and export of articles. The oranges were rotting on the trees because the annual Liverpool market was closed to Palestine, and other crops were in similar case. The country was short, too, of petroleum, sugar, rice, and other supplies, and even of matches.[15]

The mismanagement of the food situation in that part of the world would only inflame the discontent that native populations felt for Ottoman rule, a discontent which T. E. Lawrence would be able to exploit the following year when he organised the Arab tribes in revolt against the Turks. Aaronsohn continued:

> Beirut is a city of about two hundred thousand inhabitants, half of whom are Christians and the rest Mohammedans and Jews. The pinch of hunger was already felt there. Bread was to be had only on tickets issued by the Government, and prices in general were extremely high. The population were discontented and turbulent, and every day thousands of women came before the governor's residence to cry and protest against the scarcity of bread.[16]

As in Austria-Hungary, by the second half of the war, much of the problem with food production in the Ottoman Empire could be laid at the door of acute shortage of labour in the agricultural areas. George Schreiner made several trips through Thrace, the part of the Ottoman Empire which

A street scene in Jerusalem. Generally speaking, the various components of the Ottoman Empire, such as Palestine, suffered food hardship in direct proportion to their distance from the hub, Constantinople. (Library of Congress)

lay in Europe, and found that its rich valleys and plains could have supplied the Turkish capital with all the wheat it needed had the soil been cultivated. This had not been done, however. The mobilizations had taken so many men from the *tchiftliks* (farms) that a proper tilling of the fields was out of the question. A shortage in grain resulted, but another traveller in this part of the world, the British author E. F. Benson, noted that there was a further flaw in the Ottoman food supply chain, in that the Germans were able to barge the local population aside and secure much of what the Turks were able to produce for their own ends. He tells us:

> In Asia Minor the acreage of cultivation early in 1917 had fallen more than 50 per cent, from that under crops before the war, but owing to the importation of machinery from the Central Powers, backed up by a compulsory Agricultural Service law, which has just been passed, it is hoped that the acreage will be increased this year by something like 30 per cent. The yield per acre also will he greatly increased this year, for Germany has, though needing artificial manure badly herself, sent large quantities into Turkey, where they will be more profitably employed. She has no fear about securing the produce. This augmented yield will, it is true, not be adequate to supply the needs of Turkey, who for the last two years has suffered from very acute food shortage, which in certain districts has amounted to famine and wholesale starvation of the poorer classes. But it is unlikely that their needs will be considered at all, for Germany's needs (she is the fairy godmother of the Pan-Turk ideal) must obviously have the first call on such provisions as are obtainable. Thus, though in February, 1917, there was a daily shortage in Smyrna of 700 sacks of flour, and the Arab and Greek population was starving, no flour at all was allowed to be imported into Smyrna. But simultaneously Germany was making huge purchases of fish, meat, and flour in Constantinople (paid for in German paper), including 100,000 sheep.[17]

In fact, the wily Turks managed to bring it about that their ally Germany always had to pay heavily and always in cash for food supplies, even although the Ottoman government itself owed millions to Germany, and got everything which it received on credit, from flour out of Romania to paper for their journals. The German influence upon Turkey was all pervasive, and Harry Steurmer commented upon the ludicrous situation, laughable if it were not so bizarre, which he encountered at the station of Haidar Pasha, whilst travelling across Turkey by train. He found that he could not get a mouthful of bread or even a biscuit, but the only

A farmer ploughing at Klistra, Asia Minor. Turkish agriculture at this time was primitive, and further hindered during the war by lack of manpower. (Author's collection)

refreshment which was obtainable was unlimited beer, produced by a local German brewery!

In many ways the Ottoman and Austro-Hungarian Empires were similar. Both possessed ample agricultural land and an almost infinite capacity to grow cereals. Yet both had been brought to their knees by bread shortages comparatively early in the war. In both cases the reasons for this were similar – mismanagement of this vital asset, official incompetence or indeed corruption, and wanton profiteering. However, the most serious failure in both cases was in managing their manpower reserves. Too many men had been conscripted from the land, without adequate means to replace them. In Britain, by contrast this manpower circle had been squared to a large extent by replacing those conscripted from the land with increased use of machinery on the one hand, and greater use of female labour on the other. Neither of these options were exploited in any meaningful way by Austria or Turkey.

Chapter 8

The United States

The United States, with its vast prairies stretching across the Midwestern states, is often perceived as a bread basket producing enormous quantities of foodstuffs, particularly cereals and also beef from the many thousands of head of cattle which roamed those prairies. Yet to some extent this is a misconception, and the food-producing capacity of the US, and its ability to feed itself, had already been in decline before the First World War. Its experience of the conflict, both as a neutral and as a combatant, was characterised by many of the same social stresses produced by unprecedented demand for food which were present in European countries. Only in the US, however, did the wartime mood swing so decisively against alcoholic drinks, and only in the US was such a profound and far-reaching attempt made to change the habits of society in this regard.

As already noted, Great Britain in particular was heavily dependent upon imported food. When, due to the war, she found that her usual sources of supply of commodities such as meat and flour in Australasia and South America were no longer within easy reach, she turned instead to the US and Canada. This had the effect in the US in particular of driving up food prices on the domestic market. One report stated that twenty-two of the most essential foods consumed by the US home market were sirloin steak, round steak, rib roast, chuck roast, plate beef, pork chops, bacon, ham, lard, hens, flour, corn meal, eggs, butter, milk, bread, potatoes, sugar, cheese, rice, coffee and tea. For the six-year period from November 1913 to November 1919, the increase in the prices of these twenty-two articles combined was 92 per cent. Articles which more than doubled in price, that is increased more than 100 per cent, were sugar, 131 per cent; lard, 129 per cent; flour 124 per cent; cornmeal, 113 per cent; potatoes, 105 per cent; bread, 104 per cent; and rice 102 per cent. By November 1918, at the time of the signing of the Armistice by Germany, the increase in the price of all twenty-two articles had reached 60 per cent, and by November a year later 84 per cent, above the 1913 average.

Thus food hardship was a phenomenon already present in the United States before she joined the war, and among the poorer New Yorkers of the

Poor New Yorkers, from the Lower East Side, protesting about the high cost of food, February 1917. (Library of Congress)

Lower East Side there were demonstrations and protests in 1916 and early 1917 about the high costs of staple foods such as bread, which was rising daily. Ordinary people at the time complained about getting much less now

Food protesters gather in a Jewish district of New York, early 1917. The woman addressing the crowd may be the anarchist leader Marie Ganz. (Library of Congress: Bain collection)

for their money than a year or so previously. For example, butchers who customarily trimmed away bone and excess fat before weighting meat had lately abandoned the practice and began charging for these parts. Working people also recognised a new trend: markets freezing vegetables in order to preserve them longer. The problem was that water condensation on the vegetables made them heavier, driving the cost-per-pound of many of these products even higher. Many people were forced to pawn family heirlooms, alter their eating habits or cut back on meals altogether. Though the cost of living went up for everyone equally, it made the most dramatic differences in the lives of Americans living in low-income districts like the Lower East Side. One resident told a *New York Times* reporter in February 1917: 'It used to cost 49 cents to provide breakfast for the four of us. Today the same breakfast would cost $1.02 . . . We haven't had an egg in months and potatoes are a luxury.'[1]

That month a crowd of women demonstrated at the New York City Hall to protest at the soaring cost of food, led by Mrs Ida Harris, president of the socialist Woman's Vigilance League, and the well-known anarchist 'Sweet Marie' Ganz. Both women were part of a newly-formed committee called the Mothers' Anti-High Price League (also referred to as the Mothers' Anti-High Cost League in some cases). Rumours spread throughout New York's poor Jewish districts about retailers conspiring to drive up prices, and a boycott of produce, as well as a series of violent attacks and incidents of vandalism directed against shops and street peddlers, began on 19 February 1917. Mobs of women targeted vendors over the next few days; throwing rocks, soaking goods with kerosene and threatening customers who failed to observe the boycott.

This American poster, in Yiddish, states 'Food will win the war'. Aimed at Jewish immigrants, it urges them to support the Allied war effort by conserving food. (Library of Congress)

On the morning of 20 February, members of the Mothers' Anti-High Price League gathered at 176 East Broadway for an advertised meeting, followed by speeches in nearby Rutgers Park. As the crowd swelled into the hundreds and spilled out onto East Broadway, Ida Harris and Marie Ganz led a spontaneous march to City Hall. Around a thousand women converged on the gates of City Hall Park, where they found just a few police officers who were unprepared and were quickly overwhelmed. Between 300 and 400 marchers broke through and made it up the steps, before the iron gates were slammed shut at the top. The by now angry women, many of whom had children with them, began shouting 'We want food for our children!' in both English and Yiddish. In an attempt to defuse the situation a mayor's representative appeared at a window and promised to allow three of the women to meet with the mayor later that day, so long as everyone went home quietly. According to subsequent reports, the women had begun to leave when a few agitators, including Marie Ganz, harangued those that were left in bitter language, inciting a minor riot. In the end, Ganz was arrested for failing to comply with police orders to stop stirring up the crowd.

Acting on the advice of Abraham Cahan (the editor of the *Jewish Daily Forward*, a Yiddish newspaper which defended trade unionism and moderate, democratic socialism) Ida Harris and the Mothers' Anti-High Price League presented a list of demands, which included an immediate request to the city, state and national governments for $1,000,000 to set up and run municipal stores and another $1,000,000 for a school lunch program in state schools. As the League grew in confidence in its battle with the government, violence increased in Jewish immigrant districts across New York. On 22 February demonstrators turned their attention away from produce retailers to poultry markets instead, attacking customers and destroying chickens on site. The *New York Times* again reported: 'Through Pitt, Ludlow, Rivington, Essex, Suffolk and all of the east side streets the crowd surged, passing from one shop to another . . . waving the heads and wings and mutilated bodies of chickens.'[2]

Perhaps as part of an official attempt to discredit the demonstrators, a rumour quickly spread that the whole protest was artificial and part of a German conspiracy, with the agitators being paid to incite the poor to riot. This rumour of a soon-to-be enemy government plot confused the issue, by leading many better-off Americans to believe that there was no real problem to be addressed. On 24 February, thousands of ordinary people from the Five Boroughs marched on Madison Square, where some high-profile speakers addressed them. At the head of the procession was carried a white flag which read, 'Starvation'. By early March, the city had responded to the crisis by purchasing large quantities of low-cost produce, and the wholesalers lowered their prices in response. Though prices fluctuated sharply throughout the war, violence for the most part was not seen again, and certainly not on this scale.

When the United States did eventually enter the Great War in April 1917, it at least had the advantage in terms of guaranteeing its food supply of more than two years of observation of the effects of war and blockade upon both Germany and Great Britain. In his speech upon US entry into the war, President Woodrow Wilson stated:

> The course of trade shall be as unhampered as it is possible to make it and there shall be no unwarranted manipulation of the nation's food supply by those who handle it on its way to the consumer. This is our opportunity to demonstrate the efficiency of a great democracy and we shall not fall short of it!
>
> This let me say to the middlemen of every sort, whether they are handling our foodstuffs or our raw material of manufacture or the products of our mills and factories: The eyes of the country will be especially upon you. This is your opportunity for signal service, efficient and disinterested. The country expects you, as it expects all others, to forego unusual profits, to organize and expedite shipments of supplies of every kind, but especially of food, with an eye to the service you are rendering and in the spirit of those who enlist in the ranks for their people, not for themselves. I shall confidently expect you to deserve and win the confidence of people of every sort and station.[3]

However, ensuring that Americans had enough to eat was not merely a case of controlling profiteers. Initially there was confusion and muddle in the American approach to food distribution, and it was not until August 1917 that the Lever Act created the federal Food Administration. American nutritionists were also acutely aware of the problems which the nation now faced in terms of supply. The uncultivated areas of the United States were great, and the areas that grew only grass for grazing were vast. The proportionate area of land under the plough was discouragingly small, and the deficiencies in farm labour were a risk. American food production had not kept pace with the growth of the population. This was not a condition caused by the war, but instead had been giving agricultural experts cause for alarm even before 1913. In the preceding thirty-five years Americans had concentrated increasingly in cities. For example, from 1880 to 1910 the increase in the urban population was 188.5 per cent. By contrast, the increase in rural population was just 39.4 per cent in the same period. This meant a decrease in the per capita production of staple food products. For

Two American women war-workers, breaking ground with a motorised plough.
(Library of Congress)

example, wheat dropped from 8.5 bushels per capita in 1884 to 7.7 bushels in 1914. This was all the more significant because the concentration of populations in cities required an increase in staple food products. Also the rate of increase of cattle, sheep and swine slowed down as the human population grew. As a consequence of this, the US had been steadily forced to decrease the amount of foodstuffs exported, and for some thirty years before the war she was steadily losing her ability to produce and to export surplus food.

However, with the coming of the war, the high prices that Europe was willing to offer for foods caused a marked increase in American export of foodstuffs once more. The 1916 exports of wheat crops and animals jumped to 177 per cent of the 1914 figures, and the manufactured foodstuff exports for the same period increased 103 per cent. These figures might indicate that American agriculture was responding to the new demands, but in fact that was not the case. The US did not increase its ability to produce food in the years 1914–16, but merely sold out of what it had, and killed off its stocks of animals. In 1916, due to bad weather conditions, the crops were generally poor, and the US domestic market went short, for instance, of

88,339,000 bushels of wheat. This was reflected in May 1917, when speculators pushed the price of Chicago wheat to three dollars a bushel. The US home market was also under supplied by 75,000,335 bushels of potatoes, and the price in February 1917 jumped as high as thirteen cents a pound, or two pounds for a quarter. That was more than eight times as much as the fixed price for potatoes in Germany. The impressive exports of 1916 were only achieved due to exceptional weather conditions in 1915; now, with poor conditions in 1916, America faced serious shortages in the spring of 1917. In other words, it was not due to any deliberate measures or any improvement in food production on the part of the US that it was able to export what it did.

Herbert Hoover, the US Food Controller. Hoover's administrative flair made him ideal for this post. He successfully ran for the Presidency in 1928. (Library of Congress)

Nonetheless, the Wilson administration was under no illusion that the United States alone had not only the ability to keep the Allies supplied with food and to keep them in the war, but also the responsibility for doing this. The US Food Controller, Herbert Hoover, perceptively assessed the situation in 1917, telling an audience of American food conservation campaigners:

> I take it that you are all possessed of the fact that there is a shortage of food in the world; but you probably don't know that the shortage is the result of a shortage of shipping, that there are in the world today three great food pools – one of them Australasia and Malaysia, the East Indies, China and Japan; another, South America; and the third, North America. Now, with the gradual shortening of shipping, what you might call the Eastern Pool has been almost totally isolated from the Allied World. There lie in Australia at the present moment probably 250,000,000 bushels of wheat; there are in Java a million tons of sugar; there are in the East Indies probably 500,000 tons of beans and a million tons of rice, and there are four or five thousand tons of vegetable oils. If we had that supply in the Allied countries at this moment . . . there would be no need for any exertion on our part. But the world simply hasn't the shipping to spend on that long voyage. The consequence is that at the present moment we have to take the place of an enormous

food supply that is isolated. . . We have to take a larger and larger proportion of the load as time goes on, because we are standing against a constant diminution in the world's shipping. We are confronted at the present moment with the necessity to take the place of those world supplies, and we have already exported from the United States practically our normal surplus.[4]

As already noted, the rural population of the US had grown only modestly in the pre-war years. The consequent shortage of labour of farms in the United States, concerning though it might have been before 1914, became a more serious problem as the war progressed. One observer noted:

[Many] farm hands have gone to work in munition plants. Near the great munition center of Bridgeport, Connecticut, it has been possible to pick up farms for ten dollars an acre. Milkers and farm hands, who formerly worked for twenty-five to thirty dollars a month, prefer to work in factories for $3.75 a day. The wages of forty-five to fifty dollars that farmers, desperate for help, have offered, do not appeal. In the munition plant a man works eight hours; on a farm, twelve or more.[5]

In order to overcome this problem and to increase agricultural production, the Federal government made an appeal to the presidents of more than 600 colleges and universities asking their help in mobilising their students on farms during the summer. To assist in farm work the Boys' Working Reserve was also created, for young men between sixteen and twenty-one years of age who were to give their spare time in work on the land, without interrupting their studies at school. Manufacturers were persuaded to dispense with the services of a portion of their employees for temporary periods of from one to four weeks, in order to assist in the cultivation of food crops. Steps were taken by the Commissioner of Indian Affairs for determining the number of Indians on reservations who could be spared for farm and other work in other localities, and who could be induced to accept employment at the prevailing wage. Sections of the immigration law were suspended by the Secretary of Labor, so as to permit the importation of labourers from Mexico during the period of the war to work in agriculture.

The people in towns also showed an admirable desire to play their part in the war, and many started vegetable campaigns. These people took advice readily, and dug up their back yards and worked on adjacent fields. They went out by the hundreds to farm land in their neighbourhood, day after day, the wet days in the spring and the hot days in the summer, acting on advice to plant the things they could grow easily, so that they could supply

In the fields outside Sugar City, Colorado, youngsters work on their father's smallholding. The family were recent immigrants from southern Russia. (Library of Congress)

their own families and their friends, and thus much more food could be conserved. In undertaking this work, many valuable social lessons were also learned, with the townspeople having a greater understanding of the effort needed to produce salads or vegetables. It was said that they were less likely to complain about the prices of these things as a result.

Some townspeople had a back yard which was not fit to grow anything in, but which would support some poultry. Small chicks were sold by agricultural colleges to people who had never before had hens or who previously didn't know how to raise them. Thousands more eggs were distributed to school boys and school girls; these easy-to-raise Plymouth Rock hens dramatically increased the production of poultry which had a significant effect in keeping the price of this food down, at a time of high prices for wheat and other foodstuffs.

In spite of all this effort, official predictions showed worrying signs that 1918 might be a year of crisis for America. Because of the difficulties in obtaining labour, US farmers increasingly resorted to killing off their animals. Therefore, the production of meat in 1916 exceeded that of 1914 by three billion pounds. The resulting shortage of livestock constituted a great danger to food supplies, and even the Chicago meat packers raised awareness of the situation by advocating meatless days for the United States, as was the norm in England, France and Germany. Supplies of food in cold storage fell off enormously. 1917 saw a decrease of 29.3 per cent in American cheese held in cold storage on the previous year. Likewise the reserves of eggs dropped 86.3 per cent; lard, 31.7 per cent; lamb and mutton, 31.1 per cent; and frozen pork, 36.9 per cent.

Other figures showed that the US was entirely dependent upon the food produced in 1917 to carry it through the winter of 1918, and she had not only to feed her own citizens but also to help feed the Allies. The Department of Agriculture in April 1917 estimated that the winter wheat crop that year would be the lowest ever recorded. This was doubly significant when one considers the fact that two-thirds of the overall wheat crop consisted of winter wheat. The poor 1917 crop followed hard on the heels of the disappointing crop of 1916, and the wheat crops of both England and France were reported as being below normal. Demand was also rising among the European neutral countries, with Holland, Denmark, Sweden, Norway and Switzerland able to produce little or no wheat. What was needed was an aggressive, constructive policy, including properly directed food production, centralised control of labour and fertiliser supplies, and utilisation of abandoned farms and waste lands. As well as guaranteed prices for farm produce set by the government, nutritionists urged controls on consumption. One of them wrote:

> Nutrition experts agree that at most the man doing ordinary sedentary work needs but twenty-five hundred calories of food a day. It will help the individual to reduce this scientific formula to something tangible. For example, Professor Irving Fisher of Yale and Doctor Eugene Lyman Fisk of the Life Extension Institute, in their book 'How to Live,' tell us that in a small lamb chop weighing about an ounce we find one hundred calories. The same number of calories are contained in a large egg, in a small dish of baked beans, in a piece of cheese about one and a half cubic inches, in an ordinary side dish of sweet corn, in a large boiled potato, an ordinary thick slice of bread, a shredded wheat biscuit, a large dish of oatmeal, a small piece of sponge cake, a third of an ordinary piece of pie, in a lump and a half of sugar, in a dozen peanuts, in eight pecans, in four prunes, in two apples, in a large banana, in half a cantaloupe, in seven olives, in a very large orange, in an ordinary pat of butter, a small glass of milk, or a quarter of a glass of cream. Each one of

Do You Know How Peanuts Grow?

PERHAPS you have thought they grow on bushes or trees like other nuts.

No! They grow in the ground, just like potatoes. -

The peanut plant is pulled up by the roots when the right time comes, and there are the peanuts, hanging to it.

All the peanuts used in making Beech-Nut Peanut Butter go through wonderful machines that clean off every speck of sand or earth. That is why Beech-Nut Peanut Butter is always so *smooth*, and spreads on bread so nicely.

TELL US WHAT *YOU* HAVE FOUND OUT

Most boys and girls love Beech-Nut Peanut Butter on bread, toast or crackers. If you have discovered some other new ways that you like to eat it, write us a letter. We will be glad to hear from you.

If you have never tasted *Beech-Nut* Peanut Butter, ask your mother to get you a jar today.

BEECH-NUT PACKING COMPANY, CANAJOHARIE, NEW YORK

Beech-Nut Peanut Butter

©B. N.P.
Co.1917

Although peanut butter was invented before the First World War, peanut farming underwent something of a boom during it. This advertisement is from 1917. (Author's collection)

these articles yields one hundred calories; twenty-five hundred calories is all that is needed on the average for one day.[6]

The eating habits of millions of Americans had to be changed, and quickly, if she were to avoid a crisis. The habit of indiscriminately feeding leftovers to chickens and pigs was discouraged. Many of the leftovers from the table could be re-used for human consumption, and campaigners and posters highlighted the waste involved in feeding food fit for humans to animals, when there were cheap foods for both chickens and pigs available upon which they could be fed instead. Still another waste occurred in many homes from the American trait of wanting to satisfy the eye as well as the appetite. The average man who was a 'good liver' liked to sit down to a table covered with dishes heaped with a variety of foods. Just as the average American liked to see plenty of food on his table, he also liked to pile the plates with it, frequently serving enough food for three persons to one individual. All of this profligacy with food had to be discouraged. One academic, Dr Alonzo E. Taylor, wrote of the need for Americans to achieve a level of 'sacrificial consciousness' before attempts at food control could even hope to be effective:

> . . . that is the reason why in this country we have, just as they had in England in 1916 and in Germany in 1915, difficulty in the program of food conservation because our people have not yet attained sacrificial consciousness for the carrying on of the war – in which we view every act of our lives and everything we do and everything we wear and everything we eat, and everything we desire, and everything we use, from the standpoint of a new rule, whether it will or will not aid in the carrying on of the war, whether it is or is not a positive military measure. That is the final step of analysis in all systems of food control. When we have reached that plane, as they have reached it in England and France, the whole problem of control becomes simplified, because the motivation is

Women in Pittsburg receive lessons in food economy and nutrition, at a War Kitchen demonstration. (Library of Congress)

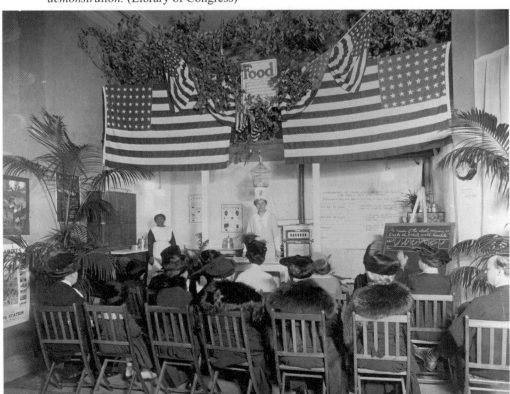

there that makes it possible to carry through a repression applied to foods in general or to any particular food.[7]

However, there was never any compulsory rationing of food in the US between 1917 and 1918. Hoover encouraged American households to consume less meat and bread, but recognised that co-operation with the Food Administration guidelines was entirely voluntary. His only police, he stated, were America's housewives. There were 'meatless Tuesdays' and 'sweetless Saturdays'. Both Mondays and Wednesday were 'wheatless', but compliance was entirely up to individual families. Only the baking industry, including hotels and restaurants, was restricted by regulations requiring the production of war bread and rolls, called 'victory bread'. Initially it was made from at least 5 per cent of grains other than wheat, and that amount increased to 20 per cent as the war continued.

American eating habits were also influenced directly by the war in other ways. Because of the large scale immigration of Germans into the United States in the nineteenth century, there were many dishes of German origin common in that country, but anti-German feeling began to grow against them. Despite being invented in the US, the Hamburger was perceived as having German origins and was associated with German immigrants. During the First World War it was known instead as a Salisbury Steak. The term 'Hot Dog' grew in popularity as against 'Frankfurter' or 'Bratwurst'. Wiener Schnitzel is now served in America as breaded veal or pork cutlet, and Rouladen have become 'roll 'em ups'. In some cases however this anti-German feeling was mis-directed, the *Washington Post* reporting that:

> On account of its supposedly German name, sauerkraut seems to be losing its popularity as an American dish. The food administration has learned that throughout the country men and women in their patriotic zeal have been spreading a strong propaganda to discourage the use of a valuable foodstuff. As a matter of fact the dish is Dutch rather than of German origin. Its wider use would stimulate a greater use of cabbage and would further the food administration's campaign for increased consumption of perishable foodstuffs and a greater saving of the staple foods needed abroad. Sauerkraut is a valuable food, and its use should not be curtailed as a result of ill-advised patriotism.[8]

Sauerkraut was not the only food product to suffer from this backlash. An interesting side-effect of the First World War in the United States was the spur which it gave to prohibition of alcohol. The subject of drink had been a contentious one in the United States almost since the first settlers of

Americans making Sauerkraut (pickled cabbage), around 1918. The dish suffered a drop in popularity at this time, due to perceptions that it was German in origin. (Library of Congress)

Puritan stock had reached the New World. However, the prohibition lobby (which represented a cross-section of interests, ranging from those with moral or religious objections to alcohol, through those with social and welfare concerns, to those manufacturers of soft drinks who cynically sensed commercial advantage in such a ban) had been gaining ground steadily since the end of the Civil War. It is a little-known fact that the Klu Klux Klan, revived in the American south around 1915, was as strongly committed to Prohibition as it was opposed to blacks and immigrants; indeed it was a central part of its agenda, and in this it made common cause with the women's suffrage movement in the US at the time. The motives of the Klan in opposing alcohol were not directly connected with the war, one of its members writing:

[In the mines] the southern [European] immigrants were the trouble makers. These undesirable employees were continually agitating strikes and walkouts, not realizing that religious holidays celebrated promiscuously, with the usual imbibing of strong liquors would not bring the same financial returns as those paid to the man who worked every day with a clear brain. The author, while at one time employed in the mines, witnessed many of these labor immigrants attempting to work in the mines, under most hazardous conditions, while still under the influence of liquor served the day previous during a foreign festival. To this economic evil can be credited the fact that many of the largest industrial groups in the country became the strongest sponsors of prohibition, realizing that the enactment of [prohibition] was their only solution for labor troubles and the creation of a stable mental attitude among the hordes of alien employees. While religious and 'dry' groups have attempted to claim all the glory for this piece of legislation, it is a well known fact that the principal part was played by industrial interests endeavoring to rid themselves of a self-inflicted plague.[9]

However, the First World War now provided both a motive and an opportunity for Prohibition. In January 1917, the 65th Congress convened, in which the 'dries' (prohibitionists) outnumbered the 'wets' by 140 to 64 in the Democratic Party and 138 to 62 among Republicans. With America's declaration of war against Germany in April, German Americans, a major force against prohibition, were side-lined and their protests subsequently ignored. It so happened that most of the major breweries in the United States were German-owned. Anheuser-Busch, founded by Germans Adolphus Busch and Eberhard Anheuser, brewed 'Budweiser' (a Bohemian-style lager) in St Louis, Missouri. Miller meanwhile had been founded in Milwauki, Wisconsin by Frederick Edward John Miller (born as 'Friedrich Eduard Johannes Müller' in Riedlingen, Germany in 1888), and Coors

An advertisement for Anheuser-Busch's Budweiser, from around 1915. An American beer brewed by Germans, it was to become a victim of the anti-German feeling during the First World War. (Author's collection)

THE GENII OF INTOLERANCE
A Dangerous Ally for the Cause of Women Suffrage

This cartoon from 1918 warns American women's suffrage campaigners to be careful who they ally themselves with. That movement was closely linked to the prohibition campaign, but the 'genie of intolerance' was already out of the bottle, for the anti-drink coalition also included the Klu Klux Klan. (From Puck magazine)

was founded in 1873, by German immigrants Adolph Coors and Jacob Schueler in Golden, Colorado. All would suffer from the anti-German backlash following US entry into the war. The Anti-Saloon League (ASL), the most successful single-issue pressure group in American history, succeeded through its relentless propaganda in equating beer with Germany

Although Prohibition did not pass Congress until December 1917, in some states pressure for the measure was so intense that they passed their own legislation to outlaw liquor. Here, the Governor of Indiana signs Prohibition into law in April 1917, rendering it a dry state. (Library of Congress)

in the public mind, and drinking it was now seen as unpatriotic. The negative stereotyping of 'Huns' as rapacious barbarians damned the brewers as guilty by association, and soon no politician dared oppose the ASL.

In addition, a new justification for prohibition arose: prohibiting the production of alcoholic beverages would allow more resources – especially grain that would otherwise be used to make alcohol – to be devoted to the war effort. A resolution calling for a Constitutional amendment to accomplish nationwide Prohibition was introduced in Congress and passed by both houses in December 1917. By 16 January 1919, the Amendment had been ratified by thirty-six of the forty-eight states needed to assure its passage into law. While wartime contingency was a spark for the movement, the First World War ended before nationwide Prohibition was enacted. Nevertheless, some states had already enacted their own legislation banning alcohol, ahead of the constitutional amendment. What had originated as a wartime measure remained in place until 1933, by which time it had become clearly apparent that the experiment had failed. Most of the big breweries survived Prohibition by producing other drinks whilst the ban was in place, including what was termed 'near beer', a drink which had been through much of the same fermentation process as beer but from which the alcohol had been removed.

Thus, whilst it was akin to Britain in that it was a *laissez-faire* capitalist economy with no great history of government intervention in food supply, in just two years the United States under Woodrow Wilson had transformed itself into a country in which the government controlled or influenced large sections of the food-producing economy. The United States, however, did not travel as far down this road as did Britain (though it may have done if the war had continued). The most significant impacts of the global conflict in America were on products of German origin, which suffered greatly during the war years, prohibition of alcohol being the most obvious and prominent outward symbol of this.

Chapter 9

The Major Neutral Countries

By the early twentieth century, international trade had reached a degree of globalisation such that any disruption caused by a major war would have far-reaching consequences, not just for the combatant nations, but also for neutral countries who had either traded heavily with the belligerents before the war and now found that trade suspended, or who depended for their economic prosperity upon the freedom of the oceans and now found that freedom curtailed. Under pressure from the Allies, as early as 1915 several neutral governments, among them the Dutch, Danish, Swiss and Norwegian, had already declared restrictions on food exported to Germany. Meanwhile, the German government had in its hands the means to coerce at least some of the neutrals most effectively. Thus, those attempting to stay out of the conflict sometimes found themselves in the unenviable position of being squeezed from both sides. This chapter examines the impact of food restriction on the major European non-combatant nations, and the ways in which their people suffered differing degrees of food hardship as a result.

Early on in the war, neutral Sweden fell under suspicion of aiding Germany. Certainly prior to the war she had been one of Germany's major trading partners, supplying her with timber and iron ore amongst other things. Sweden's imports of grains and other necessities from the United States, prior to the entry of the latter into the war, showed a considerable increase over the preceding years and this was taken by the Allies as prima-facie evidence that she was supplying the Germans with large quantities of goods. This was, however, true only in part; Sweden was compelled to purchase more abroad to replenish her own supplies, dangerously depleted in the early part of the war. Furthermore, the other markets in which grain and various supplies had been bought before the war were now closed to her, and so naturally she was forced to buy more in the only markets open to her; namely, in the United States. British interference with Swedish maritime commerce became increasingly active as the war went on, and soon huge quantities of goods of every kind assigned for Sweden were held up in Britain. Finally Britain declared that she had the right to stop all trade with her enemies which passed through neutral countries, and that anyone among the latter which was not ready to acquiesce in this ruling would no longer be looked upon as neutral. This, in effect, meant that neutrals were henceforth subjected to a rationing system as far as goods from outside were concerned. The rule violated the provisions of international law, and Sweden opposed it until the spectre of starvation, appearing towards the end of the conflict, and the creation of a new ministry which was friendly to the Entente, brought a change of policy. Sweden was obliged to introduce rationing during the First World War, and as in other countries, failure to enforce it rigorously led to inequality. Journalist Madeleine Doty visited the country during the course of the war and noted:

Madeleine Doty. The American pacifist travelled extensively in Europe during the First World War, reporting upon the conditions which she found. (From Doty, Behind the Battle Line)

> In Sweden it was hopeless. It took a page, written in the Swedish language, to get to a building around the corner. The war has been a tragedy for Sweden. Much of her physical luxury has had to go. Fuel and food are scarce. In the hotels only one electric light is allowed in a room, and the temperature kept at 60. With the food it is even worse. Sweden has reached the stage of Germany in 1916. There is little fat or food that has substance. Two hours after eating I was hungry. Yet Sweden still clings to luxuries. It was possible to buy at exorbitant prices poor pastry, cream for your coffee, and a tiny bit of candy. There was no butter; the supply of bread was low, and all the necessities rationed. The rich were thriving at the expense of the poor.[1]

As the tightening of the Allied blockade seriously reduced the supply of food in Sweden and rationing was resorted to in increasing degree, opposition to Prime Minister Hammarskjöld gathered force. It was felt that he was too doctrinaire and too stubborn in his opposition to the high-handed methods of Britain. As supplies dwindled still more and business interests found themselves in a worse situation than ever, the rumblings of discontent grew deeper and louder. Nor was the ministry itself united, Wallenberg, the minister of foreign affairs, favouring a larger degree of co-operation with Britain. The ministry therefore tendered its resignation in March 1917 and

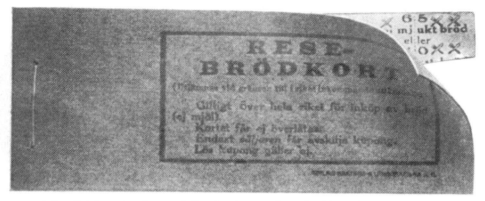

A Swedish bread ration card. Sweden imported much of her wheat from the USA, and in an effort to prevent her re-exporting it to Germany, her supplies were closely controlled by the Allies. (From Therese, *With Old Glory in Berlin*)

was succeeded by one headed by Carl Swartz, a moderate conservative. Swartz left office after his policies had failed to win the approval of the electorate in the autumn of 1917, and he was succeeded by Professor Nils Edén, whose incumbency of the Prime Minister's office saw some of these momentous issues resolved, as a trade agreement was reached with Britain which assured the Swedes increased food supplies.

Although always neutral, politically Norway had leaned towards the cause of the Allies, and indeed the sentiments of the bulk of the population lay in this direction. As the conflict progressed the attitude of Norway gradually shifted from one of strict neutrality to that of being virtually a non-combatant ally of Great Britain. The war did much to enhance Norwegian prosperity. During those years, commerce and industry developed on a quite unprecedented scale: foreign competition was reduced to a minimum; fisheries and shipping made unexampled profits; industry found a ready market, where purchasers were not too particular how much was paid. It is true that the cost of living increased to a greater extent than was the case in other neutral countries, and that, after the entry of America into the war, the difficulty of obtaining supplies led to the introduction of rationing from the end of November 1917; from that date until the conclusion of the Norwegian-American agreement negotiated by Dr Nansen on 30 April 1918, the situation gave rise to considerable anxiety, and indeed some internal unrest. It is also fair to say that the uncertainty of the situation, the expense of measures for the preservation of neutrality, and of encouraging agriculture with a view to rendering the country self-supporting, combined with the high cost of living and rising wages to bring about heavy taxation; Madeleine Doty was in the country in the early spring of 1918, and was unimpressed by what she found, writing:

> Norway was intolerable. The people were hungry. The Allies had stopped supplies, and the Germans had nothing to give. The friendly little land had grown ugly. She begrudged her visitors each mouthful of food.[2]

She found the country bleak, short of fuel for cooking and heating, and the people on the verge of starvation, adding:

> Bergen dripped moisture. The land was covered with melting snow. The streets were sheets of ice and streams of water. The houses were damp. They had the foul, cold smell of prison. It was impossible to get a square meal. There was no butter, no sugar, and little bread. Daylight lasted from eight to four. Bergen was as ugly in winter as it was enchanting in summer. For Norway is a land of extremes. Ice-bound in winter, it has in summer a long delirium of golden sunshine.[3]

Before the war, the consumption of alcohol in Norway had been low, and the figures for this country were almost the lowest in the statistics of Europe. Although from 1907 onwards the level of consumption had increased, at the outbreak of the war there certainly existed no apparent need for drastic legislation. During the war, however, it was thought advisable to pass a temporary measure of prohibition. The reasons for this were to a large extent independent of considerations of temperance. Partly it was desired to promote economy and discourage luxury; partly the object was to preserve food supplies normally used in the distillation of spirits; and to some extent, the Norwegian government wished to take no chances with the preservation of public order in such critical times. The scope of the restriction varied somewhat from time to time, but for the most part besides spirits it included wines and other drinks containing more than 12 per cent volume of alcohol. The prohibitionists in Norway were quick to seize the opportunity afforded to them, and exerted their efforts to convert this temporary war measure into a permanent law. Accordingly, in 1917 it was enacted that a referendum of the whole people should be held in 1919 on the question of whether spirits and strong wines should be permanently prohibited. Somewhat to the surprise of many anti-prohibitionists, the referendum resulted in a considerable majority for prohibition, on a turnout of about two-thirds of the voting population. The proportions for and against the proposed measure were about two to one. In these circumstances, the legislature felt itself committed to passing a prohibition law, and this was done on 16 September 1921.

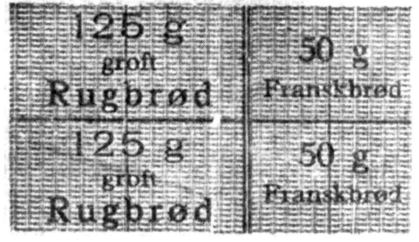

A Danish bread card. Rationing was introduced here in 1917, and caused considerable unrest. (From Therese, *With Old Glory in Berlin*)

Before 1914, Spain and Portugal constituted Norway's most important market for dried cod; but, in retaliation for the exclusion of their wines during the war, these countries proceeded to subject imports of Norwegian fish to prohibitive duties. This had such a damaging effect on the Norwegian economy that by the early 1920s, Norway was forced to repeal parts of its prohibition legislation, in order to allow wine from these countries to be imported once more. However, even now, Norway remains possibly the most restrictive country in Europe in terms of sale of alcohol, with strict limits on the times of day at which beer and wine can be purchased, and with stronger drink only available from government-controlled outlets.

The economy of the third Scandinavian country, Denmark, was heavily regulated through the so-called August Laws of 1914, and the Price Regulation Commission, which sat until 1921. The country maintained trade with both warring parties, and was one of several neutral countries which exported canned meat to the German army. Some speculators made considerable fortunes in the rapidly growing canning industry, producing products of mostly mediocre quality, and which earned them the popular but disparaging nickname of 'gullaschbaroner' or 'stew magnates'. The period 1917–18 saw shortages reach a point at which the first Danish issue of ration cards took place for staple foods. In those years there was significant social and political unrest in the country as a result of shortages. Josephine Therese arrived in Denmark from Germany in 1917, and wrote:

> . . . the story of the five days that I spent in Copenhagen might almost be written in the one word, 'eating'. Unlike Sweden and Norway, the smaller Denmark seemed to me to have an ample supply of food, and a goodly variety; but this may have been by comparison with what I had become accustomed to. Bread I found to be the exception; it was mostly black, and cards were required for the white variety. But there was plenty of meats, fats, butter, fresh fruit and vegetables, and I did full justice to all of them, and came back for more. If the variety was large, so were the prices, however. Our comparatively simple breakfast, the following morning, cost five krona (about a dollar and thirty cents) and dinner twice that.

A crowd gathers outside a butcher's shop in the hope of food supplies, watched by Danish police. Copenhagen 1918. (Det Kongelige Bibliotek)

In one of the restaurants which we frequented was a young waiter, scarcely more than a boy, who could not refrain from speaking to us delightedly when he heard us talking English. We learned that he had been educated in America, and still received newspapers from my country, and from England. As a result, he was rabidly anti-German; but he told us, with a sorrowful shake of his head, that he feared for what the future held for Denmark. Like the other Scandinavian countries, it was between the Prussian devil and the deep sea, he said, and had been so hard hit by America's edict, ending the exportation of foodstuffs to all of them, that the feeling of bitterness toward the United States was growing apace.[4]

Perhaps none of the neutrals felt the effects of the war more severely than Holland. It was virtually surrounded on all sides by belligerents; on three sides it was bordered by Germany or German-occupied Belgium, and on the fourth side by the North Sea, which, infested by mines and submarines, was very much a war and a danger zone. Although Holland was ultimately to be affected by food shortages and food riots, at the beginning of the war she was cautiously optimistic, and initially at least the advantages of the situation appeared to outweigh the disadvantages. One British author, writing in late 1914, found the Dutch hopeful that the war would pass them by without too much adverse effect:

'To keep our army mobilised, our whole community going,' writes a Dutch journalist, 'we want supplies and we want trade.' 'England,' says another writer, 'cannot wish to starve us, or to starve our cattle, which produces any amount of butter and cheese for the English market. We are now eating "war bread".' It is, we know very well, not at all the intention of Great Britain to interfere with the food supplies of a friendly nation which needs to import a third of its wheat. This is now understood in Holland. Indeed, [Britain's] action has been described by an eminent Dutchman as 'very liberal.'[5]

However, the Dutch had also to look towards Germany, their powerful neighbour. Another British observer wrote:

If Holland is 'the most neutral of neutral States', it does not mean that the war is not felt financially in the country. In Amsterdam a member of the Chamber of Commerce told me that Holland's trade since the war began has been reduced gradually by more than 65 per cent., and that this figure is continually mounting higher. Moreover, the refugees from Belgium who have found asylum in the western provinces cost the nation a fair amount of money, not to consider the expense of the fully-mobilised army's upkeep and the high prices paid for the hurried fortification works carried out since the beginning of the war. 'Dutch people are said to have made a good deal of money out of Germany, up to December or even later, by selling her food-stuffs and other articles at very high prices,' I remarked, remembering what I had heard both in England and Germany. 'Somebody certainly has,' admitted the Dutchman. 'Since August, 1914, our Government has stopped the exportation of wheat, etc., but some German private agents used to buy it and send it to private addresses in Germany; we really don't know what happened to that stuff, and as the prices offered by the Germans were very good, I know that a lot of merchants here were only too glad to make business with them. Now the new customs regulations have completely stopped this, and I can tell you that lately Germany has not managed to get anything through the frontiers.'[6]

As the war progressed, the Dutch government tried to diversify the eating habits of the people, in an effort to lessen the impact of food shortages. An official report noted:

Only a small quantity of certain kinds of fish is consumed in The Netherlands, where so far fish cannot be called a 'national dish'.

Dutch women at work in the fields, 1914. (Stadsarchief Amsterdam)

The war, however, has caused a rise in the price of meat, and so the 'Central Bureau for the sale of fish', called into being by the abnormal state of affairs, is trying to meet the exigency by introducing fish as a cheap food for the people. In 1915 the municipalities of numerous towns established markets or shops for the sale of fish.[7]

In tandem with this, the Dutch government also tried to develop Holland's fishing industry, which at the outset of the war was small, though as time went on the increasing danger to be found from mines in the North Sea would mitigate against major expansion. As previously noted, a feature of the Allied blockade system was the rationing of the border neutrals. In implementing this policy, the Allied governments concluded many treaties with trade associations in Holland. By these agreements the Allies permitted restricted amounts of imports into Holland, subject to the guarantee of home consumption. The first of a series of these arrangements was the general agreement concluded on 20 July 1915, between the British government and the Dutch. Various special agreements were entered into with respect to particular commodities such as metals, rice, tyres, jute, tinplate and hides. By the agricultural agreement of November 1916, between the British and General Trading Association and the Dutch Agricultural Export Bureau, strict limitations were placed upon the exportation of foodstuffs from Holland to the Central Powers. However, Holland was dependent upon Germany as well, and in exchange for such essential imports as coal, iron, and potash, the German government demanded a large part of the Dutch surplus of agricultural produce. The American journalist George Schreiner travelled through Europe, including Holland, in 1915 and wrote subsequently:

[The Dutch] government had reduced the export of food to Germany to a veritable minimum even then, as I learned on a trip to The Hague in December. That was well enough, but not without consequences. Holland has in Limburg a single mine of lignite coal. The output is small and suited for little more than gas production. But the country had to get coal from somewhere, if her railroads were to run, the wheels of industry to turn; if the ships were to steam and the cities to be lighted and heated. Much of the coal consumed in Holland in the past had been imported from Belgium. But that country was in the hands of the Germans. The British government had made the taking of bunker coal contingent upon conditions which the Dutch government thought unreasonable. The Dutch were between the devil and the deep blue sea. Coal they had to get, and Germany was the only country willing to supply that coal – provided there was a 'quid pro quo' in kind. There was nothing to do but accept the terms of the Germans, which were coal for food. The bartering which had preceded the making of these arrangements had been very close and stubborn. The Dutch government did not want to offend the British government. It could not afford, on the other hand, to earn the ill-will of the Germans. I had occasion to occupy myself with the case, and when my inquiry had been completed I had gained the impression that the German government had left nothing undone to get from the Dutch all the food that could be had.[8]

After the entrance of the United States into the war, the Allies demanded that Holland should drastically reduce these exports to Germany. Holland's refusal to accede to these demands was met by the General Embargo on trade, and finally by the requisitioning of Dutch vessels in American and British ports. Holland's transit traffic, an important national industry, was now brought to a standstill. Dutch exports from Holland to Germany were cut to less than a seventh of the annual pre-war average, and the same was true of the export of herrings. The export of cattle to Germany had ceased

In an effort to prevent attack by U-boats, a Dutch merchant ship proclaims her neutral status in large letters. However, as the war went on, the Dutch faced greater harassment at sea from the British and American navies. (Library of Congress: Bain collection)

completely by 1917. In the case of thirty-eight out of forty-four leading commodities, or groups of commodities, the imports had fallen in 1918 to less than the average annual net imports during the three years from 1911 to 1913. Practically no grain was imported into Holland during 1918, and the country was compelled to ration its food supply almost as rigorously as any of the belligerent countries. A Dutch street rhyme ran:

> Everything on the ticket:
> A voucher for tea, a ticket for coffee,
> A voucher for buttermilk porridge,
> A voucher for fat, a voucher for flour,
> A receipt for every bite,
> Also a voucher for a sweet little baby,
> That the Stork has to offer,
> But if you can give him no voucher,
> You will not get love.
>
> A voucher for soap,
> A voucher for onions,
> Potatoes and fresh fish,
> Coal and brown beans,
> If they are in stock . . .
> Soon you'll get coupons,
> for cigarettes and for beer.
> And you'll soon need a voucher,
> for the girls of pleasure.

This street song was an ironic take on the major problems that the scarcity of basic necessities caused, especially in the last years of the war. Though it raged beyond Holland's borders, it created increasing problems within them, which made it necessary for the Dutch government to intervene in the daily life of the citizen. During the war the central government together with the local authorities ran a large number of institutions dealing with the crisis. The national industries which depended upon foreign raw materials suffered severely, in many cases shutting down completely and causing much unemployment. The distressing conditions forced numerous new duties upon the Dutch government. Before the war was over it had assumed the functions of importer and miller of wheat, and retailer of breadstuffs, of ration-master of nearly all necessaries of life, of arbiter in the fixing of rents and of maximum prices for such commodities as were not placed on the distribution list, of underwriter of insurance against unemployment and war risks at sea, of controller of national shipping with power to decide to which

A Dutch cartoon: 'How to order a serving of potatoes in Amsterdam in 1917.' (From *De Amsterdammer*)

port each ship should sail, and to requisition part of her tonnage on the home-bound voyage. That is not to say that the public institutions were the only players in this. Civil society and the private sector also played a prominent role during the war in relieving hardship, both at central and local levels, both independently and partly in co-ordination with the government, not least of these players were the churches. There was still however much civil unrest. In Amsterdam in 1916, women looted coal from barges, and in the summer of 1917 potato riots took place. In 1917 and 1918 there were regular disturbances in many municipalities. Demonstrations, hunger marches and processions were common expressions of public discontent. Also, in Utrecht in the summer of 1918, the potato shortage led to an incident in which a group of dissatisfied people arbitrarily grubbed up the potatoes being grown on a piece of arable land by the municipality.

Because of the scarcity of certain products, surrogates began to appear on the market such as imitation tea and coffee, and wooden shoes instead of leather. Newspapers carried 'alternative recipes' and tips on how to economise. An example of one, regarding careful husbanding of sugar was published in Rotterdam in August 1918; it advised readers that often unused sugar remained at the bottom of a cup of tea or coffee and was thus wasted. If on the other hand, sugar was placed in a strainer and tea or coffee poured through it, waste would be kept to a minimum. An American in England wrote in 1918:

I am getting very gloomy direct reports of the food situation in Holland. It is represented as terrible, owing to the shortage of American importations of wheat and flour. My correspondent writes: 'If Mr. Hoover could only come over to Holland he would read on the pale faces of the workmen and other inhabitants that they are all suffering from lack of food. It

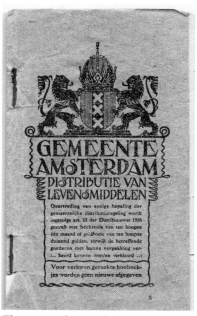

The cover of a Dutch ration book, issued by the city of Amsterdam, 1916. (Courtesy of Jori Wiegmans)

Dutch ration tickets. (Courtesy of Jori Wiegmans)

cannot possibly be the intention of the United States government to withhold from us the very necessities of life. If they only knew the situation!' Unfortunately, it is not within the power of Mr. Hoover to relieve this condition, nor can the United States take any chances of permitting cereals to enter Holland that may be re-exported to Germany, either as flour or its equivalent in meats, created by feeding American cereals to animals subsequently sold to the enemy. The question of transportation also enters into the problem of furnishing food to Holland. It is to be hoped, however, that the two governments will speedily arrive at some basis of understanding, satisfactory to both, whereby flour or wheat sufficient for the needs of the good people of Holland will be forthcoming. Common humanity should forbid that they be denied the necessaries of life as long as there is enough and to spare for the allies.[9]

In medical circles there were concerns about the impact that the shortages in Holland might have on human health. As early as 1915, the Central Health Council had suggested a special commission to study this subject. After the war, this committee issued a report entitled 'On the

Dutch soldiers guard a barge containing potatoes, after several such barges were looted by hungry women. (Stadsarchief Amsterdam)

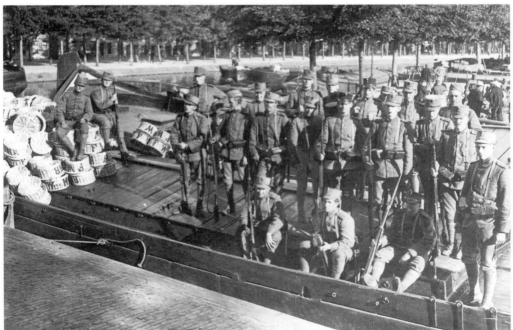

influence of the state of war on the health status of the Dutch People'. There was no universal agreement on whether malnutrition had existed in the country or not. There were even doctors who believed that the health situation was actually more favourable then than it was before the war, arguing that, '. . . in peacetime many in and outside of the working class had indulged in overfeeding, so the forced moderation in recent months was currently benefitting [their] health'.[10] However, there were clear signs at the end of the war, that had it continued for much longer then malnutrition would surely have been the inevitable consequence.

Highly-industrialised Switzerland was in a similar position to that of Holland, having belligerent nations on all sides. For the Swiss the war brought shortages of both food and commodities, and a slump in tourism, one of their country's major industries. Switzerland depended upon imports for 40 per cent of its food and energy supplies; through negotiations with the warring parties a minimum supply was ensured, and in 1915, the state introduced a grain monopoly for better coordination of supply. Charles H. Grasty, a journalist who visited the country in the middle part of the war, observed that conditions there were tolerable:

> In Switzerland oranges are plentiful from Italy, so one is not limited there, though the price is high. But of bacon I could have only three very small bits; of butter, three slivers, equal to about one ordinary piece; and of sugar, one piece broken in the middle to look like two. The bread allowance was equal to about two rolls. This is enough breakfast for anybody, and it was all anybody could get.[11]

From March 1917 to April 1920 rationing measures were in place within the country, but in spite of these measures, by 1918 Switzerland was experiencing a food emergency. The American diplomat Lee Meriwether was posted to Berne in August 1918 and noted that despite the fact that food shortages in Switzerland were becoming serious, conditions were still better than those in neighbouring Germany. Indeed, many Germans had gone there for a respite from their own food regime:

> . . . I came to Switzerland on a mission which has afforded an opportunity to see a lot of Germans at close range. The German Embassy in Berne has 700 attaches and in the Sweitzerhof Hotel, where I am writing these notes, are scores of Germans who, having enough money and enough political 'pull' to get them to Switzerland, have come here to buy a square meal and such few clothes as they are permitted to purchase. In comparison with Paris, food and clothing here are scarce and dear, but in comparison with

Germany both are plentiful and cheap, hence Germans flock to Berne to get at least temporary relief from the near-famine prevailing in their beleaguered land. I have seen here a dozen shop windows filled with bonbons and cakes over which is the announcement: 'Kucken sind verkaueflich ohne Karten' – Cakes are sold without cards – about the only thing one can buy without a card. Police permits are necessary for the purchase of shoes, clothing, etc., as well as food. Marie Antoinette has been derided for telling the French fish-wives to eat cake, if they could get no bread. She would not be mocked for making such a remark in Berne where cake is the one thing that is plentiful, and bread the one article of food hardest to find. The two exceedingly thin slices one is given at each of the three daily meals are not at all satisfying, and seem meager indeed in comparison with the generous portions one

Lee Meriwether, the American diplomat who observed social conditions in a number of European countries. (From Meriwether, *The War Diary of a Diplomat*)

gets in France; but the Germans at the tables about me appear more than satisfied – from which it would seem things in Germany are not so rosy as the Kaiser wants the world to believe.[12]

However, the situation in Switzerland deteriorated to such an extent that by the end of the war there were even riots there. Journalist Will Irwin was an eyewitness to one:

First came men and boys, roughly arranged four abreast. They were singing the International; and singing it, somehow, as though they meant business. At the head of each section floated the red flag of Socialism; here and there a particularly nasty-looking loaf of gray, hard war bread was carried aloft on a pole, by way of showing what it was all about. Behind the men straggled hundreds of women, some carrying empty market baskets, some dragging children. So far, though everything was grim and businesslike, there was perfect order. The policemen, strung along the pavement one or two to each block, regarded the affair languidly. I had half a notion to break my engagement and follow; but there seemed little possibility of interesting events.

By making this decision I missed a good deal of action. Fifteen minutes later, as the procession approached the Hotel de Ville, a tramcar drove across its path. Taking this as an affront, the crowd charged it, pulverized its windows with paving stones, damaged the conductor and the motorman, and resisted with stones and fists a charge of the police. I arrived on the scene of action in time to behold a street strewn with broken glass, and a crowd of people who looked as though they were suffering from emotional strain drifting backward before the steady pressure of the police . . . I could not help but sympathize with this demonstration; for the cost of living is ruinously high. It goes without saying that Switzerland has more food and better prospects of getting food in the future than Germany. But the prices of most commodities are higher here than across the Border. This is because the German Government has taken hold of the situation and enforced maximum prices for many standard commodities.[13]

Meanwhile, in the Iberian peninsula, bordering France but somewhat distanced from the Central Powers, lay Spain. Thanks to its declaration of neutrality when war broke out in 1914, the ensuing conflict produced significant economic development in that country. The belligerent countries needed food, weapons, uniforms, metal and coal, which Spain was able to supply. There was notable growth especially in the chemical industry, in the Catalan textile sector, the Asturian coal mining industry, the Basque iron

A scene during the general strike against food shortages, Zurich 1918. (Wikipedia Commons)

and steel industry and in agriculture with the production of cereals. Spanish industries also benefitted from the reduction in foreign competition. Shipbuilding grew, due to increased demand for the transportation of goods in Spanish ships under the protection of the flag of a neutral country. As consequence of all this, Spain's balance of payments improved significantly. Thanks to the war, the Spanish foreign debt was eliminated and gold was accumulated at the Bank of Spain, in Madrid. For the first time in its modern history, Spain was not in a trade deficit with regard to her commerce with the rest of the world.

Yet in comparison with the other major European countries, in many ways Spain remained locked in the Middle Ages. Even the capital, Madrid, could not be compared with London, Paris or Berlin. An American journalist, visiting Spain during the First World War, described scenes that he witnessed there in 1917, scarcely believing that he was in a major European city:

> The vegetables all come to the door on donkey-back. The huckster slings four or five wide panniers across his fireless steed, fills them to running over with lettuce, carrots, onions, and radishes, and seats himself cross-legged on top of the pile. The general effect is an inverted pyramid, the apex the little feet of the burro. So milk is delivered in two great egg-shaped cans, also on each side of the patient ass. The milkman, his measure slung across his back, sits just over the donkey's shoulders. Often the little dog that guards the milk while he is making the deliveries perches himself on the lid of one of the cans. Every day at sunset there move down the Prado – the Upper Fifth Avenue, the Euclid Avenue, the Van Ness Avenue, of Madrid – herds of goats, driven by a rough-looking herder or an old woman with a red handkerchief bound round her head. They pass from door to door; and the goats are milked to the proper measure in the presence of young mothers who are bringing up delicate children.[14]

The war favoured the industrial and commercial bourgeoisie and the landed oligarchy, because the escalating prices it produced were not accompanied by similar increases in wages for the labouring poor. Whilst the benefits to Spain nationally were dramatic, the war significantly decreased the standard of living of the working classes, primarily the urban industrial proletariat, which kept up more or less constant pressure for wage increases. In the countryside, the situation was different: the inflationary effect was greater, but the more direct availability of food softened its impact on the peasantry particularly in the case of small landowners and tenants (who predominated in the agrarian structure of northern Spain). In some cases they could even have benefited from the situation, being suppliers of food, but on the contrary the landless labourers, the bulk of the working population in the southern half of Spain (especially in Andalusia and Extremadura) had reaped no such benefit. Furthermore, rural Spain was in no measure able to intensify its farming to increase the yield from agricultural land to meet the demands of the war. A report published shortly after the Armistice stated:

> The true sources of [Spain's] wealth are its agriculture and pasture (industria agropecuaria). They are precisely those sources which have been the most neglected. Agriculture has suffered chiefly from systems of land tenure which have militated against good cultivation. Among them the most injurious have been the excessive sub-divisions of the soil, due to divisions, not of ownership of land, but of rights held under heritable or perpetuable leases. The cultivation of the land is left to men who are too poor, as well as too ignorant, to do it justice. Even where large estates (latifundia) are in the power of the owner, as in Andalusia, things are no better. The proprietor is an absentee who leaves the management to agents and middlemen. The land is worked by gangs brought from outside. In these conditions the agriculture of Spain is inevitably bad. Except near the French frontier, and in one belt of the Mediterranean coast, it is given up to antiquated routine. The total production is far below what it might be. Eleven bushels of wheat to the acre is the average, and the total output of the 4,000,000 hectares devoted to foodstuffs is not sufficient to feed the population; the 31,000,000 quintals grown in a good year fall about 2,000,000 short of what is needed. Where little is produced by hard labour with poor instruments, the poverty must needs be great . . . The conditions are worst in the south of Spain, and, perhaps, worst of all in the province of Jaen. The labourers (braceros) are huddled in squalid outhouses, are paid very ill (about 1s. 3d. a day), and are fed on inferior bread mixed in salads with vinegar, a little oil, and vegetables. Agrarian outrage is naturally more common here than elsewhere; it was in Andalusia that the outbreak of Agrarian Socialism, known as the 'Black Hand', took place.[15]

The effects of this process of rising prices and static wages (particularly rural wages) were sharply visible by 1917, with a significant redistribution of national income (both between social classes and between territories), with progressive worsening of the rural exodus to the towns, and tension

Crowds overturn a bus in Barcelona, during the Spanish general strike of 1917.
(Ollaparo.com)

between industry and agriculture. Furthermore, from 1917 onwards Spain entered a period of turmoil, due to the deficiencies caused by the war. Exports generated food scarcity inside the country, and domestic prices raced ahead of wages. The shortage of food was a fundamental cause of the Spanish Crisis of 1917, a constitutional emergency in which a growing socialist movement was met by a body within the army which forced the resignation of the liberal prime minister, and his replacement by a more hard-line candidate. The result was a general strike, which was mostly organised by socialists, but with notable anarchist activity, particularly in Barcelona, where barricades were built, and strikers tried to stop trams from running. The government responded by using machine guns in the streets, and the fighting left seventy people dead. In spite of the violence of the government response, the striker's demands were moderate, and not untypical of a socialist strike of this time. Popular protest had been crushed by military force, but the ensuing political standoff was resolved only when a government of national unity was formed with the brokerage of the King of Spain.

The report quoted above went on to observe that during the crisis, the only reason for which Spain had avoided a dislocation on the scale of that seen in Russia, was that her communications and infrastructure were so primitive that disaffected peasants remained isolated in their rural communities, and were unable to act in unison. One might go further, and argue that the circumstances in which Spain found itself in 1917 were in fact the precursors for the Spanish Civil War of 1936, in which once again a reformist and left-leaning government was crushed by conservatives within the armed forces.

Despite their geographical differences, from sunny Spain to cold and wet Norway, the neutral countries in Europe all found it difficult to stay entirely out of the First World War, in spite of their non-combatant status. In all of them, to a greater or lesser extent, external pressures translated into internal ones. Food shortages or rising food prices were common factors, touching off popular protest and disturbances from Berne to Madrid. Holland was perhaps hardest-hit of all the neutrals, but managed to contain public unrest successfully. In Spain by contrast the pressure of the war opened up deep divisions in society, which would take many decades to resolve. However, perhaps only in Norway can it be said that the lingering shadow of the restrictions of First World War may still be observed, in that country's strict controls on alcohol.

King Alphonso XIII of Spain, who brokered the government of national unity following the Spanish Crisis of 1917. (Library of Congress)

Epilogue

The world's first global conflict was one in which not just armies, but entire economies – indeed entire populations – were pitted against one another. In order to wage war on this scale, the whole of society in the various combatant nations would need to swing behind the war effort in that country. Indeed, perhaps for the first time, food was to become a weapon of war, as food supply could have a critical influence over the effectiveness of individual soldiers or indeed the performance of whole armies, as Chapters 1 and 2 of this book explore.

In part, this book has sought to chart the differing approaches taken by a variety of countries, combatant or neutral, Allied and Central Powers, towards the problem of food supply created by the First World War. What strikes the observer most is perhaps how different the various approaches were. Germany's efforts, in spite of her rigidly structured society and her attempts to impose food controls from the earliest days of the war, were among the least effective. Britain by contrast, although slow to introduce food control initially, became one of the most effective nations in husbanding her resources. The French paid only lip-service to food control and never approached it in any serious way, yet were able to avoid many of the hardships and internal disruption experienced by other nations. Perhaps most to be pitied are the people of the neutral countries, caught as they were in a vice between the two warring coalitions. It is hardly surprising that frustrations boiled over into disturbances, among peoples as normally placid as the Dutch and Swiss.

The central thesis of this book is that the Allies won the First World War chiefly because they were better able to organise their food supply than were the Central Powers. It is no coincidence that the only Allied country to completely collapse during the war – Russia – was the one which was most disorganised in terms of her food supplies, and the one which most resembled the Central Powers in this respect.

Notes

Chapter 1

1. Stewart, *From Mons to Loos*, p. 25.
2. *London Gazette*, 5 August 1915.
3. Liddle Collection, University of Leeds, John Trusty, tape-recorded recollections.
4. Bolwell, *With a Reservist in France*, p. 27.
5. Storch, *Vom feldgrauen Buchhändler*, p. 39.
6. Quoted in Manz, *Von Flandern bis Polen*, p. 184.
7. Dupont, *In the Field, 1914-1915*, p. 102.
8. Höcker, *An der Spitze meiner Kompagnie*, p. 211.
9. Cornet-Auquier, *Soldier Unafraid*, p. 10.
10. Longley, *Battery Flashes*, p. 94.
11. Roujon, *Battles & Bivouacs*, p. 159.
12. Morgan, *Leaves From a Field Note-book*, p. 28.
13. Beatson, *The Motor-bus in War*, p. 50.
14. Ibid, p. 52.
15. *Oxbow Herald* (Saskatchewan), 17 February 1916.
16. Doudney, *Best of Good Fellows*, p. 149.
17. Hall, *Kitchener's Mob*, p. 85.
18. McClintock, *Best O'Luck*, p. 54.
19. Empey, *Over the Top*, p. 51.
20. Fred Smith, tape-recorded interview 1989, author's collection.
21. Jack Horner, typescript memoirs, author's collection.
22. Fox, *Behind the Scenes in Warring Germany*, p. 114.
23. Empey, *Over the Top*, p. 51.
24. Waddington, *My War Diary*, p. 348.
25. Holmes, *A Yankee in the Trenches*, p. 52.
26. Empey, *Over the Top*, p. 298.
27. Wells, *From Montreal to Vimy Ridge and Beyond*, p. 258.
28. Holmes, *A Yankee in the Trenches*, p. 56.
29. Knapp, *Cocoa and Chocolate*, p. 174.
30. Ettighoffer, *'Wo bist du, kamerad?'*, p. 216.
31. Richards, *Old Soldiers Never Die*, p. 130.
32. Meriwether, *The War Diary of a Diplomat*, p. 95.
33. Clarke, *My Round of the War*, p. 211.
34. Richards, *Old Soldiers Never Die*, p. 165.
35. Ibid, p. 167.
36. Lafond, *Covered with Mud and Glory*, p. 126.
37. Gu, *Ou zhan gong zuo hui yi lu*, p. 25.
38. Trueblood, *In the Flash Ranging Service*, p. 3.
39. Ibid, p. 4.
40. De Varila, *The First Shot For Liberty*, p. 61.
41. Ibid, p. 113.
42. Typescript diary of William Scroby, courtesy of Ray Scroby.
43. Crowell, *America's Munitions 1917-1918*, p. 45.
44. Katharine Duncan Morse, *The Uncensored Letters of a Canteen Girl*, p. 128.
45. Hoffman, *I Remember The Last War*, p. 183.
46. Ibid.

Chapter 2
1. Palmer, *Letters from Mesopotamia in 1915 and January, 1916*, p. 48.
2. Ibid.
3. Mousley, *The Secrets of a Kuttite*, p. 53.
4. Ibid, p. 68.
5. Ibid, p. 73.
6. Ibid, p. 86.
7. Ibid, p. 103.
8. Ibid, p. 123.
9. Ibid, p. 124.
10. Ibid, p. 125.
11. Murray, *Gallipoli As I Saw It*, p. 92.
12. Ibid, p. 93.
13. Sparrow and Macbean Ross, *On Four Fronts With the Royal Naval Division*, p. 78.
14. Murray, *Gallipoli As I Saw It*, p. 94.
15. Vassal, *Uncensored Letters from the Dardanelles*, p. 79.
16. Ibid, p. 88.
17. Liddle Collection, University of Leeds. C. J. Walsh, diary 14 December 1915.
18. C. J. Walsh diary 15 December 1915.
19. Crawshay-Williams, *Leaves from an Officer's Notebook*, p. 136.
20. Patterson, *With the Judæans in the Palestine Campaign*, p. 63.
21. Aaronsohn, *With the Turks in Palestine*, p. 13.
22. Kemal Pasha, *Memories of a Turkish Statesman*, p. 149.
23. Vassal, *Uncensored Letters from the Dardanelles*, p. 255.
24. Rattray, *Further Recollections of 107 Field Company*, p. 34.
25. Lake, *Campaigning in the Balkans*, p. 147.
26. Ibid, p. 116.
27. 'Nutrition-related problems in the Serbian Army on the Salonika Front', *Vojnosanitetski Pregled*, Strana 74, Volumen 65, Supplement, November 2008, p. 70.
28. Ibid.
29. Von Lettow-Vorbeck, *My Reminiscences of East Africa*, p. 66.
30. Ibid, p. 160.
31. Ibid, p. 261.
32. Young, *Marching on Tanga*, p. 124.
33. Ibid, p. 195.
34. Downes, *With the Nigerians in German East Africa*, p. 90.
35. Ibid, p. 90.

Chapter 3
1. McCormick, *With the Russian Army*, p. 164.
2. Lobanov-Rostovsky, *The Grinding Mill*, p. 9.
3. John Morse, *An Englishman in the Russian Ranks*, p. 84.
4. Iogolevitch, *The Young Russian Corporal*, p. 22.
5. John Morse, *An Englishman in the Russian Ranks*, p. 105.
6. Ibid, p. 106.
7. Turczynowicz, *When the Prussians came to Poland*, p. 129.
8. Ibid, p. 145.
9. Ibid, p. 152.
10. Lobanov-Rostovsky, *The Grinding Mill*, p. 79.
11. Kournakoff, *Savage Squadrons*, p. 267.
12. Stenbock-Fermor, *Memoirs of Life in Old Russia*, p. 166.

13. Liddell, *Actions and Reactions in Russia*, p. 79.
14. Ibid, p. 182.
15. Hindus, *The Russian Peasant and the Revolution*, p. 15.
16. Pierce, *Trapped in 'Black Russia'*, p. 8.
17. Poole, *'The Dark People'*, p. 114.
18. Graham, *Russia in 1916*, p. 40.
19. Gordon, *Russian Prohibition*, p. 34.
20. *Vestnik Finansov*, No. 27, 1918.
21. Graham, *Russia in 1916*, p. 43.
22. Yarkovsky, *It Happened in Moscow*, p. 70.
23. Ibid, p. 83.
24. Ibid, p. 84.
25. Iogolevitch, *The Young Russian Corporal*, p. 253.
26. Stenbock-Fermor, *Memoirs of Life in Old Russia*, p. 159.
27. Poole, *'The Dark People'*, p. 162.

Chapter 4
1. Salter, *Allied Shipping Control*, p. 1.
2. Beveridge, *What is Back of the War*, p. 335.
3. *Isle of Man Examiner*, 21 August 1915.
4. *Leicester Mail,* 7 January 1915.
5. Jones, *London in War Time*, p. 3.
6. Ibid, p. 8.
7. Ibid, p. 91.
8. Foley, *A Bolton Childhood*, p. 78.
9. O'Brien, *Food Preparedness for the United States*, p. 62.
10. *Mona's Herald*, 14 March 1917.
11. Knapp, *Cocoa and Chocolate*, p. 157.
12. Ibid, p. 161.
13. Ministry of Food, *The Win-The-War Cookery Book*, frontispiece.
14. Ibid, p. 2.
15. Ward, *Towards the Goal*, p. 223.
16. Manx National Heritage, Patrick Cadogan letter, MS 06573/2.
17. *Isle of Man Family History Society Journal*, May 1997.
18. Burnett-Smith, *An Englishwoman's Home*, p. 146.
19. Ibid.
20. Ibid, p. 148.
21. Ibid, p. 151.
22. *Leicester Daily Mercury*, 5 February 1918.
23. East Midlands Oral History Archive LO/069/020B Winnifred Taylor.
24. Extract from unpublished notes on her family and early life by Margaret 'Margot' Elaine Cliff (1911–94) – Gillian Lighton family papers.
25. *Leicester Daily Mercury*, 4 February 1918.
26. Modern Records Centre, University of Warwick, *Annual Report of the Workers' Union 1918*. MSS.126/WU/4/1/13, p. 23.
27. Edgar, *England During the Last Four Months of the War*, p. 51.
28. Ibid, p. 22.
29. Ibid, p. 51.

Chapter 5
1. Littlefair, *An English Girl's Adventures in Hostile Germany*, p. 57.
2. Emmel, *Die massenspeisungen im weltkrieg*, p. 32.
3. Beveridge, *What is Back of the War*, p. 150.

4. Gerard, *My Four Years in Germany*, p. 291.
5. Ibid, p. 295.
6. Ibid, p. 297.
7. Report of 17 February 1915, quoted in Davis, *Home Fires Burning*, p. 1.
8. Bullitt, *An Uncensored Diary from the Central Empires*, p. 14.
9. McAuley, *Germany in War Time*, p. 58.
10. Blücher, *An English Wife in Berlin*, p. 77.
11. Ernest H. Starling, 'The Food Supply of Germany During the War', *Journal of the Royal Statistical Society* (1920) 83#2, pp. 225–54.
12. Curtin, *The Land of Deepening Shadow*, p. 140.
13. Blücher, *An English Wife in Berlin,* p. 122.
14. Hereward Thimbleby Price, *Boche and Bolshevik*, p. 49.
15. Beveridge, *What is Back of the War*, p. 90.
16. Doty, *Short Rations*, p. 122.
17. Ibid, p. 141.
18. Gerard, *My Four Years in Germany*, p. 297.
19. Curtin, *The Land of Deepening Shadow,* p. 144.
20. Blücher, *An English Wife in Berlin*, p. 127.
21. Ibid, p. 135.
22. Ibid, p. 143.
23. Bullitt, *An Uncensored Diary from the Central Empires*, p. 47.
24. Blücher, *An English Wife in Berlin*, p. 152.
25. Therese, *With Old Glory in Berlin*, p. 98.
26. Ibid, p. 99.
27. Curtin, *The Land of Deepening Shadow,* p. 156.
28. McAuley, *Germany in War Time*, p. 64.
29. Ibid, p. 59.
30. Blücher, *An English Wife in Berlin*, p. 163.
31. Schreiner, *The Iron Ration*, p. 136.
32. Blücher, *An English Wife in Berlin*, p. 176.
33. Curtin, *The Land of Deepening Shadow*, p. 292.
34. Hammerton, *I Was There!*, p. 1748.
35. Ibid, p. 1747.
36. Blücher, *An English Wife in Berlin*, p. 205.
37. Ibid, p. 225.
38. Ibid, p. 224.
39. Ibid, p. 231.
40. Ibid, p. 239.
41. Ludendorff, *My War Memories Vol I*, p. 349.
42. Blücher, *An English Wife in Berlin*, p. 292.
43. Gardiner, *What I Saw in Germany*, p. 39.

Chapter 6
1. United States War Labor Policies Board, *Report on Labor Situation of Italy*, p. 15.
2. Ibid, p. 16.
3. Truitt, *Wartime Letters from Italy*, p. 40.
4. Ibid, p. 49.
5. Report from the Ufficio Vigilanza Igienco-Sanitaria, quoted in Cecil and Liddle, *Facing Armageddon*, p. 581.
6. Quoted in Cecil and Liddle, *Facing Armageddon*, p. 583.
7. Gómez de Baquero, *Soldados y Paisajes de Italia*, p. 141.
8. Julius M. Price *Six Months on the Italian Front*, p. 123.
9. Ibid.

10. Liddle Collection, University of Leeds. Charles Carrington papers.
11. Dalton, *With British Guns in Italy*, p. 31.
12. Ibid, p. 193.
13. Quoted in Cecil and Liddle, *Facing Armageddon*, p. 583.
14. Collins, *My Italian Year*, p. 48.
15. Meriwether, *The War Diary of a Diplomat*, p. 195.
16. Irwin, *A Reporter at Armageddon*, p. 281.
17. Bakewell, *The Story of the American Red Cross in Italy*, p. 47.
18. Ibid, p. 73.
19. Coffee, *The Cooperative Movement in Jugoslavia, Rumania and North Italy*, p. 76.
20. Collins, *My Italian Year*, p. 148.
21. Press Office of the Italian Bureau of Public Information in the United States, *Italy Today*, New York, 1918, p. 27.
22. Gibbons, *Paris Reborn*, p. 42.
23. Waddington, *My War Diary*, p. 40.
24. Ibid, p. 73.
25. Hopkins, *Over the Threshold of War*, p. 314.
26. Gibbons, *Paris Reborn*, p. 212.
27. Hopkins, *Over the Threshold of War*, p. 323.
28. Gibbons, *Paris Reborn*, p. 291.
29. Waddington, *My War Diary*, p. 196 .
30. Rimbaud, *In the Whirlpool of War*, p. 166.
31. Sutton-Pickhard, *France in Wartime*, p. 31.
32. Guard, *The Spirit of Italy*, p. 220.
33. Waddington, *My War Diary*, p. 235.
34. Meriwether, *The War Diary of a Diplomat*, p. 82.
35. Gibbs, *The Soul of the War*, p. 242.
36. Doty, *Behind the Battle Line*, p. 162.
37. Adam, *Paris Sees It Through*, p. 109.
38. Putnam, *On Duty and Off*, p. 34.
39. Gregg, *Three Months in France*, p. 8.
40. Ibid, p. 30.
41. Meriwether, *The War Diary of a Diplomat*, p. 263.

Chapter 7
1. Schreiner, *The Iron Ration*, p. 41.
2. Ibid, p. 46.
3. Kitchen, *After Dark in the War Capitals*, p. 34.
4. Heylis, *My Secret Service*, p. 35.
5. Schreiner, *The Iron Ration*, p. 60.
6. McAuley, *Germany in War Time*, p. 256.
7. Schreiner, *The Iron Ration*, p. 65.
8. Ibid, p. 104.
9. Ibid, p. 152.
10. Ibid, p. 216.
11. Ibid, p. 329.
12. Heylis, *My Secret Service*, p. 85.
13. Schreiner, *The Iron Ration*, p. 53.
14. Stuermer, *Two War Years in Constantinople*, p. 113.
15. Aaronsohn, *With the Turks in Palestine* p. 46.
16. Ibid, p. 62.
17. Benson, *Deutschland über Allah*, p. 18.

Chapter 8
1. *New York Times*, 23 February 1917.
2. Ibid.
3. Bodmer, *What Are You Doing To Help?*, p. 16.
4. Guerrier, *We Pledged Allegiance*, p. 69.
5. O'Brien, *Food Preparedness for the United States*, p. 45.
6. Ibid, p. 53.
7. Kelsey, *Mobilizing America's Resources for the War*, p. 156.
8. *Washington Post*, 31 May 1918.
9. Winter, *What Price Tolerance*, p. 261.

Chapter 9
1. Doty, *Behind the Battle Line*, p. 139.
2. Ibid, p. 151.
3. Ibid, p. 152.
4. Therese, *With Old Glory in Berlin*, p. 274.
5. Robertson Scott, *War Time & Peace in Holland*, p. xxii.
6. Piermarini, *What I Saw in Berlin and Other European Capitals London 1915*, p. 247.
7. Netherlands Ministry of Agriculture, Industry and Commerce, *A General View of the Netherlands* no.7-15, Leiden, 1915, p. 25.
8. Schreiner, *The Iron Ration*, p. 48.
9. Edgar, *England During the Last Four Months of the War*, p. 52.
10. http://www.wereldoorlog1418.nl/lokale-noden/
11. Grasty, *Flashes From the Front*, p. 221.
12. Meriwether, *The War Diary of a Diplomat*, p. 299.
13. Irwin, *A Reporter at Armageddon*, p. 220.
14. Ibid, p. 29.
15. Foreign Office Historical Section, *Spain,* London, 1920, p. 43.

Bibliography

Aaronsohn, Alexander, *With the Turks in Palestine*, Boston, 1916.

Adam, H. Pearl, *Paris Sees It Through – A Diary 1914-1919*, London, 1919.

Anon, *What Italy Has Done For the War*, sl, 1918.

Bakewell, Charles Montague, *The Story of the American Red Cross in Italy*, New York, 1920.

Beatson, A. M., *The Motor-Bus in War; Being the Impressions of an A. S. C. Officer During Two and a Half Years at the Front*, London, 1918.

Benson, E. F., *Deutschland über Allah*, London, 1917.

Beveridge, Albert J., *What is Back of the War*, Indianapolis, [c1915].

Blücher, Princess Evelyn, *An English Wife in Berlin*, New York, 1920.

Bodmer, Rudolph John, *What Are You Doing To Help?*, Washington DC, sd.

Bolwell, Frederick, *With a Reservist in France*, New York, 1917.

Bullitt, Ernesta Drinker, *An Uncensored Diary from the Central Empires*, Garden City, NY, 1917.

Burnett-Smith, Mrs A. [Pseud. Annie S. Swann], *An Englishwoman's Home*, New York, 1918.

Butcher, Gerald W., *Allotments For All; the Story of a Great Movement*, London, 1918.

Cecil, Hugh, and Liddle, Peter H., *Facing Armageddon*, Barnsley, 1996.

Clarke, Basil, *My Round of the War*, London, 1917.

Coffee, Diarmid, *The Cooperative Movement in Jugoslavia, Rumania and North Italy During and After the World War*, New York, 1922.

Collins, Joseph, *My Italian Year; Observations and Reflections in Italy During the Last Year of the War*, New York, 1919.

Cornet-Auquier, André, *A Soldier Unafraid, Letters From the Trenches on the Alsatian Front*, Boston, 1918.

Cotillo, Salvatore Albert, *Italy during the World War*, Boston, 1922.

Crawshay-Williams, Eliot, *Leaves from an Officer's Notebook*, London, 1918.

Crowell, Benedict, *America's Munitions 1917-1918*, Washington DC, 1919.

Curtin, Daniel Thomas, *The Land of Deepening Shadow; Germany-at-War*, New York, 1917.

Dalton, Hugh, *With British Guns in Italy, a Tribute to Italian Achievement*, London, 1919.

Davis, Belinda J., *Home Fires Burning: Food, Politics, and Everyday Life in World War I Berlin*, Chapel Hill, NC, 2000.

De Varila, Osborne, *The First Shot For Liberty*, Philadelphia & Chicago, 1918.

Doudney, Charles Edmund, *Best of Good Fellows: Diaries and Memoirs of the Rev. Charles Edmund Doudney, M.A., C.F.(1871-1915)* , sl, 1995.

Doty, Madeleine Zabriskie, *Short Rations: An American Woman in Germany 1915 . . . 1916*, New York, 1917.

_____, *Behind the Battle Line*, New York, 1918.

Downes, Walter Douglas, *With the Nigerians in German East Africa*, London, 1919.

Dupont, Marcel, *In the Field 1914-1915: the Impressions of an Officer of Light Cavalry*, London, 1916.

Edgar, William C., *England During the Last Four Months of the War*, Minneapolis, 1919.

Emmel, Johanna, *Die Massenspeisungen im Weltkrieg*, Apolda, 1919.

Empey, Arthur Guy, *Over the Top*, New York, 1917.

Ettighoffer, P. C., *'Wo bist du, kamerad?' Fronterlebnisse unbekannter soldaten*, Essen 1942.

Fischer, Eugen [und] Bloch, Walther, *Die Ursachen des Deutschen Zusammenbruches im Jahre 1918. Im Auftrage des 4. Unterausschusses unter Mitwirkung*, Berlin, 1928.

Foreign Office Historical Section, *Spain*, London, 1920.

Foley, Alice, *A Bolton Childhood*, Manchester, 1973.

Fox, Edward Lyell, *Behind the Scenes in Warring Germany*, New York, 1915.

Fried, Alfred H., *Mein Kriegs-Tagebuch*, Zurich, 1918.

Gardiner, A. G., *What I saw in Germany: Letters from Germany and Austria*, London, [1920?].

Gerard, James W., *My Four Years in Germany*, London, 1917.

Gibbons, Herbert Adams, *Paris Reborn: a Study in Civic Psychology*, New York, 1916.

Gibbs, Philip, *The Soul of the War*, New York, 1915.

Gómez de Baquero, Eduardo, *Soldados y Paisajes de Italia*, Madrid, 1918.

Gordon, Ernest, *Russian Prohibition*, Westerville, OH, 1916.

Graham, Stephen, *Russia in 1916*, New York, 1917.

Gramberg, Eugen, *Pilze der Heimat; eine Auswahl der Verbreitesten, Essbaren, Ungeniessbaren und Giftigen Pilze Unserer Wälder und Fluren in Bild und Wort*, Leipzig, 1921.

Grasty, Charles, *Flashes From the Front*, New York, 1918.

Gregg, William C., *Three Months in France*, New York, 1919.

Gu, Xingqing, *Ou zhan gong zuo hui yi lu*, Changsha, 1938.

Guard, William J., *The Spirit of Italy*, New York, 1916.

Guerrier, Edith, *We Pledged Allegiance*, Stanford, CA, 1941.

Hainlen, Luise, *Schwäbisches Kriegskochbuch, Stuttgart, 1916*

Hall, James N., *Kitchener's Mob, the Adventures of an American in the British Army*, Boston, 1916.

Hammerton, Sir John, *I Was There!*, London, sd.

Hélys, Marc, *My Secret Service*, London, 1916.

Hindus, Maurice G., *The Russian Peasant and the Revolution*, New York, 1920.

Höcker, Paul Oskar, *An der Spitze meiner Kompagnie*, Berlin, 1915.

Hoffman, Bob, *I Remember The Last War*, York, PA, 1940.

Holmes, Robert Derby, *A Yankee in the Trenches*, Boston, 1918.

Hopkins, Nevil Monroe, *Over the Threshold of War; Personal Experiences of the Great European Conflict*, Philadelphia and London, 1918.

Iogolevitch, Paul, *The Young Russian Corporal*, New York, 1919.

Irwin, Will, *A Reporter at Armageddon; Letters From the Front*, New York, 1918.

Jarves, Elsie Deming, *War Days in Brittany*, Detroit, 1920.

Jones, C. Sheridan, *London in War Time*, London, 1917.

Kelsey, Carl, *Mobilizing America's Resources for the War*, sl, 1918.

Kemal Pasha, *Memories of a Turkish Statesman 1913-1919*, New York, 1922.

Kitchen, Karl, *After Dark in the War Capitals*, New York, sd, [c1916].

Knapp, Arthur W., *Cocoa and Chocolate, their History from Plantation to Consumer*, London, 1920.

Kournakoff, Sergei, *Savage Squadrons*, Boston, sd [c1935].

Krebs, Engelbert, *Der Ruhige Gott: Vierte Reihe der Gedanken über den Grossen Krieg*, Freiburg im Breisgau, 1917.

Lafond, Georges, *Covered with Mud and Glory*, Boston, 1918.

Lake, Harold, *Campaigning in the Balkans*, New York, 1918.
Liddell, R. Scotland, *Actions and Reactions in Russia*, London, 1917.
Littlefair, Mary, *An English Girl's Adventures in Hostile Germany*, London, 1915.
Lobanov-Rostovsky, Andrei, *The Grinding Mill; Reminiscences of War and Revolution in Russia, 1913-1920*, New York, 1935.
Longley, Cecil W., *Battery Flashes, by 'Wagger'*, New York, 1916.
Ludendorff, Erich, *My War Memories Vol I*, London, 1919.
Lynch, Reah Jeannette, *'Win the War' Cook Book*, St Louis, MO, 1918.
McAuley, Mary Ethel, *Germany in War Time; What an American Girl Saw and Heard*, Chicago, 1917.
McClintock, Alexander, *Best O' Luck; How a Fighting Kentuckian Won the Thanks of Britain's King*, New York, 1917.
McCormick, Robert Rutherford, *With the Russian Army*, New York, 1915.
Macnaughtan, S., *My War Experiences in Two Continents*, London, 1919.
Manz, Gustav (ed.), *Von Flandern bis Polen; Feldpostbriefe der Täglichen Rundschau aus dem Weltkriege*, Berlin, 1915.
Meriwether, Lee, *The War Diary of a Diplomat*, New York, sd [c1919].
Ministry of Food, *The Win-The-War Cookery Book*, London, 1917.
Morgan, John Hartman, *Leaves From a Field Note-book*, London, 1916.
Morse, John, *An Englishman in the Russian Ranks*, London, 1915.
Morse, Katharine Duncan, *The Uncensored Letters of a Canteen Girl*, New York, 1920
Mousley, Edward Opotiki, *The Secrets of a Kuttite*, London, 1922.
https://www.archive.orgMurray, Joseph, *Gallipoli As I Saw It*, London, 1965.
Norris, Armine, *Mainly for Mother*, Toronto, sd [1920?].
O'Brien, Charles William, *Food Preparedness for the United States*, Boston, 1917.
Olson, Mancur, *The Economics of the Wartime Shortage, a History of British Food Supplies in the Napoleonic War and in World Wars I and II*, Durham, NC, 1963.
Palmer, Robert, *Letters from Mesopotamia in 1915 and January, 1916* sl, sd (1916?) [private pub.].
Pankhurst, E. Sylvia, *The Home Front; a Mirror to Life in England During the World War*, London, 1932.
Patterson, J. H., *With the Judæans in the Palestine Campaign*, London, 1922.
Pierce, Ruth, *Trapped in 'Black Russia': letters, June-November, 1915*, Boston, 1918.
Piermarini [pseud.], *What I Saw in Berlin and Other European Capitals*, London, 1915.
Poole, Ernest, *'The Dark People': Russia's Crisis*, New York, 1918.
Press Office of the Italian Bureau of Public Information in the United States, *Italy Today*, New York, 1918.
Price, Julius M., *Six Months on the Italian Front*, New York, 1917.
Price, Hereward Thimbleby, *Boche and Bolshevik: Experiences of an Englishman in the German Army and in Russian Prisons*, London, 1919.
Price, Julius M., *Six Months on the Italian Front, from the Stelvio to the Adriatic, 1915-1916*, New York, 1917.
Putnam, Elizabeth Cabot, *On Duty and Off; letters of Elizabeth Cabot Putnam, Written in France, May, 1917—September, 1918*, Cambridge, 1919.
Rattray, M. J., *Further Recollections of 107 Field Company*, Darlington, 1920.
Reichsgesundheitsamtes, *Schädigung der deutschen Volkskraft durch die feindliche Blockade*, Berlin, 1918.
Richards, Frank, *Old Soldiers Never Die*, London, 1933.
Rimbaud, Isabelle, *In the Whirlpool of War*, London, 1918.
Robertson Scott, J. W, *War Time & Peace in Holland*, London, 1914.
Roujon, Jacques, *Battles & Bivouacs: a French Soldier's Note-book*, London, 1916.
Rubmann, Max, *Hunger. Wirkungen moderner Kriegs-Methoden*, Berlin, 1919.
Salter, James Arthur, *Allied Shipping Control*, Oxford, 1921,

Schreiner, George Abel, *The Iron Ration – Three Years in Warring Central Europe*, New York, 1918.

Schwarte, Max, *Der Weltkrieg in seiner Einwirkung auf das Deutsche Volk*, Leipzig, 1918.

Sparrow, Geoffrey and Ross, J. N. Macbean, *On Four Fronts With the Royal Naval Division*, London, 1918.

Spriggs, E. I., *Food and How to Save It*, London, 1917.

Starling, Ernest H., 'The Food Supply of Germany During the War,' *Journal of the Royal Statistical Society* (1920) 83#2, pp. 225–54.

Stenbock-Fermor, Ivan, *Memoirs of Life in Old Russia, World War I, Revolution, and in Emigration*, Berkley, CA, 1986.

Stewart, Herbert Arthur, *From Mons to Loos, Being the Diary of a Supply Officer*, Edinburgh, 1916.http://www.jstor.org/stable/2341079

Storch, Karl, *Vom feldgrauen Buchhändler: Stimmungsbilder, Briefe und Karten von Karl Storch*, Magdeburg, 1917.

Stuermer, Harry, *Two War Years in Constantinople*, New York, sd [c1917].

Sutton-Pickhard, Maud Fortescue, *France in Wartime*, London, 1915.

Taylor, Alonzo, *War Bread*, New York, 1918,

Teichman, Oskar, *The Diary of a Yeomanry MO: Egypt, Gallipoli, Palestine and Italy*, London, 1921.

Therese, Josephine, *With Old Glory in Berlin, the Story of a Young American Girl . . .* , Boston, 1918.

Tinley, James Madison (ed), *Food in Wartime*, Berkeley, CA, 1942.

Trueblood, Edward Alva, *In the Flash Ranging Service*, Sacramento, CA, 1919.

Truitt, Charles, *Wartime Letters from Italy*, New York, 1915.

Turczynowicz, Laura (Blackwell) de Gozdawa, *When the Prussians came to Poland; the Experiences of an American Woman During the German Invasion*, New York, 1916.

United States War Labor Policies Board, *Report on Labor Situation of Italy*, sl, sd [1919?].

von Lettow-Vorbeck, Paul Emil, *My Reminiscences of East Africa*, London, sd.

Waddington, Mary Alsop King, *My War Diary*, New York, 1917.

Ward, Mrs Humphrey, *England's Effort: Six Letters to an American Friend*, London, 1916.

_____ *Towards the Goal*, New York, 1918.

Warne, Frank Julian, *The Workers at War*, New York, 1920.

Wells, Clifford A., *From Montreal to Vimy Ridge and Beyond*, New York, 1917.

Winter, Paul M., *What Price Tolerance*, New York, 1928.

Yarkovsky, Jan M., *It Happened in Moscow*, New York, 1961.

Young, Francis Brett, *Marching on Tanga: (with General Smuts in East Africa)*, London, 1917.

Index

Page numbers in **bold** refer to illustrations.